WOMEN AND
CIVIL WAR

D1475755

WOMEN AND CIVIL WAR

Impact, Organizations, and Action

edited by
Krishna Kumar

LYNNE
RIENNER
PUBLISHERS

BOULDER
LONDON

Published in the United States of America in 2001 by
Lynne Rienner Publishers, Inc.
1800 30th Street, Boulder, Colorado 80301
www.rienner.com

and in the United Kingdom by
Lynne Rienner Publishers, Inc.
3 Henrietta Street, Covent Garden, London WC2E 8LU

Library of Congress Cataloging-in-Publication Data
Women and Civil War : impact, organizations, and action / edited by
    Krishna Kumar.
    Includes bibliographical references and index.
    ISBN 1-55587-953-5 (hc)
    ISBN 1-58826-046-1 (pb)
    1. Women—Government policy—Case studies. 2. Women in
development—Case studies. 3. Women and war—Case studies.
4. Women and the military—Case studies. I. Kumar, Krishna.
HQ1236 .W58517 2001
305.4—dc21   2001019618

British Cataloguing in Publication Data
A Cataloguing in Publication record for this book
is available from the British Library.

Printed and bound in the United States of America

The paper used in this publication meets the requirements
of the American National Standard for Permanence of
Paper for Printed Library Materials Z39.48-1984.

5 4 3 2 1

Contents

Foreword

This book is the fourth in a series of publications coming out of the on-going evaluation studies directed by Krishna Kumar at USAID's Center for Development Information and Evaluation (CDIE). In *Rebuilding Societies After Civil War,* Kumar presented a set of case studies, illuminating the different dimensions of transition from civil war to fledgling peace. In *Bullets to Ballots,* Kumar and coauthor Marina Ottaway underscored the problems and challenges of postconflict elections. *Postconflict Elections, Democratization, and International Assistance* further elaborated issues surrounding international assistance for postconflict elections. Now Kumar has produced *Women and Civil War,* based on USAID's fieldwork in Bosnia, Cambodia, El Salvador, Georgia, and Guatemala. While the book presents thoughtful findings on a wide range of issues, I would highlight three that corroborate my own experience in many war-torn societies.

First, despite the popular stereotype, women are not passive spectators in civil wars. Rather, they are active participants; they assume new roles and responsibilities both during and after conflict. They valiantly look after their families in the most trying of circumstances. They shoulder new economic burdens and responsibilities and play vital roles in the community. Many join military operations on both of sides of the conflict. I have found women to be survivors, demonstrating remarkable perseverance and initiative in the tragic conditions of war.

Second, women's organizations often play an important role not only in dealing with the challenges created by civil wars, but also in transforming traditional male-female relations. In many countries, these organizations have provided vital services to needy populations in the health, education, and economic sectors. More important, they have helped push gender issues onto the national agenda, facilitating the increased participation of women in social, economic, and political affairs, as documented in this volume.

Third, the international community has assisted women and women's organizations in war-torn societies in a variety of ways. Its timely assistance has helped alleviate the suffering of women and opened new opportunities for them. However, the effectiveness of international assistance has often been limited by the lack of a coherent framework and innovative programming. *Women and Civil War* outlines a framework for international assistance and makes useful recommendations for international donors.

I hope the analyses, lessons, and recommendations presented in this book will serve as a catalyst for a continuing dialogue on the subject. I congratulate Krishna Kumar and CDIE for this book and the effort it represents toward illuminating a complex subject that has been long obscured.

Andrew S. Natsios
Administrator
U.S. Agency for International Development

Acknowledgments

Women and Civil War originated from a study on women and women's organizations in postconflict societies that I directed at USAID's Center for Development Information and Evaluation (CDIE). In preparing this volume, I very much benefited from the advice of my three CDIE colleagues, Jean DuRette, Joseph Lieberson, and Ross Bankson. Dayton Maxwell, special advisor to USAID's administrator, read the entire manuscript and offered useful comments. Tom Buck assisted me during each stage of the process; without his scholarly help this book would not have seen the light of day. My daughters, Sonia and Sanaz, two articulate crusaders for human rights, gave me many valuable suggestions. Bridget Julian and Steve Barr of Lynne Rienner Publishers did an outstanding job in producing this volume. I am grateful to all of them.

Krishna Kumar

Introduction

Krishna Kumar

Since the end of the Cold War, civil wars (intrastate conflicts) have come to dominate the international landscape. These conflicts have caused massive death and destruction, uprooting of the populations, and erosion of social capital. A wide range of factors and conditions have contributed to their growth. They include poverty and the struggle for scarce resources in a period of rising expectations, rapid economic modernization, ethnic rivalries and divisions, political repression by authoritarian governments, arbitrary national boundaries imposed by colonial powers, support to certain political–military groups by outside powers, and the erosion of the international architecture created during the Cold War. Often, civil wars occur during natural calamities and disasters, contributing to "complex emergencies." Some examples of recent civil wars are Angola, Bosnia, Cambodia, El Salvador, Georgia, Guatemala, Liberia, Mozambique, Sierra Leone, Somalia, and Rwanda. Although many of these conflicts have been resolved, others continue unabated, perpetuating human misery.

This book explores the impact of these conflicts on women and gender relations and the ways in which women respond to them. More specifically, it tries to answer the following three sets of questions:

1. What has been the impact of civil wars on women and gender relations? How did these conflicts affect women's economic, social, and political roles and responsibilities?
2. What types of women's organizations have emerged in the postconflict era to address the problems and challenges women face and to promote gender equality? What activities do these organizations

I

undertake? How successful have the organizations been in empowering women?

3. What has been the nature and focus of assistance provided by international and other donor agencies to women's organizations? What are some of the major problem areas in international assistance?

This volume is based on a multicountry study of women and women's organizations in postconflict societies that the editor directed for USAID. The purpose of this investigation was to generate a body of empirical knowledge that could inform the policy and programs of USAID and other international donor agencies.

Three criteria were used in selecting the countries for field studies. First, to avoid duplication of effort, the study team should use the findings of existing empirically grounded studies, rather than launch fresh investigations. Second, the investigation should span the globe, including Africa, Asia, Europe, and Latin America. Third, the security conditions in the chosen countries should permit unfettered movement by the team. After extensive consultation with the regional bureaus of USAID and outside experts, the Center for Development Information and Evaluation decided on eight countries: Afghanistan, Bosnia and Herzegovina, Cambodia, El Salvador, Georgia, Guatemala, Rwanda, and Sierra Leone. Unfortunately, political developments in Afghanistan and Sierra Leone prevented any fieldwork there, and the study settled on the remaining six countries.[1]

The study followed a simple methodology. The work started with a review of academic literature, project and program documents of the international donor agencies, and articles from newspapers and professional journals. This review culminated in the development of a study proposal outlining the critical issues to be investigated, the methodology to be followed, and a schedule. The editor then organized a workshop for scholars, policymakers, and practitioners, who discussed and evaluated the proposal. The proposal was then revised in light of comments generated at the workshop. Teams consisting of one to three members were sent to each of the six countries to collect information. However, the teams faced serious problems in gathering the necessary data. Often government departments and struggling women's organizations did not keep precise records. When kept, records were difficult to reproduce or were not readily available to the teams. Moreover, inadequate communication and transportation systems prevented teams from visiting remote areas where many grass-roots women's organizations operated. Language was frequently a barrier. Hence, the teams relied largely on qualitative information gleaned from prolonged interviews or group meetings, reports on ongoing and past programs, and their own observations. Individual case studies were developed for all six countries. Finally, the editor prepared a synthesis document, drawing from the field investigations as well as other studies and investigations done by individual scholars or by national or international organizations.

The book, drawn from the research described above, discusses the nature of civil wars and the ways they affect women and gender relations. It recounts the impact of these conflicts on women and gender relations under the three broad categories of social and psychological, economic, and political effects. The book also presents brief profiles of Rwanda, Cambodia, Georgia, Bosnia and Herzegovina, and Guatemala, which illustrate these impacts. It also discusses the experience of women in refugee camps and its impact on their subsequent reintegration into their societies.

The core of the book presents a series of case studies on women's organizations in five postconflict societies—Rwanda, Cambodia, Georgia, Bosnia and Herzegovina, and El Salvador. These case studies focus on a wide range of topics: the nature and emergence of women's organizations, their activities and their contributions to women's empowerment, their sustainability and the myriad of problems and challenges they face. Each chapter discusses the nature and impact of international assistance on women's organizations and describes a few problem areas.

Chapter 8 discusses the nature and impact of international assistance on women's organizations and mentions a few problem areas that deserve to be considered by the international community. Finally, the last chapter presents general lessons and recommendations for the international community. It also identifies a strategic framework for international programs and interventions in postconflict societies.

• Note

1. The authors of the country reports are Martha Walsh (Bosnia and Herzegovina); Krishna Kumar, Hannah Baldwin, and Judy Benjamin (Cambodia); Kelley Ready, Lynn Stephen, and Serena Cosgrove (El Salvador); Thomas Buck, Alice L. Morton, Susan Allen Nan, and Feride Zurikashvili (Georgia); Virginia Garrard-Burnett (Guatemala); and Catharine Newbury and Hannah Baldwin (Rwanda). Their reports are cited in the references.

I

Civil Wars, Women, and Gender Relations: An Overview

Krishna Kumar

This chapter explores the impact of civil wars on women and gender relations. It begins with a brief description of a few characteristics of civil wars that affect women and gender relations. It then categorizes and analyzes various kinds of impacts, and mentions the nature of programs and projects supported by the international community to deal with some of the harmful consequences. At the end of the chapter, five country profiles—Rwanda, Cambodia, Georgia, Bosnia and Herzegovina, and Guatemala—written by country experts, illuminate these impacts in much more detail.

Several terms used throughout this chapter—and indeed the entire volume—require some clarification to avoid confusion. The expression *civil war* is defined broadly to include both high- and low-intensity conflicts in which insurgents seek regime change, often resulting in new constitutional arrangements and/or change in national boundaries. Thus insurgencies and wars of secession are covered by the definition. *Intrastate conflict* (or just the word *conflict*) is used as a synonym for *civil war* in this volume. The expression *international community* includes multilateral and bilateral agencies, intergovernmental international or regional organizations, transnational nongovernmental organizations, charitable foundations, and even private firms involved in development and humanitarian assistance. *International assistance* refers to the economic, technical, and political-assistance programs funded by the international community. Finally, *case-study countries* refers to the six countries in which the study was conducted.

• Relevant Characteristics of Civil Wars

All intrastate conflicts share five broad characteristics relevant to women and gender relations.

First, belligerent parties deliberately inflict violence on civilian populations. In fact, according to the Organization for Economic Cooperation and Development about 95 percent of the casualties in civil wars are civilians, a trend that alters a country's demographic composition and social relations. In traditional wars between nations, warring parties are obliged to follow international norms to minimize direct harm to civilian populations. Although these norms are never fully enforced or practiced, they exist nonetheless and may circumscribe combatants' behavior. This is not the case in intrastate conflicts. In all countries studied in this assessment, at least one party of the conflict—and, in most cases, both parties—directed violence against innocent civilians. In Bosnia and Herzegovina, Cambodia, and Rwanda, state-supported groups carried out ethnic cleansing with impunity.

Second, civil wars displace substantial numbers of people. The wholesale destruction, physical insecurity, disruption in livelihoods, and shortages of food lead people to flee from their homes and seek refuge in other parts of the country or in neighboring countries. In the aftermath of genocide in Rwanda, 2 million citizens fled across the borders to adjacent countries. In Cambodia the Khmer Rouge, under leader Pol Pot, forced all city dwellers to move to remote rural areas for political and ideological reasons. Massive displacements of people also took place in Bosnia and Herzegovina, El Salvador, Georgia, and Guatemala. Women and children generally constitute a majority of refugees and internally displaced populations. The displacement of people to refugee camps or settlements, frequently in inhospitable environments, profoundly affects gender relations. Often the traditional roles of men and women are redefined, and the family institution comes under severe stress, resulting in divorce and desertion.

Third, women's own participation in civil wars contributes to the redefinition of their identities and traditional roles. In El Salvador, 25 percent of the forces of the Farabundo Martí National Liberation Front (FMLN) were women. In Bosnia and Herzegovina and in Rwanda, women participated in ethnic cleansing. In many case-study countries women performed important roles in military operations, particularly in medical care, transportation, communications, and intelligence. In Georgia and Guatemala, women's participation was more limited. Women's motives for joining war efforts were often the same as men's, but some felt compelled to support the conflict because of their husbands' positions or political pressure. Culture, ethnicity, class, and age affected the nature and extent of women's involvement in war, but like men, women were both the perpetrators and the victims of violence.

Fourth, there is usually a conscious attempt to destroy the supporting civilian infrastructure during civil wars. Warring factions lay waste to buildings, factories, and roads and even destroy crops and agricultural facilities to create economic and political instability. Such activities inevitably increase poverty and starvation, clearly affecting women and children as much as, or more than, men. In Cambodia and Rwanda the conflicts created food insecurity and significant malnutrition. Only the timely help of the international community prevented even greater death and destruction.

Finally, such conflicts leave a legacy of anger, bitterness, and hatred among the belligerent groups that is difficult to heal. An important difference between intrastate and interstate conflicts is that once an interstate war is over, citizens in the warring countries live separately, and their interaction is usually limited. In intrastate conflicts, unless the country is partitioned, the formerly warring populations continue to face each other daily. In Cambodia and Rwanda, perpetrators of atrocities often continued to live with their victims in the same villages. Conditions were only marginally better in Bosnia and Herzegovina. In many countries, former combatants of opposing groups settled in the same communities, keeping alive bitter memories.

These characteristics of intrastate conflicts profoundly affect the social, economic, and political status, roles, and responsibilities of women and alter their relations with men during and after conflict. Not all these effects are necessarily harmful and undesirable. As discussed later, intrastate conflict also creates opportunities for change, because the very fabric of social life is torn by violence against civilians and massive displacement. Although it imposes severe hardships and deprivation, conflict also provides space to develop gender equality and can pave the way for women's empowerment in the social, economic, and political lives of their countries.

• Impacts of Civil Wars on Women

The impacts of civil war can be classified in three broad categories: social and psychological, economic, and political. Of course, the nature, intensity, and breadth of the effects of conflict on women's lives and relations between men and women vary with each country's social, economic, and political milieu. Much depends on the nature, location, and duration of the conflict and on class and caste differences within the populations.

◦ Social and Psychological Impacts

> "What security are you talking about? The conditions [law and order] have gone bad after the peace accord. I do not feel safe in my own home."—A Mozambican woman

Physical Insecurity

In all case-study countries, women suffered from physical insecurity throughout the civil wars. But the plight of women in the war zones was the worst. They lived in constant terror. Consequently, in many communities, they felt trapped in their homes. Fear of violence and sexual abuse prevented women from moving about freely, restricting their social and economic activities. Women were afraid to go to their farms or collect firewood for cooking in rural areas. There was no law and order.

What was more surprising is that these conditions improved only marginally when hostilities ceased. Early in the postconflict transition, the presence of demobilized soldiers and unemployed militia posed a serious threat to the life and property of innocent people, particularly in rural areas. The behavior of military and paramilitary organizations, long accustomed to abusing power and violating human rights, did not always improve when fighting ceased. Security-sector reforms, if introduced at all, produced results only slowly. The social disorganization and erosion of the authority of traditional institutions of social control, coupled with abject poverty, usually contributed to an increase in crime and delinquency. Many societies had to cope with a large reservoir of unemployed young men who had become accustomed to using violence and brutality during the war. These men formed gangs, particularly in urban areas, and posed a constant threat to the security of women and children.

In El Salvador and Guatemala, although human rights violations decreased with the end of civil war, violent crime increased, posing risks for women who worked late in the evening. Rural women were at risk from civil action patrols, death squads, and, in fewer instances, armed guerrillas. In Cambodia many families chose not to send their girls to school because they feared for their safety. In Rwanda high levels of interpersonal violence (although not necessarily of a criminal nature) continued.

The continuing animosity and distrust among former belligerent ethnic groups compounded the problem of physical security in many countries. In Rwanda, Hutu women who had fled their homes encountered social ostracism and physical violence when they tried to return. Hutu women whose spouses were imprisoned for alleged participation in the genocide felt socially stigmatized. In mixed ethnic communities in Bosnia and Herzegovina, minority women did not feel safe. Conflicts shattered local friendship networks in the community that had previously provided women emotional and social security.

The international donor community has not paid adequate attention to physical security issues. Development and relief agencies lack technical expertise in this area, and some agencies, particularly the U.S. Agency for International Development (USAID), are constrained by legislative mandates that restrict involvement in police and military affairs. Nevertheless, international donors have expended considerable resources on the demobilization of ex-combatants and their reintegration into civilian society. Some donors, including USAID, promoted police reforms in Bosnia and Herzegovina, El Salvador, and Guatemala. Although these efforts reduced government-perpetrated human rights violations, they failed to make a dent in the growing problem of lawlessness and violence.

Psychosocial Trauma
The brutalities of war—separation from loved ones, forced migration, sexual abuse, starvation, and extreme violence and cruelty—left deep scars on both women's and men's psyches. Anecdotal data suggest that significantly high numbers of women were traumatized by conflict in all case-study countries.[1] Women in Bosnia and Herzegovina, Mayan women in Guatemala, and Rwandan women experienced high levels of stress and anxiety in their daily lives. These women displayed symptoms typical of trauma, including listlessness, chronic fatigue, anguish, recurrent recollections of traumatic incidents, and depression. These symptoms are commonly associated with posttraumatic stress disorder (PTSD), an age-old disabling psychological condition given new prominence—and a clinical name—through its high incidence among U.S. combat veterans of the Vietnam War.

Although not denying the presence of symptoms associated with PTSD among men and women in postconflict societies, many researchers question the application of the concept to the conditions of war-torn societies. They point out that PTSD assumes that traumatic events have ended and victims have returned to a normal living environment. In postconflict societies, however, many conditions that contributed to trauma—such as physical and psychological insecurity, separation from loved ones, and threats of violence—persist for some time. These researchers also argue that the PTSD construct ignores the cultural and social context of perceptions and behaviors. Belief in karma, afterlife, and ancestral and malevolent forces can affect the way individuals experience and overcome traumatic events in different societies. Critics also argue that Western notions of trauma and therapy are alien to other societies. Western hubris has sometimes led to international assistance for trauma victims before a thorough examination of the local cultural context has been undertaken. In Rwanda, for example, where impassivity is a highly prized characteristic, the use of Western-style therapy was deemed inappropriate by many observers.

Despite severe emotional wounds, women in the case-study countries have demonstrated remarkable resilience and courage in surviving. Their suffering often remained unvoiced, though, and sometimes was expressed through abusive relationships with spouses or children. Most of these women continued performing their normal tasks, and their clinging to routine work may have helped them cope with trauma. In Georgia, internally displaced women appeared to adjust better than their male counterparts. Although men became passive and moody, women took outside work to feed their families. Some observers attributed the women's behavior to their nurturing nature. Others suggested that their comparatively low status made women more willing to work below their skill level.

The international community tested a variety of programs to deal with psychological trauma and associated problems, particularly in Bosnia and Herzegovina, Cambodia, and Rwanda. These programs included training caregivers, teachers, health workers, and others to identify the signs and symptoms of trauma, establishing mental-health programs in hospitals, and developing counseling programs at women's healthcare centers. Other programs—usually those associated with children—used sports or arts as methods of psychological healing. In a few cases, nongovernmental organizations (NGOs) promoted traditional ways of dealing with trauma. For example, USAID supported projects in Angola and Mozambique, where indigenous healers performed ritual purification ceremonies to help traumatized children. In both countries, the therapy seemed effective, at least in the short term.[2]

International programs addressing trauma generally suffered from three limitations. First, they were based primarily on Western notions of

trauma and treatment, which were inappropriate if they failed to consider the local cultural context. Unfortunately, little data exists on the best practices of more adaptive psychosocial assistance. Second, interventions were often brief, providing only short-term training and support to local entities. Because trauma counseling is a relatively long-term need, positive outcomes were often lost. Third, most of the programs concentrated on women and children, excluding men. Unless men—especially young men exposed to the brutalities of war—are treated, women and children are bound to remain victims of aggression.
• *For more illustrative and detailed information, see profiles of Cambodia, Georgia, and Guatemala*

Sexual Abuse and Exploitation
Closely related to psychological trauma is the problem of sexual abuse and exploitation of women during and after conflicts. Soldiers in belligerent groups violated women as a tactic of warfare. Security forces in El Salvador and Guatemala often abused young women suspected of rebel sympathies. In Bosnia and Herzegovina and in Rwanda, rape was an essential tactic of ethnic cleansing. Women were raped—often in the presence of their spouses, parents, or other family members—to humiliate and terrorize members of particular ethnic groups. Rwandan women were also forced to have sex with the members of the military as "payment" for victory. In practically all war-torn societies, young women living in combat zones were victims of sexual abuse by rebel forces and by the soldiers assumed to be guarding them.[3]

Little research exists on the extent of abuse and the number of female victims in the case-study countries. Victims hide the crimes and suffer silently because of the associated shame and humiliation. Even so, conservative estimates of rape victims ran in the thousands in Bosnia and Herzegovina, El Salvador, Guatemala, and Rwanda. In Rwanda, researchers estimate that more than five thousand women were impregnated through rape; most are now raising children fathered by those who killed their spouses or family members.[4] Little is known about these mothers and children, but their social and psychological agony is beyond imagination. Guatemala's Commission for Historical Clarification recorded the testimony of thousands of abused women but hesitated to delve deeply into issues of rape.

Intrastate conflicts and the resulting poverty, family disintegration, and erosion of community contributed to the growth of prostitution in many postconflict societies, particularly Bosnia and Herzegovina, Cambodia, Georgia, and Rwanda. In Cambodia economic desperation led some families to sell their daughters, and in Bosnia and Herzegovina and in Rwanda some wives engaged in prostitution. Trafficking in women grew as part of the postconflict increase in crime, the drug business, and other denigrating activities. Women in many postconflict societies were abducted or lured into prostitution with false promises and became slaves to their male bosses. Conflict undermined family institutions, so families could not control their male or female members who were involved in sex rings. The large-scale migration associated with intrastate conflicts further eroded community ties, contributing to deviant behavior and the spread of prostitution.

War often created a demand for prostitution by separating families and stationing young male soldiers far from their homes. In the post-conflict era, the presence of international peacekeeping forces increased demand for sexual workers in many countries. In Cambodia, institutionalized prostitution began when a large group of male expatriates, particularly members of UN peacekeeping forces, arrived to enforce the cease-fire agreements and organize elections. Local entrepreneurs set up lucrative brothels. Eventually the local elite—particularly military and police officials, senior government servants, and affluent business owners—began frequenting the brothels. As of 1998 more than fourteen thousand women worked as prostitutes in brothels in Cambodia.[5] Intrastate conflicts also led to increased prostitution in Bosnia and Herzegovina, El Salvador, and Rwanda, but not always on the same scale.

The international community has called attention to the sexual abuse of women in a variety of ways. USAID and other international donor agencies funded projects to assist and rehabilitate abused women. International NGOs worked with local groups to counsel prostitutes, hoping to limit the spread of HIV/AIDS. International organizations also strengthened legal and institutional mechanisms to punish sexual criminals and marketers of sex. However, many social, cultural, and even political barriers stood in the way of national and international efforts to curb prostitution and trafficking of women. Victims were not forthcoming, often fearing retribution from their bosses, and the male bosses were reluctant to forfeit their livelihoods. Communities did not want to draw attention to the problem, and government officials wanted to continue to reap financial benefits in the form of kickbacks. Finally, the international donor community lacked the technical and organizational experience needed to deal with this delicate issue.

• *For more information, see country profiles of Rwanda, Bosnia and Herzegovina, and Guatemala*

> ### Sexual Predation
> "In Cambodia, more than 25 years of civil war and the consequent social disruption have torn apart bonds of families and communities alike, so that the demands of survival often take precedence. Family disruption, abusive behavior, and death of one or both parents, step-parents with weak attachments, and the larger issue of social and community disruption are all risk factors that may propel women and children into the commercial sex industry."
> —*Commission on Human Rights and Reception of Complaints* (1997)

Family Roles and Responsibilities

"We are dead tired like a dead snake." "We work mad like a mad cow."—Two Cambodian women

Intrastate conflicts profoundly affected families, often increasing women's household burdens. The numbers of households headed by single women increased, as men were disabled, imprisoned, dead, or away fighting. Such households transformed the traditional division of labor between men and women, with women assuming male roles, including disciplining male children, building and repairing houses, dealing with community leaders and government officials, and fulfilling religious and social obligations. Most important, women had to feed and support their families alone.

Growth in the number of orphans and separated children[6] also added to women's burdens. Orphan populations increased to hundreds of thousands in some countries. Many children lost their parents during conflict. Others were separated from their families during conflict and forced migration. Still others were abandoned by parents because of severe economic or psychological stress. The burden of raising these children fell on extended families or neighbors, with women shouldering most of the responsibilities. In Rwanda the exodus of hundreds of thousands of people left thousands of separated children. Women throughout the country immediately volunteered to care for them.

Women typically assumed greater economic responsibilities during and after conflict. These additional responsibilities did not necessarily result in a corresponding decline in their household chores. In all case-study countries women continued to cook, wash clothes, and care for children despite spending more hours on farm work and other jobs. This "double shift" for women often led to tension within families. For example, in Georgia many internally displaced women who started working in the informal sector to feed their families complained that their unemployed spouses refused to seek work and wasted their meager resources on cigarettes and vodka.

Intrastate ethnic conflicts often created problems for families of mixed ethnicity. In Rwanda and Bosnia and Herzegovina, interethnic couples were targeted during ethnic cleansing. Those who survived came under intense pressure to separate or assume false identities. In Rwanda, Hutu women married to Tutsi men were accepted neither by their own parents nor by their in-laws. Mixed marriages were a priority category for asylum seekers from Bosnia and Herzegovina. Under these conditions, some men and women voluntarily left their spouses and some women were forced to leave.[7]

Finally, conflict also contributed to a decline in the status of women in some countries. Several researchers observed this phenomenon in Cambodia, where bride prices declined despite general inflation. Cambodian men could divorce their spouses and find new ones more easily than before the conflict. Polygamy is reported to have increased in Cambodia since the wars ended, forcing single women in desperate situations to enter into marital arrangements, both formal and informal, with married men.

• *For further information, refer to the country profiles of Cambodia and Bosnia and Herzegovina*

Domestic Violence

> "After 1979, men changed. Nine out of ten men are broken, nasty. During the Khmer Rouge period they had no happiness. So now that they are free, men do what they want. . . . When a husband dislikes something, even the smallest thing, he will become violent. He will hit his wife."—A Cambodian woman

Anecdotal evidence indicates that, for several reasons, domestic violence by men against women and by women against children increased in many war-torn countries. The conflicts generated a subculture of violence—one that condoned violence and viewed violent behavior as normal. Moreover, both men and women were traumatized by war, heightening family tensions. Alcohol consumption increased in nearly all countries, contributing to the increased domestic abuse of both women and children. Since women's status within the family often declined, women became more susceptible to maltreatment by male members. Finally, during the prolonged wartime absence of men, some women became more independent and self-reliant. Some returning men resented that independence and resorted to violence to assert their authority.

The international community supported programs (albeit on a modest scale) designed to assist victims of domestic violence. The programs counseled victims and arranged for legal assistance when necessary. In addition, they provided for temporary shelters and often arranged vocational training so that victims could learn skills to earn a living. They also undertook public education activities. But these projects faced social and cultural obstacles. In many countries, domestic violence is considered normal, which prevented such interventions from attracting more resources. Moreover, women are often unaware of the help available from donor-funded interventions. Even when they have known about such programs, women often have not sought help for fear of being subjected to more violence. Finally, programs rarely targeted men, who must be counseled and educated to stop the cycle of domestic violence. Consequently, only a small minority of women victims benefited from international interventions in domestic violence.

◦ **Economic Impacts**

> "I cannot inherit land. If I stay on my father's land, I am put in prison.
> I have already been beaten. My life is very bad since my parents died.
> I cannot even grow a potato or cut down a tree."—A Rwandan woman

Woman-Headed Households
As already suggested, intrastate conflicts contributed to an increase in woman-headed households in practically all case-study societies. Although rare before the war in Cambodia, woman-headed households now constitute 25–30 percent of all families in the country.[8] In the Ixcan region of Guatemala, woman-headed households were not uncommon before the conflict, but their proportion increased during the war, and they now constitute 30–50 percent of all households in the region.

There are obvious reasons for this development. More men than women were killed in the conflicts, resulting in demographic imbalances. Many women were widowed, while others of marriageable age could not find suitable husbands. Conflict also led to large-scale movements of populations, social and economic stresses, and the prolonged absence of men, which contributed to the breakdown of families, permanent separation, and divorce. In El Salvador a significant portion of the male population left the country in search of income and employment, leaving their families behind. In Georgia many men were so ashamed of not being able to provide for their families that they abandoned them.

Woman-headed households faced new economic and social challenges during the postconflict transition. A major problem was the lack of property rights. In Cambodia, El Salvador, Mozambique, and Rwanda, widows faced obstacles in acquiring legal rights to the land owned by their husbands. Until this past year, Rwandan women could not inherit land and property under customary law. As a result, thousands of war widows were deprived of the legal ownership of their husbands' or parents' farms. The situation was different in Cambodia, where laws provided for the legal ownership of land, but widows encountered problems gaining legal possession because of their low social status and the indifference of local authorities. In El Salvador, women were denied fair allotments in the postwar redistribution of land.[9] In Guatemala, women had difficulty exercising newly legislated land ownership and inheritance rights because of ignorance of those rights, institutional negligence, and pervasive machismo.

Woman-headed agricultural households, particularly those headed by widows and divorcées, often lacked the resources to purchase seeds, pesticides, fertilizers, and starter livestock. In Cambodia and Rwanda, international donors provided seeds and simple implements to subsistence farmers. These efforts, though not always adequate, gave relief to many women farmers. However, except in Rwanda, such assistance was not available to all women farmers. Moreover, because of food shortages, some women farmers consumed the seeds instead of planting them. When harvest season arrived, women farmers often had to sell their agricultural surplus locally because they lacked transportation to take the goods to larger markets, thus depriving these producers of higher prices.

Women farmers also experienced shortages of farm labor. Lacking the resources to hire workers, women often had to depend on the generosity of their relatives and friends, which was not always forthcoming. In some countries, traditional gender roles hindered women further. In Guatemala, tradition forbade Maya women from cultivating corn, and many had to force their young sons to perform the necessary work. Finally, new women farmers in most postconflict societies found it difficult to get technical advice for their agricultural operations. Agricultural extension services did not exist in most cases, and when available the services rarely reached women farmers.

A substantial number of woman-headed households in the case-study societies did not own land or other assets. Women heading such households worked as landless laborers or sharecroppers. They received minimal compensation for their hard work and barely managed to feed their families. In urban areas most women worked in the informal sector, carving out a living through petty trading. Because many women lacked marketable skills, experience, and education, only a small portion could secure employment in the organized industrial and service sectors. Women were easy targets for labor contractors who recruited for low-paying sweatshops in Guatemala and other countries.

In most case-study countries, woman-headed households were among the poorest of the poor. But some woman-headed households included males who worked in other towns or other countries and regularly sent money home. Such households were often in a better economic position than other woman-headed households.

The international community has learned that programs targeted exclusively to woman-headed households are not highly effective. Precise information about such households often is lacking, and the cost of identifying them is high. Targeted programs may create dissension locally between woman-headed households and other poor households because the poor resent special treatment of any specific group. In addition to creating such animosity, the cost of delivering targeted assistance can be high. Nevertheless, experience also shows that programs targeted toward women are necessary to provide them adequate assistance. Thus, the international community has followed a twofold strategy in post-conflict societies. First, international donors have provided assistance to all women, not exclusively to woman-headed households. Second, international organizations have supported expanded property rights for women, which would directly benefit woman-headed households.

• *For further information on this topic, please refer to the profile of Rwanda*

Poverty and Its Consequences

In all case-study countries, intrastate conflicts contributed to a marked increase in poverty. In Cambodia and Rwanda, conflicts also led to severe food shortages in certain areas. There is evidence that the number of women living in poverty increased disproportionately compared with the number of men living in poverty, but reliable data are not available.

The consequences of poverty were invariably worse for women than for men in all case-study countries. As the traditional nurturers of their families, women usually sacrificed their own welfare for that of other family members during periods of economic adversity. Because men controlled most of the assets, the household allocation of food and

> **War Widows in Guatemala**
> "Among the woman-headed households, those headed by widows face a series of particular problems and hardships. Widows are disadvantaged by virilocal residence patterns, the tendency to patrilineal inheritance, the sexual division of labor, and a lack of employment opportunities for women. The high level of loss of male kin suffered by some households only exacerbated these problems. The war widow, and those close to her, became stigmatized and isolated; her children often labeled as 'children of the guerrilla.'"
> —*Loughna and Vicente* (1997, p. 41)

resources was often biased toward men and boys. Women's intake of nutrients declined more than men's during and after conflict, and girls' health and education needs received lower priority than those of boys.

The economic conditions of three categories of women—returning women refugees, women who had depended on public assistance, and members of woman-headed households—worsened during the postconflict transition. While they lived in camps, women refugees received food and shelter and had access to health and education facilities.[10] But after repatriation, women were on their own, with less consistent or greatly reduced outside assistance. In many cases, their standard of living declined.

Poor women who had depended on food subsidies and social services (particularly health and education) before the conflict often suffered when the government reallocated resources toward the military during the civil war. In many cases, the lives of these poor women worsened—at least in the short term—during the postconflict transition because of economic reforms. International financial institutions insisted on economic stabilization through monetary and fiscal discipline, resulting in cuts in social expenditures. Although such reforms were essential to put economies on sound footing, vulnerable groups—particularly women—bore the majority of sacrifices. The social safety-net programs funded by the international community were insufficient to make up the loss. As a woman refugee in Mozambique lamented, "My children and I came back to my village. We had no food, nothing. . . . Our neighbors took pity and gave us some food. We often went to bed without food."

The economic challenges faced by woman-headed households were discussed in the previous section. Additional burdens, including separated children, HIV/AIDS, and mental and physical stress, all contributed to the problems of women who headed households.

The international community supported an array of programs to relieve extreme poverty and deprivation in postconflict societies. International donors provided food aid to Bosnia and Herzegovina, Cambodia, El Salvador, and Rwanda and tried to ensure that women and woman-headed households received a fair share of food assistance. The international community also funded social safety-net programs to alleviate economic hardships and promoted income-generating activities among women through microcredit. Job training and healthcare projects—including reproductive and mental-health programs—were developed. Finally, the international community also supported legislative and administrative reforms to increase women's access to productive assets. For example, in practically all case-study countries, international donors and NGOs funded projects to guarantee property rights for women and to end discrimination in labor markets.

• *For further information, please refer to the profiles of Bosnia and Herzegovina and Georgia*

Labor Force Participation

> "When government sold the factory, I lost my job. Now, I work as a housemaid."—A woman in Cambodia

Desperate economic conditions and the increasing numbers of woman-headed households forced more women to enter labor markets. Conflicts eroded the traditional social and political order, leading women to assume new economic roles and responsibilities.

In all countries except Bosnia and Herzegovina, women's participation in agriculture increased. In the absence of men, women performed many tasks that previously had been done only by men. Women worked on their own family farms, on others' land as sharecroppers, and as landless laborers. In some countries, including Rwanda, the government made surplus land available to women for cultivation. In Guatemala and El Salvador, women found work in the growing nontraditional agricultural export sector. Women's employment in labor-intensive agricultural exports increased their family incomes and provided a modicum of economic security and social freedom.

Because of the shortage of labor during conflicts, women could work in many industries and occupations previously unavailable to them. These openings provided them with experience and confidence to help them during postconflict transition.[11] In Cambodia, women worked in textile factories, construction, and salt and rubber production during the conflict and have been working in them ever since. Women workers in textile factories gained experience as well as good reputations, which facilitated their employment in the garment industry after the war. Women currently make up more than 80 percent of the workers in Cambodia's garment industry. In El Salvador and Guatemala, most of the employees in assembly plants that process exports are women. The increased presence of the international community during and immediately after conflict also created significant employment opportunities for women. International organizations recruited women in large numbers as secretaries, translators, office managers, and professional staff. However, employment by the international community declined over time.

As economies shrank during the early phases of the postconflict transition, female workers in the organized sector suffered. Often women were the first to be laid off during retrenchment and were replaced by returning combatants. This was particularly true if a woman was associated through her husband with the "losing side." Women workers also suffered from the privatization of state-owned enterprises in former communist economies. The experience of Bosnia and Herzegovina, Cambodia, and Georgia shows that women frequently lost their jobs during privatization because of the reinstatement of former employees or the closing of the enterprises themselves. Even when they continued working in privatized firms, women often lost medical and other benefits.

Women generally faced job discrimination in both the public and the private sectors. Women received lower wages than men for the same work, and they were less likely than their male counterparts to advance. Women were likely to be employed in menial jobs in which men had little interest. Although many countries passed legislation or formulated rules prohibiting discrimination against women, such measures were not enforced rigorously. Indifference, bureaucratic inertia, political confusion, and the low social and economic status of women all contributed to weak enforcement of the laws.

Most women in the case-study societies worked in the informal sector, earning their living by selling cooked foods, vegetables, fruits, clothes, or other household items. Although women were a significant part of the informal sector before the conflicts, their numbers increased during the postconflict transition. This increase reflected the addition of women who had lost jobs in the formal sector, as well as the wives of men who had lost jobs. In fact, a "feminization" of the informal sector took place in all the case-study countries.

The international community supported microcredit programs targeting women. Loans were advanced to small groups ranging from five to eleven borrowers. They required no collateral, or only minimal group collateral. The international community was imaginative in using microcredit in postconflict settings. For example, in Cambodia and Rwanda international donors supported "cow banks," a successful program that provided cows to women who used them to produce milk and cheese for income. The program stipulated that each woman turn over her cow's first calf to the project. Once those calves were returned, the women were free to keep or sell any additional calves.

Microcredit programs were generally successful in the case-study countries. An overwhelming majority of borrowers used loans for productive purposes. Although interest charged did not always cover the total cost of lending, rates of loan repayment were high and most costs were recovered. In Bosnia and Herzegovina, some microcredit programs grew into communal lending services, creating local businesses. The most important result of microcredit programs was much-needed relief to vulnerable female populations in rapidly changing environments. Many illiterate and inexperienced women started their own businesses with microcredit, and although their income and profit margins were low, these women were able to survive. As one observer noted, "Some women in Mozambique have attained relative economic and political autonomy from male domination. This has been primarily through entrepreneurial activity in the grass-roots war economy."
• *For further information, refer to the profiles of Bosnia and Herzegovina, Cambodia, and Georgia*

∘ Political Impacts

Expansion of Public Roles
All case-study countries saw an expansion of women's public roles and responsibilities during conflict. The challenges of surviving the absence of men and the opportunities created by conflict contributed to this expansion.[12]

Many women became active at the community level during conflict. They organized formal and informal local groups to provide relief to vulnerable populations. Women in Bosnia and Herzegovina managed day-care facilities and voluntary health services in seized communities. Women participated in the distribution of food aid in Rwanda, and in El Salvador they founded organizations to press for the release of political prisoners and to provide relief to families of the victims of political repression. In most case-study countries, women became more engaged in churches, schools, hospitals, and private charities, usually volunteering their services. They also established self-help groups in urban and rural areas.

In the absence of men, women often took charge of local political institutions. During 1985–1988 in El Salvador, 33 out of 262 mayors elected (nearly 13 percent) were women. Because they had organized politically before the peace accords and the formation of political parties, women also won seats in the Parliament. After the fall of the Pol Pot regime in Cambodia, women's representation in village councils increased dramatically. Other countries, including Lebanon and Mozambique, witnessed a similar phenomenon.

Women also entered the public arena to support war efforts. They raised funds, organized public meetings and marches, and mobilized public opinion for war in the name of ideology, ethnicity, and nationalism. Women joined militias in Cambodia and El Salvador, and they played supporting roles in military operations in other countries by managing auxiliary services such as health and intelligence operations. Some women rejected military solutions and founded organizations to end warfare, becoming powerful voices in the peace process.

In many cases, the expansion of women's public roles enhanced their social and political positions in their countries. Women activists represented a new vision of gender equality. They redefined traditional roles, and they projected a new self-confidence. The number of committed and politically perceptive women leaders increased, and many assumed leadership roles in the postwar era.

Other women became disillusioned with mainstream political parties and broke ranks. For example, women leaders who had worked hard for the FMLN in El Salvador felt that the FMLN's leadership was not committed to gender equality. The women founded Women for Dignity and Life (Dignas) to promote a feminist agenda outside the FMLN. The organization established close working relationships with a variety of governmental and voluntary institutions to promote women's empowerment.

In Cambodia, women refugees who had gained skills and organizational experience in overseas refugee camps returned to play prominent roles in grass-roots advocacy organizations. In Rwanda, women's leadership in the microcredit activities of rural women's associations led directly to the elections of women to both reserved and open seats in local government councils.

Postwar Retrenchment and Political Participation

"If women continue to perform the public functions that they assumed during the crisis, the men will have nothing to do, and we will end up

> taking care of lazy men who become yet another dependent [child] for
> us to look after."—A woman leader from Somalia[13]

Once hostilities ceased, most case-study countries witnessed a retreat of women from public life. This was most visible in postconflict elections held to establish democratic governments. Although women made up at least half of the electorate, they were represented only marginally in national legislatures. For example, five women were elected to the National Assembly in Cambodia, representing only 6 percent of elected representatives. The situation was similar in Guatemala, where women held only 7.5 percent of the seats in the Parliament. In Bosnia and Herzegovina the House of Representatives seated only one woman in the forty-two-member chamber. Women's representation was better in El Salvador and Mozambique, where women occupied 11 percent and 25 percent of the seats, respectively.

Three factors seemed to have contributed to this postwar retrenchment. First was the psychological stress of war, which generated nostalgia for the traditional social and political order in which women enjoyed only marginal roles in public life. After the peace accords in Cambodia, for example, some of the Cambodian elite clamored for the old order, which was seen as free from social and cultural strife. A few social and religious leaders in Bosnia and Herzegovina and in Guatemala demanded a return to traditional values and norms. The most vivid contemporary example of the return to tradition is Afghanistan, where women are deprived of all political and social rights.

Second, war fatigue gripped some women leaders and workers and contributed to their decisions to leave public life. Women who had shouldered heavy public burdens in addition to their familial responsibilities were physically and emotionally exhausted by the end of the conflict and were relieved to give up public activism.

The third—and perhaps the most significant—factor in women's retreat from public life was that men sought to reassert their authority once they were freed from preoccupation with war. Although they regarded women's participation in politics as a necessity during conflict, many men considered such activism inappropriate in the postconflict era.

However, other factors contributed to increasing women's political participation. First, the establishment of democratic systems opened new political space for women. As a part of the peace accords, many war-torn societies (Bosnia and Herzegovina, Cambodia, and Guatemala) drafted new constitutions based on the principles of democracy and equality. In El Salvador the existing constitution was revised to pave the way for democracy. The preamble to the Eritrean constitution now reads, in part: "Noting the fact that Eritrean women's heroic participation in the struggle for independence and solidarity based on equality and mutual respect generated by such struggle will serve as an unshakable foundation for our commitment and struggle to create a society in which women and men will interact on the basis of mutual respect, fraternity and equality."

One distinguishing feature of the revised and new constitutions was the explicit recognition of gender equality. All constitutions provided equal political rights to women, and a few tried to establish quotas for them in local and national legislative bodies. Thus new opportunities for women were codified as part of the postconflict societies, and women responded with enthusiasm.

Second, the growth of women's organizations further expanded women's public roles during the postconflict era. To promote women's welfare and gender equality, women leaders and workers founded many new organizations and revitalized existing ones in all case-study countries. Women's organizations have emerged as powerful forces in Bosnia and Herzegovina, El Salvador, Guatemala, and Rwanda, but their influence has been much more limited in Cambodia and Georgia.

Finally, the international community influenced the political aspirations and behavior of women in the case-study countries by advocating their social, economic, and political empowerment. Many multilateral and bilateral donors funded visits by women leaders to international meetings and conferences on gender issues. International women's NGOs established branches in postconflict societies or affiliated themselves with indigenous groups. The activities funded by international donor agencies to promote democracy, although not concentrating exclusively on women's political participation, also helped struggling women's groups and organizations assume new political roles and responsibilities.

Despite a brief era of disfranchisement, women in postconflict societies have made headway in the political arena. For example, the percentage of women members in national legislatures increased after the first postconflict elections in Bosnia and Herzegovina, Cambodia, El Salvador, and Georgia. The representation of women in ministries of national governments also improved over time in case-study countries, and women gained seats in elections to local government bodies. For example, the percentage of women city councilors in El Salvador increased from only 3 percent during the conflict to 14 percent in the 1993 elections. By the 1999 elections, the percentage of women had almost doubled from the 1993 percentage.

• *For more country-specific information, refer to the country profiles of Bosnia and Herzegovina, Cambodia, Georgia, and Guatemala*

The above discussion indicates that civil wars profoundly affect women's personal well-being, their status and role in the family, their access to economic resources, their political participation, and their general attitudes and perceptions. While these conflicts impose massive miseries and hardships on women, they also open new opportunities for changing existing gender stratification. It is up to women, women's organizations, and other concerned leaders to seize upon these openings to solve the problems faced by women in postconflict societies and promote gender equality.

• Notes

1. Women are often reluctant to participate in surveys and research, or to seek therapy, especially relating to incidents of sexual abuse or rape. This is due to the social stigma attached, lack of exposure to the issues, and a general fear of becoming the object of unwanted attention. Therefore it is difficult to collect data, and many researchers suspect that the incidence of trauma is dramatically greater than what is quantifiable.

2. Green and Honwana, "Indigenous Healing of War-Affected Children."

3. Rebel militia in Liberia, Mozambique, and Sierra Leone abducted young women and kept them as sexual slaves. When the conflict was over, these women were abandoned. Most of them had difficulty adjusting afterward. Often their families and communities spurned them. Without resources or work experience, they became destitute beggars or prostitutes. In Rwanda women were forced to have sex with members of the military as "payment" for victory or were raped by men of the enemy group in revenge.

4. This is cited by El-Bushra and Mukaruguga, "Women, War, and Transition." Abortion was not an option for these women. Many have since remarried. Often other family members have accepted the children.

5. United Nations Development Program, *Cambodia Human Development Report*.

6. The term "separated children" refers to those who have lost their parents during the fighting or while migrating. Children are not considered orphans unless their parents are confirmed dead.

7. It is interesting to note here that in Somalia, where people married into different clans, couples whose clans later became enemies had to divorce. Women returned to their parents while children remained with their fathers.

8. United Nations Development Program, *Cambodia Human Development Report*.

9. Women's land in El Salvador was the first to be confiscated during the land reform effort.

10. Some refugees living abroad sought shelter with family, ethnic communities, or others. These refugees found their own means of survival without the assistance of the international community.

11. In examining increased participation in the labor market, it is important to note the difference between rural and urban women. Rural women who had taken over male roles were often simply more tired; urban women, on the other hand, tended to gain status in society. It also is important to point out that the results depend on the stage of the postconflict period: as the economic situation changes, so does the availability of jobs for women.

12. Although women's participation in the political process increased during conflict, there were instances when conflict undermined participation. Somalia provides an interesting case. With the breakdown of political authority, political power passed into the hands of clan elders. Councils of elders, which replaced government officials and party functionaries, consisted of male members only. Thus, women were deprived of any say in community affairs.

13. Lewis, *Women in Transitioning Societies,* p. 23.

Profile: Rwanda

Catharine Newbury and Hannah Baldwin

Before 1994, few people outside the region knew much about Rwanda, a small, densely populated country in the center of Africa, where more than 7.5 million people inhabited a land area about the size of Vermont. Violent conflicts marked Rwanda's transition from colonial rule to independence in the early 1960s: a revolution involving the overthrow of the Tutsi-dominated monarchy, and subsequent episodes of violence, created a large refugee population in surrounding countries. The 1994 genocide led to the murder of more than five hundred thousand Tutsi by the extremists belonging to the Hutu majority. The genocide ended when the Rwandan Patriotic Front (RPF), a primarily Tutsi political movement and army based in Uganda, established control over the country. Fearing reprisal, more than 2 million people, mostly Hutu, sought refuge in Zaire and Tanzania.

During the first two years after the genocide, about eight hundred thousand former Rwandan exiles, mostly Tutsi, returned to Rwanda from neighboring countries and other parts of the world. Large numbers of Hutu refugees from Zaire and Tanzania started returning in November 1996. This massive influx of people placed an enormous strain on social services in Rwanda. By the end of the 1990s, postgenocide Rwanda contained a very heterogeneous mix of people, each with its own experiences of violence and sorrow, with all trying to rebuild their lives in a time of uncertainty and, for most, desperate poverty.

• Effects of the Conflict on Women

In previous episodes of violence in Rwanda, men had been the main targets while women and children were usually spared.[1] Also, in the past, churches had been places of refuge for those threatened with violence. But in 1994, churches became chambers of death, and the perpetrators of the massacres targeted women and children as well as men. All Tutsi women were targeted, simply because they were Tutsi, and large numbers were killed, often after having been subjected to sexual violence and torture. Educated, elite women were attacked by marauding militia gangs, regardless of their ethnicity. Some Hutu women were subjected to violence by RPF soldiers, in revenge for the violence perpetrated by

Hutu men.[2] Whether sexually violated or not, Rwandan women of all groups and social strata saw their lives, their families, and their tenuous hold on economic security disrupted by the conflicts.

Individual women were at risk simply because of their gender, while certain categories of women were targeted because of their actual or presumed membership in particular groups.[3] Tutsi women in general were at risk, even those married to Hutu men, as were Hutu women married to Tutsi men, Hutu women who tried to protect Tutsi, and Hutu women associated with groups seen as opponents of the Habyarimana regime. For example, one of the first women killed in the massacres that began on 7 April 1994 was Agathe Uwilingiyimana, a Hutu leader in the Mouvement Démocratique Rwandais party and Rwanda's first woman prime minister.

Almost every Rwandan woman has a dramatic story—of hunger and deprivation, fear, flight, and loss of family and friends. The ubiquity and the depth of suffering are striking, even five years after the war and genocide.

Voices of Rwandan Women

"We have suffered [*twarababaye*]. The men made war, and the women suffer."

"We felt as if we had lost all, as if we had been stripped of our skin. People lacked food, clothing, housing."

"The social fabric was ripped apart; indeed, the person herself had been torn apart."

○ **Destruction of Trust**

The war and the genocide shattered the dense local friendship networks and community solidarity that had traditionally provided solace and support for women. Family members and friends fled or were killed, and neighbors and former friends sometimes turned into enemies. What was left was not only social dislocation, but also a legacy of fear, insecurity, anger, and, for some, a desire for revenge. Under these conditions, social trust dissolved, and many women came to feel isolated, alone, and abandoned; they found it difficult to trust others beyond members of their immediate families.

Many women who survived the war and genocide experienced serious economic deprivation. Not surprisingly, female-headed households were vulnerable. This is a worldwide phenomenon, but in this case the "normal" net of social networks was also frayed and unstable. After the genocide, this vulnerability was particularly severe and affected a large proportion of Rwandan women. Many women were left completely destitute, without even a place to live. Extreme poverty made it difficult for women to care for children and other relatives who had survived, and legal constraints hampered efforts to obtain access to property and land belonging to their deceased husbands or other relatives.

War and genocide intensified existing differences among women while creating new ones. The current government claims that ethnic distinctions are no longer meaningful and expresses a commitment to transcending them. Public discussion of ethnicity is discouraged. But in the years since the genocide, ethnic distinction and discrimination have hardly disappeared.

Tutsi women survivors often distrust or fear Hutu neighbors whom they suspect of involvement in the violence. Many other genocide survivors do not want to return to their previous residences because of bad memories and suspicions about former neighbors.

Many Hutu women in both rural and urban areas feel insecure under the postgenocide government because public discourse tends to label all Hutu as *génocidaires*. In particular, women who returned from the refugee camps in Zaire or Tanzania in 1997 found themselves not only economically destitute but also socially stigmatized as complicit in the genocide.[4] Another particularly vulnerable group are women whose husbands are in prison, accused of involvement in the genocide. In addition to caring for their children, these women are expected to provide food for their husbands in prison. They also are sometimes ostracized in the localities where they live.

Hutu and Tutsi women involved in mixed marriages bear a special burden. A Hutu widow whose Tutsi husband was killed in the genocide may find herself rejected by her in-laws and denied access to her husband's land and property. Likewise, a Tutsi woman married to a Hutu man often encounters similar problems with her husband's relatives. The daughters born of such mixed marriages also have difficulties.[5]

The experiences of women who grew up in Rwanda before and during the genocide differed from the tens of thousands of Rwandan women who returned from exile as adults. Often referred to as "59ers" (because they or their parents fled during the Rwandan revolution, which began in 1959), these returned exiles are not a homogeneous group. Exiles who lived in Uganda or Tanzania speak a different language (English) and have experienced a different social environment from those who lived in Burundi or the Congo, both Francophone countries. And those who lived in the Congo grew up in a different political and social situation from those who were socialized in the polarized ethnic atmosphere of Burundi. There are differences and sometimes tensions among these returnees from different places, as well as between them and Rwandan women survivors who lived in the country before the genocide.

Under these conditions, rebuilding social trust among women and in the broader society is no small challenge. Some women's organizations in Rwanda have taken steps to rebuild this trust, but much work remains to be done.

○ Sexual Violence and Social Stigma

An estimated two hundred thousand Rwandan women or more were victims of some form of sexual violence during the genocide. All women were at risk, but the militias and soldiers carrying out the genocide targeted Tutsi women and subjected them to particularly brutal treatment. As Binaifer Nowrojee has documented in *Shattered Lives: Sexual Violence During the Rwandan Genocide and Its Aftermath,* sexual abuse was used as a weapon to humiliate the Tutsi as a group by destroying their women.[6] The survivors of this brutal treatment have been described as the "living dead." Some were sexually mutilated. Others have had to deal with chronic pain, in addition to the risk of AIDS and other sexually transmitted diseases and the fear of pregnancy. The psychological burdens are severe as well. The Interahamwe militia often sexually abused women in public, even in the presence of their own families. Some women were forced to serve as "sex slaves" for Hutu men.

Elite women, regardless of ethnicity, were at risk as the militias acted out class anger against the privileged. Some reports indicate that Hutu women were also targeted, first in northern areas of Rwanda controlled by the RPF and later during and after the genocide. "Hutu women were made to pay for what Hutu men had done."[7]

In Rwanda, because the stigma of rape is enormous, women who have been violated often hesitate to talk about it. Psychological trauma is thus compounded by social isolation. As a Rwandan testifying at the Fourth International Conference of Women at Beijing explained:

> Raped women are doubly punished by society. First, judicial practice does not grant them redress for rape as long as graphic evidence is not brought out into the open. Second, from society's point of view there is little sympathy, for at the moment that men and children died without defense, these women used the sex card, "selling their bodies to

save their lives." Thus, they are judged from all sides, and even among their families they are not easily pardoned. Even worse, people reproach them for having preferred survival through rape.[8]

The Stigma of Rape

A secondary school student, forced to be a sex slave of a Hutu militiaman for several weeks during the genocide, found it difficult to continue her studies after the conflict ended. A tall, beautiful woman, she formed a friendship with an RPF soldier, and they were engaged to be married. But a few days before the wedding, when she told her fiancé of her rape during the genocide and that one of her parents was Hutu, he called off the wedding and ended the relationship. She was devastated, pondering what kind of future she had.

Women raped in this fashion are victims of political struggles and war, yet they are denigrated by society. Their chances for marriage may be destroyed, and some have given birth to children who themselves are scorned. It is estimated that up to five thousand children have been born as a result of rape during the genocide. Some women chose not to keep their babies born of rape. Many who decided to keep these children encountered resistance and reprobation from their families and the local community. The terms used to describe these offspring reflect such reprobation: "children of bad memories," "devil's children," "little Interahamwe."[9]

The incidence of sexual violence against women in Rwanda diminished after 1994, but patterns of violence continued. After the RPF victory, young Tutsi women survivors of the genocide were reportedly pressured at times to accept relationships with RPF soldiers, in recognition of the soldiers' sacrifices during the war. Some Hutu women were beaten, raped, or otherwise humiliated by RPF soldiers. In some areas, Tutsi women who had survived the genocide were targeted in grisly attacks carried out by Zaire-based Interahamwe guerrillas, who sought to eliminate witnesses.[10] A report on the growing incidence of prostitution in Rwanda during the period after the genocide mentions the particular vulnerability of women who experienced sexual violence. Apparently, some local officials in the postgenocide government have pressured such women into sexual liaisons on the grounds that they were already social outcasts because of their experiences.[11]

◦ Woman-Headed Households

Tens of thousands of Rwandan children lost one or both parents during the war and the genocide. To care for these orphans, many women have taken in children other than their own—often, the children of relatives or friends, but also sometimes unknown children needing help. In addition to fostering orphans, many Rwandan women are caring for elderly or infirm relatives. And there is pressure on women of childbearing age to produce offspring to replace those lost during the war and the genocide.[12] In the refugee camps, a pattern of child marriages developed, linking young girls with teenage boys or older men. Such marriages were seldom durable; when they ended, the young wife found herself abandoned, with few prospects of finding another husband.[13]

Clearly, women have had to shoulder enormous burdens, particularly since, in addition to caring for the surviving members of their own nuclear families, many women are providing food, clothing, and school fees for orphaned children.

Although some women have the assistance of a male relative, many women in postconflict Rwanda do not. Widows of the genocide, women whose husbands are in prison, and teenage girls heading households are particularly vulnerable. In such conditions, women have had to assume responsibility for activities previously carried out by men or by a husband and wife together. Rural women have long participated actively in cultivating food and cash crops. But they normally relied on men to build and repair the house, track household finances, devise income-earning strategies, tend the banana grove, and care for cattle. Where men are absent in postconflict Rwanda, rural women have had to take over such activities. In urban areas, women find it particularly challenging to

---

The Plight of Widows: Large Burdens, Limited Resources
A middle-aged widow lost her husband and her four youngest children in the genocide. She now lives in Kigali with her three remaining children and several orphans she has adopted. She loves children. Though caring for these orphans cannot replace the children she lost, she feels less sorrow. While having a salaried job, she is not secure. She fears a younger person with higher educational qualifications may replace her. Losing her job would make her situation much more difficult. With her modest income and help from a relative, she regularly provides meals daily to more than fifteen people in her household.

secure rights to housing, obtain resources for rent, and find employment or other income-earning activities. Before the war and genocide, women did not work as day laborers on construction sites; this has now become a common sight in Kigali.

The number of woman-headed households increased dramatically because of the war and genocide. A demographic survey conducted by the government in 1996 estimated that 54 percent of the population was female and that 34 percent of households were headed by women.[14] The latter figure is significantly higher than the 25 percent of female-headed households before 1994. Yet 34 percent probably underestimates the actual number, because of reluctance on the part of those surveyed to claim that status. Moreover, the 1996 figure does not include the large numbers of refugees who returned at the end of 1996 and during 1997.

Of the 34 percent of households headed by women, many were headed by widows. Widows headed an average of 60 percent of the female-headed households, although regional figures varied considerably. In six of Rwanda's twelve prefectures, the percentage of widows heading households was higher than 60 percent: Byumba (66.5 percent), Kibungo (65.7 percent), Butare (65 percent), Gisenyi (63.5 percent), Ruhengeri (62.9 percent), and Cyangugu (61 percent). The 1996 "Enquête socio-démographique" also confirmed that women who are separated, divorced, or widowed usually remain single, whereas men who are separated, divorced, or widowed tend to remarry. For example, in 1996 women constituted 85.5 percent of those separated or divorced, and 89 percent of widows/widowers. Most of these widows were over thirty years old.[15]

These figures show the importance of taking gender into account in efforts to reconstruct Rwanda after the genocide. The evidence on poverty serves to reinforce this point. In 1999, five years after the genocide, the World Bank estimated that 70 percent of the population in Rwanda was living below the poverty line.

Visits to rural communes provide graphic examples of what poverty means in terms of people's lives. First, housing remains a serious problem. As of 1999, an estimated three hundred thousand people, many of them women, still needed housing.

Food is another problem. The poorest households in Rwanda experience regular food deficits. In 1995–1996 the government estimated that 10 percent of households needed food aid on a permanent basis and an additional 2.2 percent needed food aid on a temporary basis. This means that 340,000 children were living in absolute poverty.[16] Interestingly, the proportion of especially vulnerable households was almost the same as the percentage of women twenty and over found to be under-nourished (13.8 percent).[17]

These statistics refer only to the most vulnerable households, which experience chronic food deficits. In the last half of 1996, 26 percent of households received food aid of some kind, and 30 percent were helped by food-for-work programs. But the problem goes beyond inadequate food. If, as the World Bank has estimated, 70 percent of Rwanda's households live below the poverty line, then even households that are able to meet their minimum food needs may not be able to obtain other basic necessities such as salt, soap, and decent clothes. Of course, healthcare and school fees are especially problematic.

Female-headed households are particularly vulnerable to poverty, as are households headed by children, the elderly, and the disabled. The main reasons for such poverty are lack of access to land, lack of live-stock, and lack of labor.

Widows and other women without partners often do not have adequate access to land. In customary legal practices in Rwanda, girls usually did not inherit land from their fathers; when a woman married, her husband was expected to provide her with land to cultivate to meet the needs of her husband, their children, and herself. When a husband died, his widow was supposed to be allowed to remain on the husband's land, holding it in trust for her male children; levirate marriage (a brother of the deceased husband marrying the widow) was sometimes practiced. If there were no children, a widow's staying on her husband's land depended on the goodwill of her late husband's kin or on whether she would have a house and land if she were to return to her own family.

In recent decades, the growing monetization of agriculture and increased population pressure have eroded widows' land-use rights. Clearly, the tenuous position of women without husbands in rural Rwanda is not new. But because of the large number of widows and other single women after the war and genocide, this problem is more serious now. It is perhaps not a coincidence that the estimated percentage of female-headed households in 1996 (34.1 percent) was almost the same as the percentage of rural households that (in 1994–1995) had only half a hectare or less of land (34 percent). A 1997 UNICEF study noted difficulties widows were encountering with regard to land, citing "anecdotal evidence that women who have been widowed are being refused access to the land that they worked prior to 1994."[18]

Upon returning from refugee camps in Congo in 1996, some widows were denied access to their husbands' land. This problem was exacerbated in some cases because the marriage had not been registered at the commune—either because the marriage had occurred in the refugee camp (so there was no record of it in Rwanda) or because, although married before fleeing to the Congo, the couple had not registered their marriage. One sign of severe rural impoverishment during the late 1980s and early 1990s was the large number of common-law unions that had not been "legally" registered. Young men lacked the where-withal to pay the bride price and other costs associated with formal registration of their marriages.

The UNICEF study observed that "households that have one economically active member are more likely to be classified as poor."[19] Since women head the majority of households headed by a single person, this burden falls particularly heavily on them. It is difficult for a woman to grow sufficient food for her family as well as do all her other chores unassisted. If the woman has inadequate land (one-fourth of a hectare or less), the way to make up for food deficits is to work for cash, often as an occasional agricultural laborer. This, too, is difficult for a woman heading a household with small children, yet the number of women working as day laborers has grown in the postgenocide era.

Widows and other women living alone lack both resources and time, and they seldom have the means to hire others. As already noted, economic difficulties are compounded because many women, both Hutu and Tutsi, are supporting not only their own children but also orphans. Family structures are thus quite dynamic, and the burden of caring for orphans strains household resources. For many such children, this situation undoubtedly plants the seeds of future problems related to education, marriage, and inheritance.

A rural woman who is supporting her children alone and who turns to wage labor finds her opportunities limited. Moreover, in some areas, wages have remained stagnant, even while food prices have increased.[20] Purchasing food is a necessary but risky strategy, and this is a serious issue for long-term self-sufficiency. Mothers experiencing such poverty are unable to ensure the basic needs of their children:

> Without sufficient land, rural mothers heading a household with small children (i.e., she [*sic*] is the only member of the household that is old enough to be economically active) could not hope to provide the basics for the children, even if she [*sic*] finds alternative agricultural income-generating opportunities.[21]

Without a house, food to eat, a goat, and decent clothes to wear, women find it difficult to participate actively in the public arena. Clothes in particular are seen as important in Rwandan culture, as reflected in the Rwandan proverb: "No one can speak publicly wearing torn clothes." Still, attaining this basic minimum is necessary but not sufficient.

Women whose husbands are in prison face particular problems. Although not technically widows, these women may lack housing. Like widows, they do not have access to sufficient labor to ensure adequate food and other necessities (let alone school fees and healthcare) for themselves and their children. Regular trips to take food to a central prison or communal lockup sap both their time and their resources. The wives of men in prison are socially stigmatized and, at times, ostracized because of their relationships to those suspected of participation in the genocide.

Women in Rwanda have always worked. Rural women remain the mainstay of food production and play a critical role in the production of cash crops such as coffee. Urban, educated women have salaried jobs outside the home, and nonelite women have performed other income-earning roles. But because of their second-class status and a variety of legal constraints in both customary law and the written legal code, few women have had much experience in state-level interactions—dealing with political authorities, taxes, banks, and large-scale commercial activities. Such concerns were normally left to the men, who paid the taxes. Consequently, many widows were ill-prepared to assume responsibilities that previously had been their spouses'.

• Notes

1. The attacks against Tutsi civilians in Rwanda in early 1964 were a major exception; at that time, political authorities of the First Republic encouraged or condoned massacres of Tutsi men, women, and children as a form of vengeance against Tutsi exiles who had carried out guerrilla incursions into Rwanda, almost reaching the capital in December 1963. In the first half of 1973, Tutsi in Rwanda were again targets of ethnic violence, amid political crisis in Rwanda and a spillover of tensions from Burundi, where the Tutsi-dominated government had carried out selective genocide against tens of thousands of Hutu in 1972. Extremists stirring up ethnic violence in Rwanda laid the groundwork for Juvénal Habyarimana to seize power in a coup d'état in July 1973.

2. Twagiramariya and Turshen, "'Favours' to Give and 'Consenting' Victims."

3. During the genocide, the militias, composed almost entirely of Hutu men and youth, committed some of the worst atrocities, treating their victims with unimaginable cruelty. Soldiers in the ex–FAR (forces armées rwandaises)

and particularly the Presidential Guard also committed violence against women. Some women managed to survive by playing dead, hiding, or running away—but often they escaped only after having been raped repeatedly and abused in other ways. Some Tutsi women were compelled by their captors to live as "sex slaves" for weeks or months. See Nowrojee, *Shattered Lives*. Additional analysis on the effects of sexual violence on women during and after the genocide is found in Twagiramariya and Turshen, "'Favours' to Give and 'Consenting' Victims."

4. Women's Commission for Refugee Women and Children, *Rwanda's Women and Children*.

5. One woman the authors met in the course of fieldwork explained that her husband, a Hutu, had been in prison for more than two years, accused of genocide. She insisted he was innocent and regularly took food to the prison for him. But she was having difficulties with her husband's family, who did not trust her. She herself is the daughter of a mixed marriage; because her father (who was killed in the genocide) was Tutsi, she is viewed as a Tutsi. She feels caught in the middle, in a liminal status without a firm social base.

6. Nowrojee, *Shattered Lives*.

7. Twagiramariya and Turshen, "'Favours' to Give and 'Consenting' Victims," p. 103.

8. F. U. Layika, "War Crimes Against Women in Rwanda," in Niamh Reilly, ed., *Without Reservation: The Beijing Tribunal on Accountability for Women's Human Rights* (New Brunswick, N.J.: Center for Women's Global Leadership, 1996), p. 40, cited in Twagiramariya and Turshen, "'Favours' to Give and 'Consenting' Victims," p. 110.

9. Twagiramariya and Turshen, "'Favours' to Give and 'Consenting' Victims," p. 104.

10. For examples of such incidents, see Twagiramariya and Turshen, "'Favours' to Give and 'Consenting' Victims," pp. 105–107.

11. République du Rwanda, "Étude sur la prostitution."

12. Twagiramariya and Turshen, "'Favours' to Give and 'Consenting' Victims"; D. Newbury, "Understanding Genocide."

13. De Smedt, "Child Marriages in Rwandan Refugee Camps," pp. 211–237.

14. République du Rwanda, "Enquête socio-démographique 1996," pp. 6, 28–29. This report found the largest proportion of female-headed households in Butare (43 percent) and Kibungo (40.1 percent), and the lowest in Ruhengeri and Gikongoro (28 percent and 28.7 percent respectively). Note that in 1995, as the country began to rebuild, it was estimated that 70 percent of the population was female and that 60 percent of households were headed by women.

15. République du Rwanda, "Enquête socio-démographique 1996," pp. 8, 29–30.

16. République du Rwanda, "Étude d'identification," cited in de Keersmaeker and Peart, *Children and Women of Rwanda,* p. 51. The proportion of households identified as vulnerable was 15 percent in 1994–1995. After 1996, with the return of hundreds of thousands of refugees from Congo and Tanzania, the proportion of households with food deficits probably increased significantly. De Keersmaeker and Peart point out that in 1994, food-crop production had declined by 525 tons from its earlier level of 1,325 tons; the available calories

were only a little more than one-third of what was needed to meet minimum caloric requirements of the population.

17. Such aggregate statistics, however, tend to mask important regional variations and differences among households within a given area. For example, in two prefectures, the percentage of undernourished women was more than 50 percent higher than the national average: Kibungo (23.3 percent) and Umutara (21 percent). De Keersmaeker and Peart, *Children and Women of Rwanda*, p. 48. (Unless otherwise noted, these and subsequent statistics cited on poverty and rural inequality are from the de Keersmaeker and Peart study.) The extent of the food shortages faced by very poor households also varied significantly within a given prefecture. A case in point is Butare, where the food deficit for those who stayed through all of 1994 was 10–20 percent; however, for those who had returned to the prefecture in March 1997 or after, the food deficit was 60–70 percent. Kibungo provides another example. Prefectoral figures on food production in Kibungo show a surplus. But for households with only one active person working, and one-quarter hectare or less of land, the annual food deficit in 1997 was 30–40 percent. Save the Children Fund (UK), "Household Food Economy Analysis," and idem, "Household Food Economy Analysis," cited in de Keersmaeker and Peart, *Children and Women of Rwanda*, p. 54.

18. De Keersmaeker and Peart, *Children and Women of Rwanda*.

19. Ibid., p. 54.

20. Save the Children Fund (UK), "Household Food Economy Analysis."

21. De Keersmaeker and Peart, *Children and Women of Rwanda*, p. 56. In addition to inadequate land, livestock, and labor, rural productivity in Rwanda is also limited by insufficient access to improved seeds and other inputs, by lack of credit, by the rudimentary nature of their tools, and by an inadequate system of agricultural extension that does little to meet the needs of most rural producers. The collapse of coffee prices (Rwanda's major export) in the late 1980s further undermined rural incomes (p. 53).

Profile: Cambodia[1]

Krishna Kumar, Hannah Baldwin, and Judy Benjamin

Cambodia, a country of 11 million people, was unwillingly engulfed in the Indochinese war. North Vietnamese regulars and Viet Cong guerrillas clandestinely used the country's eastern borders as sanctuaries to launch attacks on South Vietnam. In retaliation, and with the tacit approval of Prince Sihanouk, the United States began secret bombing of communist bases in 1969. The bombing continued until 1973. As bombing increased, the communist forces moved deeper into the countryside, which in turn led to more bombing in the interior. The escalation uprooted millions of people, who flooded the cities in search of protection and peace.

A Maoist insurgency movement, the Khmer Rouge, gained ground in the countryside and took complete control of the country on 17 April 1975. The Khmer Rouge implemented the most radical and brutal restructuring of Cambodian society in the country's history. The regime evacuated all cities, abolished money, closed schools and monasteries, and severed links with the outside world. It also sought to undermine the institution of the family. It executed officials of the previous government and the educated strata—teachers, doctors, and other professionals. The regime forced men, women, and children to work daily from eleven to fifteen hours. The Khmer Rouge carried out systematic ethnic cleansing (against ethnic Vietnamese and Chinese) and what has been termed autogenocide. Estimates of the dead during the Khmer Rouge's sanguinary forty-two-month reign range from 1 to 3 million, out of a 1975 population of 7.3 million.

Vietnam toppled the regime on 7 January 1979 and installed a new, essentially totalitarian government friendly to its interests. However, the Khmer Rouge, supported by China, continued war for another nine years. With the end of the Cold War, the major powers finally initiated diplomatic efforts to bring peace to Cambodia.

• Effects of the Conflict

Before discussing the effects of three decades of war and genocide on women, three general observations should be made. First, the tragedy has profoundly affected both men and women. They have suffered from the poverty, pain, and brutal violence inflicted upon them. However, because of traditional hierarchical structures, sexual division of labor, and differential access to economic and political power, the war has in some ways affected men and women differently. Second, the effects of the conflict on men and women have been mediated by a number of interacting factors and conditions. For example, the abject poverty exacerbated by the war has compounded many adverse effects of the conflict, but poverty itself was a contributing factor to the war. Finally, the conflict has had both positive and negative effects for women. While the conflict has caused vast suffering among women, it has also led to new opportunities for some. In particular, it has undermined the traditional hierarchical structure of the society, opening the way for more balanced gender relationships.

◦ Trauma and Disability

Hundreds thousands of women have personally experienced and been traumatized by the brutalities of war, such as cruelty, extreme violence, forced migration, sexual abuse, and separation from loved ones. Women who witnessed the deaths and torture of their loves ones are haunted by their memories. Many women were unable to hold funerals for their dead ones and, without an opportunity for closure, could never fully grieve. Others did not know the fate of their lost husbands and thus experienced extreme difficulty in accepting their disappearance. Although many wished to search for their disappeared relatives, some recognized the futility of searching for a lost spouse; as one women remarked, "Pouring water on a dead tree is useless."

Psychologists debate whether Cambodians show the symptoms of what is commonly called posttraumatic stress disorder. Such symptoms typically include depression, listlessness, chronic fatigue, mental anguish, psychological disabilities, and recurrent recollection of traumatic incidents. Some experts have observed an absence of these symptoms among Cambodians, and they have concluded that posttraumatic stress disorder has not affected the postconflict population. Others, however, have suggested that trauma is widespread but that its behavioral manifestations differ dramatically from society to society. In Cambodia, religious beliefs, the notion of karma, societal relationships, and other cultural norms have tempered the most extreme expressions of posttraumatic stress disorder.[2]

In interviews and focus groups, women mentioned their high levels of stress and the profound sorrow they experienced. They were deeply moved by the recollection of traumatic war experiences and often were

> ### Teeth of the Dead
> "I was in my house and heard gunshots and shouting and I came running. I saw the dead bodies of my two daughters. . . . My third daughter came running and shouted, they shot her in her mouth as if she was shouting. Her teeth fell out and I took them. They saw me and asked me to give them. I was not allowed to preserve them. I kept one daughter in my arm and the other on my lap and I could only cry. They were all dead."
>
> *—Quoted by Wijk* (1997)

unable to contain their emotions. Despite these problems, women have been valiantly trying to take charge of their lives. They have found solace in religion, in public rituals, and in family. Some women who experienced sexual assaults have regained self-esteem by performing a culturally approved cleansing ceremony in Buddhist temples. For others, the challenges of survival have helped them overcome their trauma.

While rape was not used as a weapon of terror and intimidation, it was not uncommon. However, two psychologists who studied the subject have concluded that rape and sexual violence were commonly practiced by Khmer Rouge officials and frequently occurred during the migration of refugees to the Thai border. Moreover, single women were highly vulnerable in the refugee camps.[3] We know little about the plight of women who were raped and sexually abused during the conflict, but most of the victims of such crimes have rarely sought outside help. They prefer to remain anonymous out of fear of social stigma.

The situation for women disabled by land mines likewise has remained tenuous. During and immediately after the war, thousands of people were killed or lost their limbs to land mines. Most were men; only 5 to 7 percent were women. Anecdotal evidence indicates that women usually face more difficulties in obtaining treatment and prostheses. Often they are too poor to travel, or family members are reluctant to take them to the city for physical therapy and rehabilitation. As they are unable to perform their personal and family chores, disabled women are not treated well by others. Often the married victims have been left by their husbands and have little or no means of support.

◦ Status and Role in the Family

The conflict affected the institution of family in at least three profound ways. First, the Khmer Rouge sought to undermine family cohesion and redefine the roles of family members. They assigned men and women the same tasks in agriculture, irrigation, and other activities. They encouraged family members to spy on one another, and in many parts of the country during 1977–1979 they even collectivized cooking and child care. They organized marriages between randomly selected people without the consent of their families. The cumulative effects of Khmer Rouge policies on the family have been devastating.

Second, the large-scale movements of populations resulting from carpet bombing, forced evacuation of cities by the Khmer Rouge, and the guerrilla war on the Thai border contributed to the disintegration of many families. Thousands of families were separated during the forced migration. Often, husbands drifted away under physical and psychological stress, abandoning their wives and children.

Finally, the high casualties of young men in combat resulted in a demographic imbalance. There was a surplus of women of marriageable age during the 1980s and early 1990s.

As suggested by two analysts, these developments led to a decline of women's status in the family.[4] Before the war, women had enjoyed an honored position in the family. Kinship was traced through both husband and wife. Moreover, after the marriage, men usually lived with the parents of their wives. Thus, women enjoyed the emotional and material support of their families and friends, strengthening their position in the marriage. The traditional status of women was damaged by the surplus of women of marriage age during and after the war. Because of the postconflict demographic imbalance, men have found themselves in a better bargaining position. They have been able to offer lower bride prices and easily divorce their spouses and find new wives.

Faced with this situation, many women have preferred to become second and third wives rather than remain unmarried.[5] The decline of women's status was repeatedly raised in focus groups and interviews. Women participants often told the Center for Development Information and Evaluation (CDIE) team that women are no longer treated the way they used to be. Many women, especially those of the war generation, are concerned about their social status and how it has changed.

High rates of domestic violence against women have been reported throughout the country. A recent survey conducted in Phnom Penh and six provinces found that 16 percent of women respondents were physically abused by their husbands, and half of them sustained injuries as a result of the abuse.[6] In another study, the Cambodian Women's Crisis Center noted that more than 27 percent of women were battered by a member of their household, usually the spouse.[7] Participants in focus groups also indicated that wife and child beatings have become widespread. Many respondents attributed the domestic violence to the prolonged bloodshed and a subsequent decline in women's status. Such a subculture condones violent behavior—so much so that people begin to view it as a normal occurrence.

The conflict also resulted in the growth of woman-headed households, a phenomenon uncommon in the past. Recent statistics indicate that women presently head between 25 and 30 percent of Cambodia's households.[8] In such households, the traditional division of labor between men and women has become blurred, as women have assumed roles normally undertaken by men. They discipline male children, build or repair houses, deal with community leaders and government officials, and fulfill religious and social obligations usually expected of the male members. More important, they have become the sole support for the family and make critical decisions about family members.

Female-headed households usually face severe economic and social difficulties. Female farmers, for example, persistently face labor shortages for heavy agricultural operations. They are rarely in a position to hire outside laborers, depending instead on the generosity of distant relatives and friends. Although traditional laws provide for the ownership of land, women tend to encounter difficulties in legitimizing their claims and in obtaining access to necessary agricultural inputs. They also find it difficult to get a fair price for the marketable surplus. Social constraints arise because the female heads of households are not readily accepted in the community. Men may be embarrassed to interact publicly with single women. Still others try to take unfair advantage of their situation. Married women in the community often look at them with suspicion, if not hostility. In focus groups, single women told the team that with the rise of polygamy, married women in the community were suspicious of their intentions and concerned they might attract their spouses.

Despite these constraints, female-headed households may be better off in their living standards than male-headed households. A recent survey found that the incidence of poverty is 37 percent in male-headed households and only 33 percent in female-headed households.[9] This finding contradicts conventional wisdom.

Several explanations have been given for this unexpected finding. Female-headed households include many that have an elderly woman as the head but also have grown sons with their wives and children, or grown daughters with their husbands and children. Hence, many "female-headed households" may include relatively prosperous extended households. In research that accounted for this, female-headed households without male labor had the smallest landholdings, the lowest income, and the smallest holdings of farm animals.[10] Moreover, lower poverty rates might reflect a lower dependency burden. In the absence of husbands, families are likely to have fewer children. Another explanation points to the fact that the average age of the female head is higher than that of a male head, and in Cambodia the incidence of poverty declines with the age of the head of the household beyond age thirty-five. Finally, women may simply be more adept at developing a wide range of economic activities in the informal sector.

∘ Labor Force Participation

Although the conflict imposed economic hardships on women, it also opened new opportunities to participate in the economic sphere. Because of the mass mobilization of men into the military, mass killing, and increased labor demand for war and rehabilitation work, women were forced to undertake activities and perform economic roles that had been restricted to men. This led to the undermining of the traditional sexual division of labor that had characterized Cambodian society.

Historically, men and women worked together in agriculture, particularly in cultivating rice. Men were generally responsible for heavy tasks such as plowing and harrowing, whereas women transplanted seedlings from seedbeds to the fields. The remaining tasks—harvesting, transporting, and threshing—were jointly done depending on convenience. Women were also responsible for grinding rice and transporting it to the mill. The temporary or permanent absence of the male members of the household during the war put a heavy strain on this division of labor. Often women had to perform all agricultural tasks by themselves. The situation has somewhat eased in recent years as the army has demobilized and young adults born in the early 1980s have entered the labor force. Still, many female heads of households with insufficient funds to hire laborers have difficulty obtaining assistance. They must plow and harrow the fields themselves.

During the conflict, women made significant employment gains in the industrial sector. Before the democratic transition, most workers in state industrial enterprises were women. According to Judy Ledgerwood, 7,137 of 10,693 employees were women.[11] Women constituted a majority of workers in textile and salt production and nearly half the employees in the rubber industry. With the transition to a market economy, the ownership of many of these enterprises passed into private hands. It is not clear how the change in ownership has affected male and female workers. Increased numbers of men did enter into the labor market. Nonetheless, in the garment industry, which has emerged as the largest industrial employer, women still constitute 90 percent of the work force.[12]

Women have traditionally dominated petty trading in Cambodia. They sell fish, vegetables, fruits and flowers, and cakes and other food cooked at home. Many women initiated such ventures, which require little capital investment. Women continued to engage in petty trading throughout the war years. (The only exception was during the Khmer Rouge era, when the leadership prohibited all economic transactions.) However, Cambodians' limited purchasing power prevented any rapid expansion of petty trading during the conflict. The situation changed with the arrival of thousands of officials and staff from the United Nations, nongovernmental organizations, and other international agencies. They dramatically increased the flow of cash into the economy. These highly paid expatriates stimulated a demand for goods and services, increasing the demand for petty trading by women. Consequently, a thriving informal sector emerged in Phnom Penh and other cities, a sector that continues today.

The presence of a large number of expatriates, especially UN peacekeepers, also led to a rapid growth in another industry—prostitution. While prostitution had existed in the past, it had been hidden. To meet the demands of the expatriates, many entrepreneurs openly set up brothels, which were soon frequented by local customers as well, institutionalizing the phenomenon. Initially, these brothels imported commercial sex workers from Vietnam and Thailand, but soon they were also recruiting from the countryside. According to a recent study, more than fourteen thousand women work as prostitutes. Girls under eighteen make up more than 15 percent of these sex workers.[13] Poverty compels many destitute women to seek their livelihood in commercial sex work. Many impoverished families sell their daughters into prostitution, sacrificing one for the survival of the family. Young women are often tricked into prostitution with the promise of good jobs and high salaries. The large number of internally displaced persons—generally people without land access, lacking community ties, and having a high proportion of female-headed families—constitutes a major vulnerable group. Such women and girls may feel that the relatively high economic returns outweigh the risks. Whatever the reason, there is no shortage of commercial sex workers for the large commercial sex industry, an unfortunate legacy of international intervention in the country.

◦ **Political Participation**

As in many war-torn societies, women's involvement in the political arena increased during the conflict. Although a few women did occupy important positions in the Sihanouk government, the Khmer Rouge were the first to organize women at the grass-roots level. Khmer Rouge leaders established a women's wing of the Communist Party of Kampuchea in the late 1960s. In turn, this wing organized women's groups in rural and urban areas. We know little about the inner workings of the women's wing and its units at the local levels. Kate Frieson, however, does state that it was responsible for "organizing women's support, taking on important rear-guard roles in the military conflict against the Phnom Penh regime."[14] Once the Khmer Rouge came to power, the women's wing assumed more power and prestige and became another instrument of political repression and intimidation.

The communist regime that succeeded the Khmer Rouge took major steps to enhance women's participation in the political process. It promoted women to leadership positions in commune solidarity groups. Some scholars have suggested that the regime did so mainly because men were reluctant to serve in these groups, as officeholders received no salary.[15]

Though perhaps true on certain fronts, this was not the only reason for granting women positions of leadership. Like many communist regimes, the government was committed to promoting gender equality. In any case, the leadership of solidarity groups conferred political and social power upon female incumbents and expanded their political horizons. In addition, women were represented at the highest levels in the Communist Party and the government. One woman served as a member of the politburo while five others participated on the thirty-one-member Party Central Committee. In addition, in 1988 there were 21 female members in the 117-member national assembly.[16] While women, like men, did not enjoy political freedom, they did have a role in the decisionmaking process at the local and national levels.

The situation began to change during the transition to democracy. In a major irony linked to the peace process, women's political participation has declined rather than increased during the transition. Only five women, for example, were elected to the new National Assembly in 1993. Although women constituted 56 percent of the registered voters, only 5 percent of all competing candidates were women. The first democratically elected government had not a single woman at the ministerial level. There were only five female undersecretaries of state. None of the provincial governments was woman-headed.[17] It is likely that war fatigue, political disenchantment, the unstable economic situation, and the assertion of the Khmer identity with its emphasis on women's traditional roles have contributed to this phenomenon.

There are signs that after the initial disfranchisement, women have begun to take a slightly greater interest in politics. They are becoming more active at the national, provincial, and local levels. During the 1998 elections, major political parties fielded more women candidates than in the previous elections, and five of the thirty-nine political parties vying for a seat were headed by a woman. The number of women elected to the National Assembly has doubled, from five to ten. There are now two women ministers in the national government and four state secretaries. At the local level, women now head nearly 10 percent of the village development councils.

• Notes

1. The U.S. Agency for International Development (USAID) team was led by Krishna Kumar and consisted of Kumar, Hannah Baldwin, and Judy Benjamin. The team visited twenty-eight organizations, interviewed more than forty key informants, and conducted four focus-group discussions with program beneficiaries. In addition, the team met with the senior officials of the Cambodian government, the U.S. ambassador, the USAID mission director, and senior USAID staff. It also collected documents, records, and other publications not available in Washington, D.C. This case study is based on the data, information, and ideas gathered from the above sources.

2. Boyden and Gibbs, *Children of War.*

3. Marcus, "Cambodia Case Study."

4. See Ledgerwood, "Politics and Gender," and Frieson, "Women's Organizations in Postconflict Cambodia."

5. Ledgerwood, "Politics and Gender."

6. Ministry of Women Affairs, *Physical Abuse.*

7. Cambodia Women's Crisis Center, *Helping Women Help Themselves.*

8. United Nations Development Program, *Cambodia Human Development Report.*

9. Ibid.

10. Ledgerwood, "Economic Transformations and Gender."

11. Ledgerwood, "Politics and Gender."

12. United Nations Development Program, *Cambodia Human Development Report.*

13. Ibid.

14. Frieson, "Women's Organizations in Postconflict Cambodia."

15. Ibid.

16. Ledgerwood, "Politics and Gender."

17. Ibid.

Profile: Georgia

Thomas Buck, with Alice L. Morton,
Susan Allen Nan, and Feride Zurikashvili

Situated on the Caucasian isthmus between the Black and Caspian Seas, the Republic of Georgia has long been ethnically heterogeneous despite its small size and a population of just 5.4 million people. Minorities constitute 30 percent of the Georgian population. By the time Georgia won independence from the Soviet Union in 1991, ethnic tension had become a part of the political discourse. The bitterly contested Ossetian and Abkhaz wars resulted in thousands of casualties and upwards of three hundred thousand internally displaced persons.

The South Ossetia conflict erupted in the months after Georgia's declaration of independence in 1991, when the Ossetian leadership announced South Ossetia's new status as a "Soviet Democratic Republic," divorcing it officially from Georgia. Invasion would soon follow. The conflict was particularly brutal for civilians. Unofficial bands of local Georgians joined the Georgian national guard and shady paramilitary groups from other parts of the country.[1] Over a thousand civilians perished during combat. Soldiers on both sides of the conflict burned more than sixty villages to the ground.[2] Fighting continued to flare sporadically until June 1992, when the Georgian government, led by Eduard Shevardnadze, signed a cease-fire agreement brokered by the Russian government, signaling the withdrawal of Georgian forces.[3]

In western Georgia, the ethnic Abkhaz government declared its intention to split from Georgia in 1992, fueling another conflict. From the beginning, violence against civilians was widespread and severe. Thousands of civilians were killed during the fighting, while a vicious pattern of assault, murder, looting, torture, and pillaging was documented on both sides. After initial success, the underequipped and poorly trained Georgian army was driven out of Abkhazia in September 1993 by motivated Abkhaz forces, with the critical support of Russian hard-liners in Moscow and volunteers from north Caucasian regions. De facto independence continues to this day.[4]

- ## Impact of Conflicts on Women

Of the five thousand Georgians killed during the fighting in Abkhazia, two thousand were women and children. In the period after the official cease-fires were signed, an additional twelve hundred women and children died as a result of forced migration, sporadic ethnic-based attacks, and other forms of ethnic cleansing.[5] Gender-based violence was common. Rape was systematic and widespread in the Abkhazian conflict, as soldiers from both sides used sexual violence as a tool of ethnic cleansing. Actual rape numbers have been difficult to access because many women have refused to seek assistance for psychological and physical trauma owing to the cultural stigma that such treatment would invite.[6] Between 55 and 60 percent of all internally displaced persons were women. Those who fled from Abkhazia in 1993 faced horrible conditions, many trekking on foot across snow-covered mountainous terrain for over a month. Among internally displaced persons themselves, this escape became known as the "death path." Although there is little in the way of official statistics, between 200 and 350 internally displaced women and children died from sickness, malnutrition, and exhaustion during the long journey. Some women were forced to give birth in inhumane conditions, and several died during childbirth. The psychological trauma suffered during this period profoundly affected displaced women in the years to come. A 1995 Oxfam survey of internally displaced women and children concluded that the internally displaced person (IDP) community suffered from posttraumatic stress disorder syndrome on a near epidemic level.[7]

○ **Traumatized Women and Men**

Various forms of psychosocial stress have long plagued Georgian internally displaced women and their families on a nearly epidemic scale. A 1995 Oxfam study rigorously examined 653 displaced women and children residing in collective centers in Tbilisi and other regions of Georgia. Its team of psychiatric specialists concluded that over 86 percent of adults suffered from posttraumatic stress disorder and its various resulting symptoms, including heart and cardiovascular diseases (21 percent), chronic migraines and long-lasting sleep disorders (51 percent), and severe depression (22 percent). Twenty-one percent of displaced women surveyed by USAID in 1999 had been clinically diagnosed with a form of neurosis.[8] Causes for psychosocial stress were both conflict- and postconflict-related. Substantial numbers of women surveyed by Oxfam were traumatized by the loss of their homes and property (91 percent), by bombings (82 percent), and by the loss of close family members during the conflict (34 percent), among many other factors. The continuing period of displacement, arduous living conditions, and deepening economic troubles has added to the stress disorders of people living in collective centers.

In a 1997 examination of 219 internally displaced families, a Georgian NGO, Foundation for the Development of Human Resources, concluded that conflict-related psychological and psychosomatic complaints among the internally displaced had decreased over the previous two years. Stress-related health problems and depression were now more attributable to factors related to the postdisplacement environment and the strains of everyday life. Many families increasingly believed themselves to be victimized, feeling ostracized and segregated by local populations unhappy with their continued presence and with the Georgian government's perceived lack of interest in their plight.[9] In addition to the heavy toll on the psychological and physical health of women, the trauma of displacement has also affected the psychological well-being of men in profound ways. Put simply, women have been much more successful at adapting to the difficult conditions and strains of everyday life in the IDP community. As humanitarian aid has dwindled, many displaced women have worked tirelessly and relentlessly to provide desperately needed income and provisions for their families through petty street trade and other menial labor. Many men, meanwhile, have largely been unwilling to trade and to find other menial methods of generating income, instead spending much time idle and loitering in housing centers. In a 1996 study of the internally displaced, the Foundation for the Development of Human Resources noted that men were much more fixed on returning to their past lives and were "paralyzed" by the problems of the present day. Their lives were often characterized by escapism, by "empty and routine time-passing," and by a growing pattern of alcoholism. Any hope they had was held out for the "magic rod" of outside help.[10]

Most displaced women interviewed by the CDIE team indicated that their husbands and other men were "double traumatized" by the conflict and its aftermath. On the one hand, many displaced men felt personally responsible for losing the war and having to abandon their homes and former lives, their families forced into exile and destitution simply through their inability to win the war. On the other hand, men have felt unable to fulfill their traditional role as leaders of their families. Worse, many were deeply ashamed that women had become more creative at finding alternative sources of income, however paltry, through trading and other ventures. Displaced men tended to shun income-generating donor programming such as microcredit out of this growing sense of shame. NGO and donor officials have indicated that up to three-quarters of internally displaced persons participating in income-generating programming have been women. Not surprisingly, these same officials increasingly agreed that programs should concentrate on the problem of displaced men.

◦ Changes in the Economic Roles of Women

As in all intrastate conflicts, the forced displacement had major economic effects on the many thousands of internally displaced women who fled Abkhazia and South Ossetia. Prewar Georgia had been one of the wealthier republics in the former Soviet Union, benefiting in particular from its agriculture-intensive position as the breadbasket of the USSR. Abkhazia itself had long had the reputation as the richest region within Georgia, with its highly fertile lands accounting for much of Georgia's agricultural output and its strikingly beautiful Black Sea coastline attracting multitudes of tourists from throughout the Soviet Union.

Most of the Georgian women who fled the region left relatively prosperous lives behind them. Many were trained professionals who had worked as teachers, as economists, and in manufacturing and healthcare, among other trades. Seventy-two percent of displaced women surveyed had been fully employed before the outbreak of war. Over 21 percent of displaced women, meanwhile, had completed higher-education degrees, while 31 percent had finished vocational or professional schooling.[11] In the years since the displacement, internally displaced women and men have struggled under the massive weight of poverty and unemployment. According to unofficial statistics, 75 percent of displaced families earn less than half the monthly subsistence income level, set by the Georgian government at US$35 per family member.[12] Unsurprisingly, physical displacement has been accompanied by widespread professional displacement. The UN High Commissioner for Refugees and the Norwegian Refugee Council concluded in 1998 that upwards of 64 percent of internally displaced persons were jobless.[13] The CDIE survey confirmed that formal employment was one of the most acute and unsolved issues for displaced women, increasingly demoralized by almost a decade of epidemic-level rates of joblessness. Of women questioned in the survey, 68 percent were without work as of late 1999.[14] Faced with such difficult living conditions, many internally displaced Georgian women have quietly taken the lead in providing basic income and food for their families. They have adapted much more readily to the extreme stresses of the life of displaced persons than have men. They have begun to alter the long-standing tradition of men as main earners and providers for the family.

According to a 1998 survey organized by the Women's Study Center of Tbilisi State University, women have come to be the main sources of income in 72 percent of Georgian displaced families. Displaced women have left their shelters and homes by the thousands throughout Georgia to squeeze out meager livings through unofficial trade and agriculture. In larger cities such as Tbilisi, they have become the backbone for much of the unofficial or gray-market trade that has flourished in recent years. They sell products in crowded bazaars, on street corners, in subway stations, peddling everything from sunflower seeds to imported electronics. Some women have opened street kiosks selling basic foodstuffs, cigarettes, and alcohol, to name but a few of the items offered. The vast majority of the trading remains unofficial; 75 percent of the women questioned in the 1998 survey had refused to register their activities with the government.[15] Trading activity was rarely considered "work" by the women themselves. Indeed, many women interviewed considered themselves unemployed even as they spent long hours laboring on streets and in markets. Others would simply not admit to their trading, even when sacks of produce were clearly visible in their living quarters. Reasons for the silence range from basic shame to the common fear that existing humanitarian aid would not be distributed to "working" women and their families. Women traders, often skilled and educated professionals or farmers during their previous lives in Abkhazia, equated trading with basic survival and were rarely proud of their activities. The large majority made barely enough to make ends meet. One woman surveyed spoke for many when she said, "We all consider ourselves unemployed, as all we can earn is the money for our daily bread."[16]

Major obstacles exist for displaced women who hope to transform trading from a method of survival into a formal venture. The 1998 survey found that 94 percent of displaced women who traded were strongly dissatisfied with business conditions. Corruption, extortion, and stifling tax levels were all cited as major impediments. Of those questioned, 93 percent claimed to have paid "tributes" to the police, local administrations, and tax collectors.[17]

Koka

Koka was the most unlikely of business ventures, made up of twenty-two women and eight men from the Gali region of Abkhazia who were increasingly fed up with their growing misery and the inability of the Georgian government to help them. Although most of the women members were professionals and knew little about farming or trading before the war, their experience with the group has provided great psychological as well as material help.

As in cities, displaced women have become increasingly active in rural areas, providing needed food and income for their families and altering traditional gender roles along the way. In western Georgia, women make up the vast majority of the seasonal agricultural work force on tea plantations and in corn farming. One group of Zugdidi-based displaced women formed a small cooperative association, called Koka, that produced basic agricultural goods including fruits and milk products on donated farmland. Food was produced both for members' families and for trading in the marketplace (see box).

Inreasing numbers of Zugdidi-based displaced women have also begun to cross the border and brave the short trip into the Gali region of Abkhazia to tend to family farms abandoned during the conflict. Known as "pendulum migrants," these women grow vegetables, fruits, and nuts both for their own family and for trading in markets. They travel to Abkhazia early in the morning, often bribing Russian peacekeepers guarding the border, and return very late the same day. Though Abkhaz authorities have tolerated pendulum migration, these displaced Georgian women work and travel in constant fear of Abkhaz reprisal.

Georgian men rarely risk the journey, so sure are they of military reprisal. From a gender perspective, this phenomenon represents yet another economic change attributable to the conflict as women have taken over the farming responsibilities reserved for men before the war. As with trading, many displaced families have come to rely on women to deliver income and food necessary for survival.[18] Donors have begun to recognize the value of internally displaced women traders as they have moved away from humanitarian assistance toward more development or "self-reliance" programming in recent years. Specifically, many desperately poor women who seek basic loans to begin or expand their trading have turned to donor microcredit programs for financing. The Foundation for International Community Assistance (FINCA), a USAID–funded international NGO, offers innovative group lending. It consists of small low-interest, short-term loans starting at US$100 to groups of traders without the need for collateral. Since most displaced persons have very little in the way of valuable possessions that could be put up as collateral, this system has quickly evolved into a critical method for assetless people to receive loans (Georgian banks customarily require collateral worth at least twice the amount of the loan). Recipients receive the money in small groups, usually no larger than seven people. Each member pledges solidarity with the group and promises to pay back as a group.

Though the program was not designed exclusively for women, 75 percent of FINCA's 4,500 clients are women, and well over 70 percent of those women are from displaced families based in the Tbilisi region.

The Norwegian Refugee Council has partnered with an indigenous Georgian women's organization, Women in Business, to create a revolving fund of microcredit for women's ventures. They have the aim of eventually transforming the fund into a credit union. In addition to trading, the fund's successful enterprises have included laundry services and bakeries. Generally, FINCA and Norwegian Refugee Council microcredit lending has been successful. Only 1 percent of FINCA's first-time "group-clients" have defaulted on loans. That represents a mere US$14,000 of the US$1.3 million invested.

The role of displaced women as leading family income earners has not led to a growing sense of empowerment within the family or IDP communities in general. On the contrary, gender roles have remained clearly delineated. Women are still expected to perform traditional household duties of feeding and caring for their children, even after long and difficult days trading on street corners and in marketplaces. Men spend much of their time in and around the household, as observed by the CDIE team, but they do little to help in chores traditionally reserved for women in Georgian society. As many surveyed women stressed, time is always in critical demand. On an average day, respondents spent seven hours working outside the home and eight caring for their children. This double burden of both caring and providing for their families has left little time for rest and has logically contributed to growing levels of stress diagnosed in displaced women.[19]

∘ Lack of Political Participation and Representation

Internally displaced women remain very much disconnected from the political processes of postconflict Georgia. As in the broader Georgian and Caucasian political world, there are disproportionately few women in positions of power. No women had central roles in the political run-up to the wars in Abkhazia and South Ossetia; likewise, no women currently participate in the ongoing political negotiations between the Georgian and separatist Abkhaz governments. Almost universally, the handful of displaced women currently in positions of power at both the national and the local levels are former communist elites with little interest in advancing women's rights—displaced or otherwise.

The main representative institution for the IDP community from Abkhazia continues to be the Government of the Abkhaz Autonomous Republic in exile, composed of the same unelected Georgian–Abkhaz party officials in power at the start of the war, though now residing in Tbilisi as a de facto shadow cabinet to the separatist Abkhaz government. Women interviewed by the CDIE team expressed almost universal disgust with this institution. They perceived it to be genuinely uninterested in and out of touch with issues and concerns of displaced people. Complaints about the government-in-exile typically revolved around nepotism and corruption.[20]

Segregation from local communities and a lack of permanent residence has had adverse effects on the political rights of displaced women. In its report to the UN Development Program, the Gender Development Association (an indigenous women's group) notes that participation of displaced women in local elections and in privatization processes has been impeded by restrictive regulations and laws unmodified in the aftermath of people settling in collective centers and with host families.[21] Many respondents in the survey voiced deep frustration with a lack of any kind of representation from local officials. Women were particularly concerned with the glaring absence of representation by the displaced in the privatization processes taking part throughout western Georgia. Those who confronted local officials about privatization issues were met with weak arguments and vague promises.[22]

Most displaced women interviewed were much more interested in everyday economic and psychosocial issues confronting their families and communities than they were in political questions. Political mobilization and motivation were rare, if not nonexistent. No survey respondents were members of political parties. Most felt betrayed and abandoned by President Shevardnadze's government, which was blamed by many for losing the war and abandoning displaced persons in their times of deepest need. Local officials, as mentioned above, tended to be distrusted. Individual leaders in the displaced-women community who have taken their concerns to local and government officials have tended to be striving in two general directions. First, leaders press officials regarding the immediate everyday needs of displaced communities. Second, they are concerned with improving and speeding the negotiation and repatriation processes with the Abkhaz government, with the ultimate goal of returning home and taking up their "real" lives once again.

Displaced women were often unaware of their rights. Of the 105 displaced women questioned in the survey, only 5 knew of their basic human rights under the UN Declaration of Human Rights and the Convention for the Elimination of Discrimination Against Women. Of those five, two were leaders of women's organizations and three had recently graduated from university. The Georgian government has recently passed laws defending the rights of women, mothers, and children, but as several displaced women leaders stressed, most displaced women remained ignorant of the laws and their legal consequences. Several displaced women's organizations have dedicated efforts and programs to educating women about their rights, in particular women residing in rural and remote regions of the country.[23]

- ## Notes

1. MacFarlane, Minear, and Shenfield, *Armed Conflict in Georgia,* p. 8.
2. See Zurikashvili, *Socioeconomic Status of Women.*
3. MacFarlane, Minear, and Shenfield, *Armed Conflict in Georgia,* p. 8.
4. For detailed reviews of the war and its effects, see Chirikba, "Georgian–Abkhaz Conflict"; Greene, "Internal Displacement"; Hayden, "Georgia"; Human Rights Watch, *Commonwealth of Independent States;* and MacFarlane, Minear, and Shenfield, *Armed Conflict in Georgia.*
5. See Zurikashvili, *Socioeconomic Status of Women.*
6. MacFarlane, Minear, and Shenfield, *Armed Conflict in Georgia,* p. 26.
7. Kharashvili, *Psychosocial Examination of IDP Children and Women;* Metonidze "Woman and War in Abkhazia"; Zurikashvili, *Socioeconomic Status of Women.*
8. Kharashvili, *Psychosocial Examination of IDP Children and Women,* pp. 24–29; Zurikashvili, "Report on a Survey of Internally Displaced Women," p. 7.
9. Foundation for the Development of Human Resources, *Psychosocial Rehabilitation of IDPs in Georgia: 15 December 1996–15 December 1997,* pp. 20–21; Kharashvili, *Psychosocial Examination of IDP Children and Women,* pp. 24–29; and Zurikashvili, "Report on a Survey of Internally Displaced Women," p. 7.
10. Foundation for the Development of Human Resources, *Psychosocial Rehabilitation of IDPs in Georgia: 15 June 1995–15 June 1996,* p. 7.
11. Zurikashvili, "Report on a Survey of Internally Displaced Women," pp. 5, 8.
12. Zurikashvili, *Socioeconomic Status of Women,* p. 8.
13. Gender Development Association, *Conditions of Women in Georgia,* p. 69.
14. Zurikashvili, "Report on a Survey of Internally Displaced Women," pp. 7–8.
15. Zurikashvili, *Socioeconomic Status of Women,* p. 8.
16. Zurikashvili, "Report on a Survey of Internally Displaced Women," p. 8.
17. Zurikashvili, *Socioeconomic Status of Women,* p. 8.
18. Zurikashvili, "Report on a Survey of Internally Displaced Women," p. 8.
19. Ibid., p. 9.
20. Ibid., p. 4.
21. Gender Development Association, *Conditions of Women in Georgia,* p. 68.
22. Zurikashvili, "Report on a Survey of Internally Displaced Women," p. 4.
23. Ibid.

Profile: Bosnia and Herzegovina

Martha Walsh

After World War II, Joseph Broz (Tito) became the head of the new Federal Socialist Republic of Yugoslavia, which incorporated the six republics of Slovenia, Croatia, Serbia, Montenegro, Macedonia, and Bosnia and Herzegovina (BiH). Bosnia was the third largest of the six republics in terms of both land mass and population. According to the 1991 census, Bosnia's population was 4.3 million, of whom 41 percent were identified as Muslim, 31.4 percent as Serb, 17.3 percent as Croat, and 7.6 percent as other. Despite ethnic identification in the census, all three populations mixed and mingled in urban and rural societies. Since World War II, 30 to 40 percent of marriages in urban areas were mixed.[1] The shared history and culture of all three groups formed the basis of a distinct and unifying identity that "straddled ethnoreligious communities, but did not subsume these differences."[2]

When Tito died in 1980, the national unity he had struggled to create began to crumble. In March 1992, Bosnia held an independence referendum that was approved by a two-thirds majority. The Republic of Bosnia and Herzegovina was recognized by the European Union on 6 April. On the same date, Bosnian Serb nationalists began the siege of Sarajevo, and the Bosnian war began. Bosnian Muslim and Croat forces originally fought a united defense against Bosnian Serb advances. However, relations broke down in 1993, engendering a "war within a war."

The Bosnian Muslim/Croat conflict was eventually resolved in 1994 through international mediation, which resulted in the creation of the Bosniac–Croat Federation. The reunification of the forces enabled a stronger resistance. In 1995, the combined forces launched a dramatic offensive, forcing the Bosnian Serbs into a negotiating position. In November 1995, the factions met and reached agreement, and a month later, on 14 December 1995, they signed the General Framework Agreement, also referred to as the Dayton Accords, which brought a halt to the hostilities. The effect of the General Framework Agreement was to create one state, Bosnia and Herzegovina, consisting of two entities. The Federation of Bosnia and Herzegovina consists of 51 percent of the territory and has a Bosniac and Croat majority among the population. The Republika Srpska (RS) has the remaining 49 percent of the territory, with a Bosnian Serb majority.

The two interrelated atrocities that became the hallmarks of the conflict in Bosnia were ethnic cleansing and the systematic rape of women. Ethnic cleansing was a process whereby towns were "purified" of the other ethnic groups through forced eviction and execution. Women were often forced into flight, while men were rounded up and executed or sent to concentration camps. Rape contributed to this process by tainting the ethnic purity of the women raped and instilling fear within the community, encouraging them to flee. Although the sexual violence against women has been widely reported, much less is known about the rape and sexual assault of men in concentration camps. The demographic, social, psychological, and physical chaos caused by this strategy of ethnic cleansing and systematic rape is the most horrifying and enduring legacy of the war.

• Impacts

The impacts of a conflict on a society depends on the nature and extent of the conflict. In Bosnia, virtually every sector was devastated, from the economy to the social fabric of local communities. Although the degree of damage varied, every village and community experienced some, if not all, of the brutality of the war. For example, Sarajevo was constantly under siege for nearly four years. Zenica, an hour away, was not heavily bombarded, but it suffered severely under a blockade in 1993. The paralysis of the state infrastructure and the health and education systems similarly affected all citizens.

All of these impacts are inherently gendered. The way in which men and women experience and deal with the consequences of conflict depends on gender roles and relations prior to the conflict and how they were renegotiated during wartime.[3] Class, ethnicity, age, and education, however, also are significant factors that determine the responses of both men and women in a postconflict situation. In some cases, intragender differences will be as significant as—if not greater than—intergender differences. It has been recognized that a scarcity of resources and ethnic tension may in fact lead to competition among women.[4] This is certainly true in Bosnia, where class, ethnicity, and residential status are key elements in determining a woman's position and have proved to be a source of conflict between women and women's organizations. The following sections address the salient effects of the conflict and their gender implications, drawing out areas of such conflict.

∘ Status and Role in the Family

Conflict creates a confusing and contradictory dynamic in which gender identities are reified and polarized while at the same time women's roles are expanded into male-dominated arenas. On the one hand, there lies the essentialist notion of men as warriors and women as victims and moral guardians of the community. On the other, at least for women, conflict necessitates a dramatic role change whereby women become the providers and, in some cases, the defenders of the family, a traditionally male role. The way this dynamic plays out and the consequences it has in postconflict development differ between types of conflict and geographical regions.

The type of role change that frequently occurs, whereby women are allowed to move into previously male-dominated sectors of work and community participation, appears to offer transformative potential for the role and status of women in the family and community. In Bosnia, this process is taking place, although at a very slow pace and to a limited extent. A number of factors may explain the difficulties in realizing the potential for change.

The gender identities of women throughout Yugoslavia were transformed by the wars: "From the idealised working woman of socialist rhetoric, she has become the equally idealized mother of the nation."[5] Pronationalist policies were adopted by all parties and embraced by some women themselves. A Sarajevo woman was quoted as saying, "I plan to fire off one baby every year to spite the aggressors."[6] Such "revenge fertility" has been found in other conflicts with strong ethnonationalist components, such as Rwanda.[7] These policies linger latently in Bosnia's labor laws and the reticence of doctors to advocate family planning, thus maintaining an emphasis on women's reproductive roles. W. Bracewell further argues that "sending women back to the home answers economic needs as well by getting rid of surplus labor and shifting the costs of welfare provision back to the family."[8] In this sense, it has facilitated a major objective of the postconflict rehabilitation, the employment of demobilized soldiers, thus solidifying the public–private dichotomy. These identities are imposed just as strictly on men as on women. Men fear being considered "henpecked" or effeminate if they break out of norms of masculinity.[9]

Although the warring factions may have manipulated gender identities to serve nationalist and economic aims, women in the immediate aftermath of the conflict sought not to challenge the imposition or reimposition of a patriarchal order in the household. For many women, the safe return of their husbands, sons, fathers, and brothers from the front was paramount. At the end of the war, most simply wanted to return to a "normal life"—that is, the life they led before the war—without questioning what their position actually was or would be. While acknowledging the home as a potential site of oppression, one researcher on Bosnia also noted the importance of recognizing "the power and autonomy certain women gain from recovering the terrain of home and family."[10]

Recent research indicates that the value women place on their domestic roles has not changed substantially in the past few years. According to Prism Research (hereafter referred to as the 1997 Prism survey), the family factored as the number-one point of pride for women of all backgrounds, although it is higher among those from rural backgrounds between the ages of thirty-five and fifty.[11] In addition, roles involving the family (mother, sister, wife) ranked highest among the level of importance placed on life roles. The mothering role ranked highest. Roles as a member of a nationality placed second, although it was less important for Croats than Bosniacs or Serbs and, interestingly, slightly more important for those in urban than rural areas. Roles and pride in work came further down the list. It is not surprising for working mothers to place family first. Yet the apparent importance of nationality may play a part in reinforcing family roles as it was noted above that gender identities are bound up with ethnonationalist idealization of masculinity and femininity.

Where women are contributing income to the household, there does not appear to be a change in the financial decisionmaking process within the household. Female market traders, for example, reported they make decisions jointly with their husbands. Only one woman said she was the chief decisionmaker, and this was due to her husband's having had a stroke. Likewise, the majority of women in the Prism survey reported that decisions are made jointly. Still, it is difficult to know from data and brief conversations what goes on inside the household.

◦ Economic Burdens and Opportunities

Economic collapse and an increased dependency ratio have combined to produce an extraordinary burden on women. Indeed, women randomly interviewed cited the economy as the biggest problem for women, and many noted that life is more difficult for women than for men because women "now have to do everything."

In 1991, women constituted 35.9 percent of the work force.[12] Currently, women account for 40 percent of persons on waiting lists of enterprises restarting after the war, although their actual employment and unemployment rates are not known.[13]

Barriers to women's employment in the formal sector are revealed through data that indicate widespread direct and indirect discrimination. One study shows that women, particularly women in female-headed households, have lower employment rates than men.[14] Moreover, those who are employed receive wages 20 to 50 percent lower than their male counterparts. Meanwhile ex-soldiers were found to have the lowest unemployment rates and the highest wages. An Organization for Security and Cooperation in Europe (OSCE) human rights report on employment discrimination found that among cases reported, gender discrimination was linked to prioritized employment for demobilized soldiers, the majority of whom are male.[15]

Both policy-oriented and social-cultural discrimination have forced women to identify alternative means for income generation. In addition, those who had previously not worked are finding it necessary to engage in economic activity to make up for the shortfall in household revenues. Much of this activity takes place in the "gray economy" of market trading. Although it provides at least a supplemental income, this is a precarious livelihood because the government is clamping down on this sector in an effort to raise revenue.

The dire economic and employment situation also has resulted in women turning to sex in various ways. A recent reporter's study on prostitution and trafficking suggests prostitution may be widespread. As noted above, displaced women may be particularly vulnerable to organized prostitution.[16] An increase in the trafficking of foreign women has had the effect of reducing local prostitutes to the most dangerous and debasing work. It also seems that job insecurity in a bleak economic environment is making women more vulnerable to sexual harassment at work.

The one area in which women have a significant advantage is employment with international organizations. Because women were more likely than men to study social sciences, and particularly foreign languages, many have been able to gain very well paid employment as interpreters, secretaries, and program assistants. Men are more often found as drivers and in lesser-paid positions within these organizations. Whether these short-term gains can be converted into longer-term advantages remains to be seen, since the pool for secretaries and administrators will soon be saturated. Long-term gains would be more certain where female staff are encouraged to develop within the organizations and acquire new skills marketable in the postinternational, nongovernmental-organization era.

The current economic era is dominated by preparations for privatization. In BiH, the process of privatization is immensely complicated. In both the RS and the Federation, it involves a system of vouchers given to individuals to compensate them for income, benefits, and pensions not paid during the war. At the same time, state enterprises are being auctioned off. Although the international community is focusing on the development of a free-market economy, little attention is being paid to the potential impact of this process on women. Experience from other former Eastern Bloc countries shows that women are likely to be disproportionately disadvantaged.[17] Specifically, they are usually the first to be "downsized." A recent UNDP publication on transition economies in Central and Eastern Europe notes that widening gender inequality has been one of the human costs of economic transition.[18] The report highlights the disfranchisement of women from politics and the economy as well as the impact of cutbacks in social welfare and an increase in domestic violence.[19]

Part of the privatization process is the acquisition of ownership rights over formerly socialized property. Before the war, state enterprises owned many apartments that were then given to workers who had tenancy rights. Now, with a chronic shortage of housing attributable to war damage and the scenario of "musical houses" caused by refugee movements, establishing ownership is extremely complex.[20] Laws have been written and rewritten a number of times. Some of these laws have negative consequences for women. The Law on the Sale of Apartments in BiH allows for a reduction in the purchase price based on percentage of number of years the buyer has worked. It allows spouses to combine their years of work to increase the deduction. Further, it enables a surviving spouse to use years of a deceased spouse. Yet there is no provision to allow a surviving spouse to combine his or her working years with the deceased's.[21] Women, by virtue of both longer life-spans and the wartime death toll among men, constitute the majority of surviving spouses. This particularly affects young widows, who have few if any working years of their own. Although a property commission has been established to address ownership issues, the gender aspects of the laws have not been fully addressed.

Although there was no bar to women owning property, women are less likely to have legal title to property than men. According to the Prism survey, 25 percent of respondents had tenancy rights to a socially owned flat, and only 3.5 percent to private property. As it stands, for a woman in a divorce case to claim rights over property of which she is not on the title, she must prove that she contributed substantial income during the marriage. Moreover, men can transfer title into the names of others (other family members, for example) so that women have no claim. These issues, along with the overall shortage of housing, pose particular problems for women seeking to leave abusive relationships.

Other forms of discrimination in the economy include the system of disability payments. In the Federation, payments are divided into three tiers: war veterans, civilian victims, and those with disabilities unconnected to the war, with war veterans receiving the most generous benefits. This creates disadvantages among most women with disabilities as well as women caring for disabled children or other family members. A network of disabled-persons associations has organized a lobbying campaign to standardize the benefits package for all disabled persons. Although women are active in disabled-persons associations, such as Parents of Children with Disabilities and Lotos, women's organizations generally have not been involved in this issue.

Relatives and other foster families have taken in a number of war orphans. However, the vast majority of municipalities are not providing support to the foster families, thus stretching both resources and patience within households.[22] As the principal providers of child care, women are particularly affected.

With the pension system in disarray and without adequate service provision, the elderly continue to constitute a large, vulnerable group. A study conducted in 1998 revealed, however, that elderly men living on their own may in fact be more vulnerable than elderly women given the men's inability to handle simple domestic tasks, such as cooking and cleaning for themselves.[23]

◦ Political Participation

As part of the socialist egalitarian system, there was a quota for women's representation in government. In 1986, women constituted 24.1 percent of the assembly of the Republic of BiH and 17.3 percent of representatives of municipal assemblies.[24] However, a number of Bosnian women commented that women elected to office under this system were politically connected and the relatively high rates of women's participation did not reflect commitment to visibility of women in politics.[25] After the first postconflict elections in 1996, there was a massive retrenchment of women from public life. In the BiH House of Representatives (which represents both entities), only one woman was elected to the 42-seat chamber (2.38 percent). In the Federation, women were elected to 7 seats out of 140 (5 percent), while in the RS Parliament only 2 out of 106 seats (1.89 percent) were won by women.[26] At the cantonal level in the BiH, women fared slightly better, averaging 6.4 percent. In the municipal elections of 1997, women's share increased only slightly. In the Federation, women held 6.15 percent of the total seats, and in the

RS 4.63 percent. In the RS assembly elections held at the same time, women marginally increased their share to 2.43 percent.[27]

In 1998, Bosnian women activists tackled the issue of women's underrepresentation head on through a process that became a USAID–funded project, There Are More of US, Let's Vote.

There Are More of US, Let's Vote

In an effort to change the gender balance in politics for the 1998 elections, there was a countrywide campaign to educate women voters and push for a quota in the electoral law. It was the first time a coalition of women's organizations had been formed around a collective advocacy initiative. There were thirteen participating groups, primarily representing groups focused on human rights and democracy activities.

The League of Women Voters began negotiations with the Provisional Election Commission to include a women's representative on the commission and then pushed for the reinstitution of a quota—this time 30 percent—to ensure a critical mass. The result was Article 7.50, paragraph f, which states that male and female candidates will be listed "so that each gender on the list has at least three candidates equally distributed among the first nine candidates on the list."

At the same time, they worked to encourage participation of women at the grass-roots level in the election and approached OSCE for support of a women's voter-education project. With assistance from USAID, the organizations sent field representatives to villages and towns throughout the country, reaching fourteen thousand women in roundtables and discussions. In addition, posters and leaflets where distributed and displayed countrywide.

Women's representation vastly improved in the 1998 elections. Women's representation in the BiH House of Representatives jumped to 26 percent, with 15 percent in the Federation House of Representatives and 22 percent of the RS National Assembly. At the cantonal level, women hold 18.46 percent of the seats, and in the ten new municipal assemblies they hold 22.66 percent. Some concern has been expressed as to the caliber of women selected. It was suggested that parties in general select "weaker" party members regardless of gender to ensure party loyalty.

A permanent election law is being drafted as of the date of this writing under the leadership of OSCE. The chair of the commission had expressed reservations about instituting quotas. However, it was the women members of the Parliament who immediately put together a statement strongly advocating the retention of the quota system. Women's organizations, including many of those involved in the voter-education campaign, also have been engaged in this issue, which has become a principal topic of ongoing roundtable discussions. Unfortunately, the electoral system is changing from a closed-list to an open-list system in which a quota is less likely to assist women. Consequently, the gains they made in the 1998 elections may be rolled back.

In 1997, during discussions on the lack of visibility of women in politics, both men and women expressed the view that "women were too emotional, not interested, and that their priority is family."[28] Although this was not a definitive study, it was perhaps reflective of the absence of women in politics. In a survey taken in June 1999 after the increase in women's representation, attitudes toward women's participation in public life were dramatically different. Of the 1,050 BiH citizens surveyed, 58 percent responded that there should be more women in elected positions. Among women, this figure increased to 73 percent. In addition, 70 percent of all respondents agreed that every registered party should be required to include a certain percentage of women as candidates. The percentage that received greatest support (33 percent) was 41 to 50 percent. Moreover, 64 percent responded that parties should be required to appoint a certain percentage of women to government positions.[29]

This last question is particularly salient because women's representation in executive positions is negligible. There are no women in the BiH Council of Ministers and out of sixty-four posts connected to the Council of Ministers, only four women have been appointed. There are no women ministers in either the Federation or the RS. In the Federation, none of the cantonal presidents, assembly presidents, or prime ministers are women.[30]

In the judiciary, women constitute the majority of municipal court judges and have significant participation in cantonal and district courts, but there are few female court presidents. There is only one female judge on the BiH Constitutional Court. The situation is worse in the RS, where no women sit on the RS Supreme Court and only one out of nine judges in the Constitutional Court is a woman.[31] The Prism study showed that 59.9 percent of respondents believed there should be more women in law. This area ranked highest in the areas of society in which women should be more involved. The absence of women in higher levels of the judiciary is problematic given the difficulties in bringing and winning cases on gender-based discrimination and prosecuting sex offenses. Even where women do preside in courtrooms, they are not necessarily gender sensitive. A woman judge in Zenica reportedly refused to give priority to cases involving domestic violence, despite the urgency of prosecuting such cases.

Despite the significant achievements of 1998, there is much room for improvement. One of the major hurdles to women's full and active participation in political life is their position in the economy. Politics and economics are inextricably linked throughout the world. However, the problem seems to be magnified in countries emerging from conflict, where the select few who profited from the war or who have emerged as political leaders control both the economic and the political landscape. It is difficult for men or women without the proper connections to break through these barriers. The challenges, however, are greater for women because they are found in the least-remunerative jobs and are less likely to have connections but more likely to have other burdens and responsibilities. Although quotas will address the short-term issue of instituting a culture receptive to women's political participation, long-term strategies to level the playing field in politics must be coupled with efforts to increase women's economic position and status.

Women in BiH are just beginning to make a link between the low levels of their participation in politics and in decisionmaking roles and their low status in the economy. As in many Central and Eastern European countries, there has been little tradition of citizen engagement in economic policy issues, except at a very theoretical level. As women's organizations begin to master skills in public policy advocacy, they are beginning to turn their attention to the practical issues of access to credit, business training, social safety-net benefits, and employment.

Although it is still too early to assess what the long-term impact of the conflict and postconflict transition will be on the men and women of BiH, it is clear that the conflict—characterized by widespread fighting, ethnic cleansing, and systematic rape—has left deep scars on almost every aspect of the society, people, and economy of BiH. This profile has tried to highlight how men and women, in general, may have experienced and dealt with the consequences of the conflict in different ways.

• Notes

1. Donia and Fine, *Bosnia and Herzegovina,* p. 9.
2. Ibid., p. 7; Bringa, *Being Muslim the Bosnian Way,* p. 33.
3. Byrne, "Gender, Conflict, and Development," p. 23.
4. Ibid., p. 42.
5. Bracewell, "Mothers of the Nation," p. 27.
6. Ibid., p. 28.

7. *Economist,* February 1997.

8. Bracewell, "Mothers of the Nation," p. 28.

9. Savjak, "Sexism and Equality."

10. Nguyen-Gillham, "Bosnian Women and Social Reconstruction," p. 196.

11. The Prism survey, which was sponsored by Delphi International STAR with funding from private foundations and international organizations, was the first effort to document the status of women and the economy and perceptions of women about opportunities for change. The study was prepared for the first conference held on this topic in Zenica, BiH, in November 1997.

12. United Nations Development Program, *Human Development Report: Bosnia and Herzegovina 1998,* pp. 72, 91.

13. Ibid., p. 72.

14. CIET Vulnerability Study in World Bank, *Bosnia and Herzegovina— Priority Reconstruction Program,* p. 16.

15. Organization for Security and Cooperation in Europe, *Employment Discrimination in Bosnia and Herzegovina,* p. 9.

16. Medica Zenica Infoteka, "A Second Look," p. 86.

17. See Einhorn, *Impact of the Transition.*

18. United Nations Development Program, *Transition 1999.*

19. Ibid.

20. Displaced persons have swapped houses on a large scale as they occupy the houses of those displaced from the area in which they now live (e.g., Bosniacs inhabiting Serb houses and vice versa).

21. International Human Rights Law Group, *Women's Rights in BiH,* p. 162.

22. United Nations Development Program, *Human Development Report: Bosnia and Herzegovina 1998,* p. 45.

23. Byron and Walsh, "Beyond Reach."

24. Organization for Security and Cooperation in Europe, *Women's Representation in Bosnia and Herzegovina,* in International Human Rights Law Group, *Women's Rights in BiH,* p. 181.

25. Walsh, *Postconflict Bosnia and Herzegovina,* p. 25.

26. International Human Rights Law Group, *Women's Rights in BiH,* p. 181.

27. Ibid., p. 182.

28. Walsh, *Postconflict Bosnia and Herzegovina.*

29. Organization for Security and Cooperation in Europe, "Survey on the Role of Women in BiH Politics."

30. International Human Rights Law Group, *Women's Rights in BiH,* pp. 182–183.

31. Ibid., p. 183.

Profile: Guatemala

Virginia Garrard-Burnett

In 1954, the leftist and democratically elected president of Guatemala, Jacobo Arbenz, was overthrown in a coup by the Movimiento de Liberación Nacional, a stridently anticommunist movement. The Arbenz overthrow and the rise of the armed opposition in 1962 set the stage for the tragic drama that become Guatemala's contemporary history, marked by the motifs of military government, Marxist armed struggle, military government, and three generations of political violence.

Although Guatemala's struggle lasted for thirty-six years, making it one of the longest uninterrupted civil wars in Latin America, the violence between 1978 and 1985 was particularly intense. Military operations were concentrated in the (primarily indigenous) departments of El Quiché, Huehuetenango, Chimaltenango, and Alta and Baja Vera Paz, as well as on the southern coast and in the capital. Within this time frame, state repression and violence accelerated sharply between 1981 and 1982. By 1983, the army had routed the Guatemalan National Revolutionary Unity and, by its own count, eliminated 440 indigenous villages entirely. An estimated twenty thousand Guatemalans died violently between 1981 and 1983.[1] Estimates of the number of displaced persons during *la violencia* range from five hundred thousand to a million and a half.

- **Effects of the Violence**

  ∘ Social and Psychological Wounds

Because most of the protagonists in Guatemala's armed conflict were men, most of the victims of state violence were men.[2] The UN Commission for Historical Clarification has noted that about 25 percent of the direct victims of human rights violations and acts of violence were women. They were raped, tortured, and killed, sometimes because of their ideals and political or social participation, but also in massacres or other indiscriminate actions. Thousands of women were widowed and thus became the sole breadwinners for their children, often with no material resources after the scorched-earth policies destroyed their homes and crops.[3]

The psychosocial effects of violence have had lasting repercussion well beyond the immediate emergency of *la violencia*. As anthropologist Linda Green has stated, "women's bodies have become repositories of the painful experiences they have been unable to articulate as a result not only of being silenced but also because of the non-narratability of atrocious experiences."[4] Women who witnessed violence or lost family members continue to suffer psychological and physical ailments *(tristeza)*, literally the embodiment of suffering, or suffering incorporated. Physical ailments such as chronic headaches, gastritis, chest pains, visual problems, respiratory infections, and psychological manifestations such as recurring dreams and nightmares, sadness, and depression are common.[5]

The Catholic Church–sponsored Recovery of the Historical Memory Project (REHMI) compiled a list of psycho-physical and emotional ailments that continued to plague witness and victims of state-sponsored violence up to two decades after the acts themselves. These included sensations of sadness, feelings of injustice and helplessness, prolonged mourning, psychosomatic problems, eating disorders (specifically, hunger), and feelings of isolation and loneliness.[6]

Tristeza is also manifested in more amorphous physical ills such as "mournful heart" *(duelo del corazón)* and sleep disturbances from nightmares and other types of compelling dreams. In the case of Mayan victims in particular, disturbing dreams have a special significance, since dreams are considered to be a form of communication with the ancestors and are a rich reservoir for cultural interpretation.[7]

Sexual violence was a common strategy of the counterinsurgency forces, as women were threatened, kidnapped, raped, and tortured by the military in the early 1980s. As M. Brinton Lykes notes, "Under conditions of . . . state-sponsored violence, violence against women takes on additional dimensions of horror," a quality that the Guatemalan army apparently understood all too well.[8] In his study of the violence in the Ixcán, Jesuit priest Ricardo Fall noted that when women were captured and raped by soldiers they were often forced to cook and clean for them afterward. In at least one case, soldiers fresh from the bloodlust of a massacre forced the surviving young women of the village to strip and dance for them; they then raped them.[9] This kind of sexually enforced servitude humiliated and broke women down both emotionally and physically. By invading their homes, their bodies, and their work, the military was able to demonstrate that it fully dominated even the most intimate spheres of the women's worlds.[10]

Rape is a source of "silent suffering," which soldiers used as a specific weapon of war against Mayan women. However, the guilt and shame of rape victims, compounded by Mayan and Latin cultural mores, prevents women from seeking help for the *tristeza* brought about by the assaults.[11] In many cases, women suffer chronic gynecological problems as a consequence of their assault, for which they are reluctant or unable to seek treatment.[12]

The victims continue to feel shame and fear recrimination from their families and communities. As a result, they are even more likely than other types of victims to feel isolated and withdrawn from everyday life. Rape victims, like women victims of violence in general, are also more likely to be sharp, impatient, and abusive toward their children, thus passing to the next generation the indirect consequences of the violence they suffered.[13]

In psychological terms, the mourning for a person who "disappeared" is more attenuated than for a person who is known to be dead, even when the known dead died a violent death. By the same token, the process of grief is more pronounced and extended for a victim of violent death than it is when a person dies of natural causes.

The process of mourning for the disappeared in a distinctly Mayan sense is an explicitly gendered, enduring reaction to the violence and relates to the indeterminate disposition of the victims' remains. Within the Mayan cosmovision, even among orthodox Catholics and Protestants, there is an ongoing relationship with the dead.[14] For survivors, this essential relationship cannot be realized fully until the lost relative is known without doubt to be dead and the remains of the loved one are put to rest properly, in a place where they can be honored. Under this cosmovision, without according the dead their proper status, survivors are unable to establish the postlife relations with loved ones that are essential to the maintenance of family and community coherence. When a Mayan *campesino* was asked why he had not sought refuge in Mexico, his answer was, "Because my father died, they killed him here and I can't leave him here alone. And I leave him cigarettes and *guaro* [cane liquor] [to honor him in death]. . . . It's important to do because he enjoyed them and that way he will be content."[15]

In particular, women report ongoing and imperative dreams of lost fathers and husbands from which they cannot find relief until the bodies are located and given proper burial.[16] Such apparitions constitute a disturbing presence for survivors. In one observer's words, "The armed forces literally expelled people from the world of the living, but as death was not expelled, the spirits cannot be disposed of—they form a new sort of patrol, becoming another terrifying presence, persecuting the living."[17] Because of such issues, the process of exhumation and proper ritualized reburial is particularly important.[18]

The cultural impact of survival has had additional implications. Traditional Mayan society, like Guatemalan society in general, tends to be extremely patriarchal, with religious brotherhoods, councils of (male) elders, and kinship networks forming the loci of local power and identity.[19] In making the transition from wife to widow, women lost their status vis-à-vis that of their husbands. Mayan widows sometimes also lost their places within the local hierarchies of kinship, which complicated issues of patrilineal land ownership and exacerbated legal difficulties tied to women's rightful ownership of titles to land. Women whose husbands have disappeared and whose deaths are not registered in town records have particular trouble in obtaining title to their husbands' plots of land.[20]

In traditional Mayan society, widows normally have a sanctioned status within the community, where they enjoy respect and support. However, the complex and seemingly arbitrary nature of the violence stigmatized many war widows who, as a result, did not receive the economic and emotional help they needed from their villages and extended families. This forced widows into a new, highly marginalized social space within their own communities, ostracizing them from their traditional networks of kinship and other forms of social organization.[21]

The violence also isolated many women from their adult sons, who were called up to serve in the civil patrols and the army, or who decided to serve as *orejas* (literally, "ears") for the military. In addition, many adult sons disappeared from the communities; they were thought to have either joined the guerrillas, abandoned their families to live abroad, or been killed by the security forces. In such cases, the sons' ambiguous status served to further isolate their mothers within the community at large.[22]

In some locations, the effects of the violence were so pervasive as to leave "cities of women," villages in which adult males were effectively absent.[23] While the effects of such a gender vacuum of men were mainly deleterious, it did in some instances help to promote the opening of new political space to fill the void left by the collapse of traditional male-dominated venues of power and authority. Generally, these took the form of widows' organizations and cooperatives that addressed some of the economic and social needs of Mayan women who were marginalized not only within Guatemalan society at large, but even within their own communities.

As a widow from Malacatán, San Marcos, reported, "They killed my husband. I was left behind, suffering like I was a little girl. I didn't know how to manage money, nor work, nor did I know how to provide for the family. See, the life of a woman is among men, and the life of a woman alone with children is hard. I was left like a bird on dry branches."[24]

Beyond the traumas brought on by life as a single woman in a highly gendered society, women continue to suffer the long-term effects of *la violencia* in family life. Married women whose husbands return from fighting with the guerrillas or from military service suffer the double burden of dealing with male family members who are also affected by trauma and who also must readapt to life within the family. Wives and husbands must readjust gender roles of day-to-day life. More often than not, a woman who ran the household single-handedly while in exile or in the immediate aftermath of the war finds herself demoted to the previous status quo when she remarries or her husband returns.

The majority of widows, however, do not remarry. Rosalina Tuyuc of Coordinadora Nacional de Viudas de Guatemala (CONAVIGUA) estimates that only ten to fifteen of the widows of the fourteen thousand members of that national organization have formally remarried, although more women, reflecting the national pattern, have entered into informal consensual unions with men. While Tuyuc's figures are only rough estimates, they nonetheless point to the low incidence of remarriage among women widowed by public violence. The reasons behind the low rate of remarriage are both strategic and circumstantial. Some women do not remarry because they did not wish to subordinate themselves to a new husband. But many others cannot find a suitable and willing mate in a pool of men that is so greatly reduced by assassination and disappearance.[25]

The use and misuse of alcohol is common in rural Guatemala and drunkenness is a customary, even sanctioned, component of the traditional fiesta system dating back to the sixteenth century. However, the excessive use of alcohol outside of traditional venues has increased in the wake of the violence of the early 1980s. This is equally true of both witnesses to violence and perpetrators of it—that is, men who have served in the civil patrols, the army, or in the guerrilla forces. A study conducted for the Guatemalan army shows that upwards of 50 percent of cashiered soldiers become full-blown alcoholics.[26]

In addition, male witnesses or victims of violence are more likely than nonvictims or females to drink heavily in order to dull the emotional and psychological aftermath of their ordeals or to help them confront tense or fearful situations.[27] The increase in male alcoholism has resulted in a concomitant rise in family violence, with an increased incidence of wife and child abuse among male victims of political violence.

Among Mayan women, alcoholism was uncommon prior to the violence. However, anthropologists began to note by the 1990s that "regular drinking to escape grief and other suffering [had become] fairly common among women."[28] In addition, REHMI also reports that the incidence of alcohol abuse among women has increased significantly since the early 1980s.[29]

Guatemala has no statistical base that keeps data on violent acts against women, nor is there one that measures violence in the families of men who have been part of the armed forces or the security forces, or of the armed opposition. Nevertheless, there does seem to be a clear, if anecdotal, increased correlation between military service and the incidence of family violence.[30] In December 1996, Guatemala promulgated a strongly worded law against family violence. It defined a man's violence against his female partner as a violation of her human rights and called for "whatever methods of protection necessary to protect a woman's right to live in security and dignity."[31]

Despite this de jure guarantee of women's rights within the legal or consensual family, there are cultural constraints that prevent these decrees from having any teeth. There is a prevailing conception among non-indigenous and Maya alike that women are, at some level, the property of men. There is also the stereotype (hardly unique to the Guatemalan milieu) that women who provoke aggression from their husbands or *compañeros* bring it on themselves, and that the aggressors should feel no responsibility toward the victims. This view "legitimizes" violence against women, even in the eyes of law enforcement officials.[32]

This manifestation of the culture of violence is particularly evident in family behavior—abuse, beating, spousal rape, alcoholism—that even the perpetrators and the victims themselves may not understand to be the embedded consequence of years of civil violence. In this regard, a gendered response is clearly called for—not only for women, but also for men—to receive the training and counseling they need to cease abusive lifestyles before they pass them along to their sons and daughters. In an unrelentingly *machista* society, such lessons will not come easily. Indeed, given the fact that most adults in Guatemala have grown up in the aberrant climate of armed struggle and institutionalized repression, the task of social reconciliation in postconflict society is unusually challenging.

One of the enduring aspects of the violence of the early 1980s is the distrust that lingers within some nuclear families. The Guatemalan army encouraged children to inform on family members, and ill-feeling still remains among family factions that supported one or another partisan faction during the war. The distrust, hate, envy, and disintegration of cultural unity that resulted from the period of violence continue to have a deleterious effect on extended and nuclear family relations.[33]

A second long-term effect of violence is evident among the children (many of whom are now young adults) who were direct and indirect victims of *la violencia*. While this issue is outside the scope of this study, the long-term effects of childhood trauma, social upheaval, displacement, hunger, embedded fear, and wounded parenting have clear implications for Guatemala's young women and men today. This is especially true for children who lost not only close family members, but also their ethnic identity, community affiliation, and spiritual grounding. Among women and men alike, this is a population that is potentially at great risk.[34]

◦ **Women in the Political Arena**

The violence of the early 1980s pushed an unprecedented number of Mayan and *ladina* women into the political arena. Overwhelmingly, the proximate cause of political mobilization was trauma: the loss or disappearance of a loved one, or the economic and social exigencies of widowhood. The most important national and local women's organizations have their origin in trauma; in contemporary Guatemala, human rights and gender are conflated issues in most, though not all, women's organizations.

The largest women's organization in the country, CONAVIGUA, emerged as a Mayan widow support group in 1986, and now has more than fourteen thousand Mayan and *ladina* members nationwide. Coordinadora Nacional de Viudas de Guatemala (GAM), a human rights organization modeled after the Mothers of the Plaza de Mayo in Argentina, includes men in its organizations, but its membership is primarily female. Its organizational prominence has catapulted one of its surviving founders, Nineth Montenegro, into prominence as an important political player in the national arena. The same process has made smaller, local organizations a greater or lesser source of women's empowerment toward social and political advancement in civil society; examples of these smaller-scale organizations are groups such as Kak'chin Konojel, Mujeres Maya Ixil, and Mama Maquín.[35]

The following table shows the number of women elected to office, and the percentage of total elected offices that they hold in each category.[36] There are proportionally a fair number of women serving in elected office at the departmental and national levels, but women are not as well represented at the municipal level of government.

	Diputadas		Governors	
1999	13/113	(11.5%)	2/22	(9%)
2000	8/113	(7%)	6/22	(27%)

Women's voter participation is relatively high. In the presidential election held at the end of 1999, the female vote accounted for 48 percent of the votes in the first round and 35 percent in the second round. Nevertheless, many women view the right to vote as an extension of their husbands' franchise, and tend to vote as their husbands instruct them.[37]

The obvious question is, what happens when the effects of *la violencia* and the long civil war dissipate. Will there be a political space for women in civil society? Without trauma to expand the parameters of politics within the boundaries the domestic sphere, will women be willing to enter politics or to take advantage of the newly opened public

---

Relevant Peace Accords

Global agreement on human rights:
- Guaranteed rights for women
- Eliminate discrimination against women
- Ensure women's right to participate in civil power

Agreement for the Resettlement of Populations Displaced by the Armed Confrontation:
- Guarantees for the resettlement of the displaced populations . . . to make particular emphasis on the promotion of families headed by women, particularly women and orphans which have been most affected

Agreement on the identity and the rights of indigenous peoples:
- Criminalize the sexual harassment of indigenous women
- Combat the discrimination against women in agrarian reform

Agreement on [the] strengthening of civil power and the rule of the military in a democratic society:
- Strengthen women's organizations in rural and urban settings

Agreement on socioeconomic issues and the agrarian reform:
- Equality of opportunities and conditions, promoting women's access to study, training, credit, land, productive and technological resources
- Participation of women in economic and social development
- Recognize the obligation of the state to promote the elimination of all forms of discrimination against women
- Recognize the undervalued contribution of women in all aspects of economic and social activity, particularly her work in favor of improving the community

Sources: Morales Trujillo, "Las obligaciones legislativas"; and Waugh, "Gender Issues in the Special Objective," p. 3.

space? Will women be willing to enter the public sphere if they no longer perceive politics as an extension of the domestic sphere?

Certainly, there is a political will from both outside Guatemala and, to a lesser extent, within, to ensure that this will be so. The peace accords include several specific agreements that specifically address the rights of women, including the establishment of a Foro Nacional de la Mujer to promote women's issues and to ensure that the terms of the accords are met.[38] As powerful Frente Republicano Guatemalteco leader Zury Ríos Soto puts it, "The accords are the floor on which a house can be built."[39]

There are nearly 150 specific accords, with hundreds of separate mandates. The examples listed in the sidebar offer an incomplete but representative selection that illustrates the tone of the peace accords' mandates that address women's rights and women's roles in postconflict Guatemalan society.

Since 1996, the National Assembly has promulgated a wide spectrum of laws regarding women's rights within the family, protection of women against family violence, and women's rights to own and sell land in their own names.[40] The government of Guatemala has also endorsed the Beijing Platform of Action and the Summit of the Americas.[41] There is some political will to create a permanent National Institute of Women (Instituto Nacional de la Mujer) to guarantee that women's rights are a priority in future legislation and policy planning on a national level.[42]

Nevertheless, female political activists across Guatemala's wide political spectrum remain dubious as to the genuine political will on the part of male policymakers toward advancing meaningful legislation and social policy furthering the advancement of women, even in basic areas such as education and women's health.[43] Nor do even prominent women political figures tend to embrace a feminist or even a specifically gender-based political vision. As Nineth Montenegro, cofounder of GAM, ex-*diputada,* and, most recently, vice-presidential candidate for the New Nation Alliance (ANN), expressed it, "I am not a feminist. . . . The priority has been social struggle, not simply the needs of women."[44]

For most of the prominent women interviewed, gender questions are most important at the points where they intersect with larger conceptions of social justice. Gender's secondary place on the agenda of priorities is evident across the political spectrum. In the view of former *guerrillera* Yolanda Colom, "the oppression of women is not separate from the revolutionary movement," but is nonetheless subordinate to the oppression of the poor inflicted by the dominant class. Nineth Montenegro of the ANN feels that "men have stereotypes of women and women have stereotypes of men. There is not solidarity, but it's the fault of the system that they haven't dropped these prejudices to be able to work with one another." For Zury Ríos, women are not proportionally active in national politics because "the work demands discipline, and many women don't have it."[45]

What is important, however, is the intersection of social reconciliation, political development, and gender. Common points of conjuncture include such issues as human rights and, most emphatically, education for girls, an issue raised by nearly every female political figure in this study. Prominent women in politics all argue that the woeful lag in fundamental education for girls is the single greatest source of gender inequity in Guatemala, and as such is a critical issue that must be addressed, even at high political cost. Nevertheless, even for women in politics, gender appears to be a secondary category of analysis, behind ethnicity or nongendered political ideology.

Despite some promising and tangible signs of advancement, there are a number of obstacles that stand in the way of vindicating women in the wake of Guatemala's long war. Despite the pivotal *Agreement on the Identity and Rights of Indigenous Peoples* in the peace accords and some significant social will toward correcting Guatemala's deep-rooted racism, indigenous women still labor under a double stigma, and this is true of no sector so much as the victims of the violence of the 1980s. However, since nearly twenty years have passed since the worst conflagrations of civil violence, it is important that policy also be directed toward the interests of those affected women whose posttraumatic stress is not so apparent in contemporary civil society.

• Notes

1. Bell, Kobrak, and Spirer, *State Violence*, fig. 4.1.
2. Ibid., chap. 15, p. 1.
3. Ibid.
4. L. Green, *Fear as a Way of Life*, p. 247.
5. Pro-Niño y Niña Centroamericanos (PRONICE), *Violencia organizada*, pp. 54–55.
6. Oficina de Derechos Humanos del Arzobispado de Guatemala (ODHAG), *Informe proyecto interdiocesano (REHMI)*, vol. 1, p. 3.
7. Ibid., pp. 45–47.
8. Lykes et al., "Human Rights and Mental Health," p. 527.
9. ODHAG, *REHMI*, vol. 2, pp. 213–214.
10. Falla, *Masacres de la selva*, p. 132.
11. PRONICE, *Violencia organizada*, pp. 54–55.

12. Rosalina Tuyuc, interview, March 2000.

13. Utz Kaslemal, inteview, March 2000.

14. See Colby and Colby, *Daykeeper.*

15. PRONICE, *Efectos psicosociales,* p. 42.

16. Priest in Alta Verapaz, interview, March 2000.

17. Zur, *Violent Memories,* p. 224.

18. ODHAG, *REHMI,* vol. 1, p. 31.

19. Zur, *Violent Memories,* p. 224.

20. Equipo de Antropología Forense de Guatemala, "Las masacres en Rabinal," pp. 287–288.

21. Winch, "Maya Women's Organizing," pp. 60–61.

22. Camey Huz, "Estrategia de desarrollo," pp. 32–33.

23. OIM, FONAPAZ, SEPAZ, USAID, "Programa de asistencia," cuadro no. 3-B, p. 38.

24. Widow from Malacatán, San Marcos, quoted in ODHAG, *REHMI,* vol. 1, p. 227.

25. Tuyuc, interview, March 2000.

26. García Aguilar, *Moral y educación militares 1988,* cited in Nájera, "Estadísticas sobre abusos," p. 67.

27. ODHAG, *REHMI,* vol. 1, p. 49.

28. Zur, *Violent Memories,* p. 212.

29. Ibid.

30. Nájera, "Estadísticas sobre abusos," p. 7.

31. "Mujer y derechos humanos," unpublished manuscript, p. 15.

32. Ibid., p. 14.

33. Camey Huz, "Estrategia de desarrollo," p. 27.

34. See PRONICE, *Efectos psicosociales.*

35. Zamora and Camey, "Informe de la organización a nivel nacional."

36. http://www.c.net.get/ceg/doctos/listadiput.html; and "Participación cívico política de las mujeres," 2000, photocopy, no attribution.

37. Ibid.

38. See Foro Nacional de la Mujer, "Plan de acción mujeres y desarrollo," pp. 1–5.

39. Zury Ríos Soto, interview, March 2000.

40. See Irwin, "Gender, Cash Cropping, and Land Purchase."

41. Asociación Mujeres Vamos Adelante, "Attachment 2."

42. "Derechos de la mujer," unpublished manuscript, p. 10.

43. Ríos Soto, Nineth Montenegro, Aura Marina Otzoy, Yolanda Colom, interviews, all March 2000.

44. Montenegro, interview, March 2000.

45. Colom, Montenegro, and Ríos Soto, interviews, all March 2000.

2

El Salvador and Guatemala: Refugee Camp and Repatriation Experiences

Patricia Weiss Fagen and Sally W. Yudelman

Throughout the decade of the 1980s (1979–1991) civil war ravaged El Salvador, and the insurgent Farabundo Martí National Liberation Front (FMLN) became the dominant force in several communities in the east and center of the country. During those same years, a cyclical conflict, which had begun in Guatemala in the 1960s, broke out again. Conflict began earlier and lasted longer in Guatemala than in El Salvador, striking different parts of the country at different times. During the conflict in El Salvador, villages and crops were razed and household members massacred, leaving survivors little choice but to flee. Consequently, during the 1980s, large areas of the countryside were almost emptied of civilians. In Guatemala during the early 1980s, the Guatemalan military targeted the highland areas with counterinsurgency campaigns. Violence was directed at both Maya and Ladinos believed to be sympathetic to the Unidad Revolucionaria Nacional Guatemalteca (URNG) insurgents, but the Mayan communities were hardest hit. An unprecedented and murderous military sweep cut through the highland and adjacent lowland areas of the country between 1981 and 1983, decimating and driving out the survivors. In El Salvador and Guatemala, as in other civil conflicts, civilians generally and women and children in particular bore the brunt of the violence and human rights violations.

A minority of the Salvadorans and Guatemalans who took flight were officially recognized and assisted as refugees by the United Nations High Commissioner for Refugees (UNHCR). Of these, the largest and most important groups were the approximately twenty thousand Salvadorans who walked across the borders into Honduras, and forty-six thousand Guatemalans who made their way to the state of Chiapas in Mexico.[1] This chapter explores the experiences of the female populations in the two refugee areas and what happened when they returned. More specifically, it describes the conditions and programs in the refugee camps that affected the self-images, technical skills, and community participation of female refugees. It then explains the constraints that prevented women refugees from applying their skills and sustaining their community participation on their return. Finally, it discusses the policy implications of its findings and conclusions.

• Women Refugees from El Salvador

◦ Conditions Prior to the War

Nearly all communities in what was to become the war zone depended primarily on subsistence agriculture. Families were large, and single-parent homes were infrequent. Male and female roles were clearly differentiated, with women rarely involved in productive work outside of household gardens. Families generally accepted the notion that girls did not need formal education, and therefore girls attended school far less often than boys. As a rule, women did not take public roles in community affairs or local organizations. To be a "good woman" implied acceding to male authority. Hard work and "earning their keep" were the most valued female virtues.[2] Although imbued with the importance of being responsible, girls were not taught the skills needed to survive and raise children on their own. Because of the political ferment and the intensive level of grass-roots organization prior to the outbreak of conflict, however, women as well as men became politically aware and committed.

◦ In the Refugee Camps in Honduras

The FMLN fighters typically brought their families to the Honduran border or provided cover so that they could cross and find safety. Consequently women significantly outnumbered men in the three Honduran refugee camps: Colomoncagua, Mesa Grande, and the smaller San Antonio. The majority of the refugees, women as well as men, belonged to or were loyal to one of the five insurgent FMLN groups. Both the FMLN and the minority of males in the camps encouraged women to work and to participate in the political sphere. Female participation was viewed as an important contribution to the shared struggle. While neither men nor women questioned the latter's exclusive responsibility in the domestic realm, domestic burdens were substantially lightened by the basic assistance provided to refugee families by international agencies and nongovernmental organizations (NGOs).

The refugee camps were enclosed spaces, heavily guarded by Honduran security forces. There was no freedom of movement and little land for agriculture, which had defined the refugees' lives prior to the war. The refugees feared and resented the constant vigilance of the Honduran soldiers surrounding the camps. However, the international nongovernmental and humanitarian organizations and solidarity groups present in the camps won the trust of the refugee population, and were sympathetic to their political objectives.

A number of NGOs contracted by UNHCR introduced productive projects in the form of *talleres* or workshops intended to partially furnish the material needs of the refugee population. These workshops often involved tasks that normally would have been defined as male pursuits, such as production of household goods or shoes, as well as carpentry and mechanics. Although most of the women preferred traditional activities (sewing, pottery making, etc.) to nontraditional activities, the international agency personnel, many of whom were women, encouraged refugee women to engage in unfamiliar projects. "When we left [El Salvador]," one woman explained, "we were very ignorant. We just knew how to have kids and cook for our husbands; we didn't understand anything about how things should be for women. . . . In the camps, there were lots of people from other countries who came to give some kind of training to the people and we got some good experiences from them." Agency personnel taught the women that they had the same rights and abilities as men. Because most workers in the refugee camps were women, the refugee population as a whole became familiar with seeing women in roles other than wife and mother.

It is not known the extent to which women refugees became genuinely skilled workers in the variety of crafts available, but women's involvement in collective work and camp organization was strong in all three camps.[3] Nearly all participated in some way in public life, though the nature of the participation varied. Many of the women had little time for the formal workshops, either because they had young children under their care or because they had other forms of engagement. Politically active women were often involved in camp organization and mobilizations that took a significant amount of time; a few of the younger women were part-time combatants who crossed the border with the men.[4] The Catholic Relief Services, which had oversight responsibility for the workshops, emphasized acquisition of administrative, managerial, and organizational capacities as much as technical skills, and reported strong refugee participation in training classes.[5] In Mesa Grande, where participation in formal workshops was smaller than in the other camps, the women formed a female battalion who stood guard in the camp and kept order among men who drank excessively or mistreated women.[6]

The women worked together and often worked beside the men in carrying out new activities and, contrary to what had been the case in home communities, they carried out many traditional tasks collectively. The international agencies left a large range of decisionmaking to the refugees, with the intention of building organizational abilities. Since women predominated in the population and fully participated in refugee committees, the self-government measures had the double effect of strengthening their organizations and bonding them further.[7] Finally and perhaps of greatest long-term importance, the refugee camps offered healthcare and educational opportunities hitherto unavailable to most of the rural poor in El Salvador. In the refugee camps, women had access to and practiced family planning. Virtually all children went to school and adult women could attend literacy classes. The women refugees treated the options open to them in different ways, some availing themselves of every opportunity to learn a skill or to gain community leadership, while others utilized health and educational services for their families but participated less in productive work or mobilizations. What was important in strengthening the feelings of self-esteem among the female population generally was the fact that these refugee women could *choose* to become laborers, community leaders, and security guards, and thereby demonstrate responsibility and female authority.

Nevertheless, living in closed camps far from home was distressing and stressful, and both women and men wished to return to El Salvador. When the FMLN promoted a return movement, very few of the refugees stayed behind. The women as well as the men were homesick, tired of the restrictions imposed on them, and eager to reclaim their citizenship and political activism. Despite opposition from UNHCR and the Salvadoran government, the women and men in the Mesa Grande, Colomoncagua, and San Antonio camps insisted on leaving in collective movements they themselves organized and to places their leadership had designated. They negotiated and organized a series of highly visible collective returns to communities they knew to be still in zones of conflict.

○ Return to El Salvador

The collective repatriations, called *masivas,* began in 1989 and continued during the last years of the war. They were, in fact, intended as part of the war effort. The FMLN had determined that its negotiating position in the peace talks would be enhanced as refugees and internally displaced groups repopulated the conflict zones. The refugees responded by claiming their right to return to contested areas, and they demonstrated their continuing revolutionary commitment by re-creating in their own country many of the organizational elements they had created in the refugee camps. The majority of the Honduras-based refugee camp population was already back in El Salvador by the time the peace accords were signed in early 1992.

Although returning to a devastated landscape and facing dire poverty, the returnees received help from many of the same groups that had shown solidarity toward them in the refugee camps. Foreign donors wishing to support the revival of civilian life in the former conflict zones provided fairly generous funding to the returnee communities (and continue to do so, albeit in declining amounts). Because of the political encouragement and material assistance, the women interviewed reported being optimistic at first that the achievements and skills they brought from the refugee camps could be utilized. Many used donor funds and invested considerable effort in establishing income-generating projects such as crafts and small stores. To their great disappointment, most of the enterprises failed within a short time, due to inadequate markets, stiff competition, and competing demands on women's time.

Before the peace accords, returnee women in El Salvador were still encouraged to be politically active. Without the basic family subsistence and support they had received as refugees, however, women's domestic duties expanded significantly upon return. They discovered that it was far more difficult to maintain forms of community involvement even while there was political support for them to do so. Meeting the challenges of family survival took precedence and the burden of doing so was almost entirely on their shoulders. Until the war formally ended, the men still considered themselves primarily as military and political actors. According to their wives and partners, the fact that men had grown accustomed to seeing the basic needs of their families met by others (i.e., the organizations in the refugee camps) caused them to devote less attention to the care and support of their children than they had prior to the war.

In early 1992, a comprehensive peace agreement finally ended more than a decade of fighting. Thereafter, male attitudes about appropriate roles for women again changed or, more accurately, reverted to what they had been prior to war and exile. Conditions did as well. The peace accords had expanded possibilities for political participation but brought no relief to rural poverty. While postconflict international support for microenterprises of various sorts did provide opportunities for female labor, these did not significantly change the very limited opportunities for income generation in rural Salvadoran communities. A combination of factors related to poverty and male resistance made it all but impossible for the Salvadoran women in returnee settlements to use the skills and organizational capacities they had recently acquired. Economic frustration and disappointment among the men caused alcoholism and violence to reemerge and intensify. Again, as before the war, the communities depended on subsistence agriculture. Men dominated public and political spheres. Collective work, political participation, and organization among women further declined.

If the lives of the refugee women and their families have returned to prewar patterns, what has changed? Clearly, the women themselves feel that they have changed significantly. Although tied to their homes by family and domestic tasks, they nonetheless welcome opportunities to meet and seek common solutions to shared problems.

With regard to education, former refugee women interviewed are adamant in their commitment to school for the girls as well as the boys in their families. Sadly, women living in poor rural communities sometimes find it difficult to realize this commitment when faced with strong economic pressures. Thus, daughters are still less likely than sons to attend school, or more likely to be taken out to help at home. Gradually, as educational opportunities expand, it is more likely girls will receive schooling. Family planning has become more prevalent in rural areas thanks to advocacy by Salvadoran women's organizations, partly influenced by the returnees.[8] Rural families, however, remain large. Given the levels of movement, migration, and communications channels in El Salvador, it is hard to imagine that even rural women will continue to willingly accept the small spaces they have thus far occupied in politics and society.

Not surprisingly, there is a continuing pattern of migration from the rural areas, including the repatriate communities. Migration is especially strong among the young women who came of age in the effectively urban environments of refugee camps, and who now prefer the crowded and dangerous urban centers to the seemingly hopeless rural poverty. These young women are literate and usually more skilled than their mothers in nondomestic tasks; hence, they consider their prospects to be relatively better than what they are leaving behind. These younger, more mobile, now-urban young women bear watching.

• Women Refugees from Guatemala

◦ Before the War

The women who became refugees were overwhelmingly of peasant origin. Two-thirds identified with one of Guatemala's twenty-two indigenous Mayan groups. The remaining third considered themselves to be Ladinas (mixed-bloods), a designation that is often culturally rather than racially defined. While most originated from towns and villages in the highland areas, over 40 percent of those who later took flight were the products of a previous (voluntary) migration to the lowlands of Ixcan and the Petén, referred to as "colonized" areas.[9] Few poor rural women in Guatemala had more than occasional access to healthcare. The women had large families but only rudimentary knowledge related to maternity or sexuality. As in El Salvador, education was neither fully accessible nor free, and was not viewed to be important for girls. Few of the women spoke Spanish well, if at all, and their Mayan languages and dialects were not mutually intelligible. Women generally married early and their activities revolved around household duties.

The people of Mayan origin who constitute the majority population in Guatemala have experienced major discrimination throughout that nation's history. This discrimination has greatly exacerbated their poverty. The cultural separateness of the indigenous groups from the social and economic mainstream was especially profound among the Mayan women. It would initially complicate relations between them and those who would be their mentors in the refugee camps in Mexico.

◦ The Refugee Experience

Most Guatemalan refugees arrived in the southernmost Mexican state of Chiapas during the early 1980s with families intact. The refugees in Mexico found themselves in areas inhabited largely by ethnic Maya, culturally similar to themselves. They were welcomed at first, but because of the scarce land and resources in the region, their presence soon became burdensome. Political tensions in Chiapas were already high, and they intensified during the 1980s and 1990s. The Mexican government believed the refugee population to be fueling the already conflictive atmosphere in the region, and treated it with hostility. On grounds that the Guatemalan guerrillas were crossing the border, the Mexican government insisted on moving about one-half the refugee population, which was then widely disbursed in settlements in Chiapas, to more concentrated settlements in the states of Quintana Roo and Campeche.

The conditions in refugee camps for Guatemalans in Mexico, as for the Salvadorans in Honduras, obliged men and women to take on new roles that broke with the traditions of their native villages. Like their Salvadoran counterparts, the Guatemalan women reported significant changes due to the refugee experience. And, in a similar fashion, they learned that they had options apart from being wives and mothers.

Schools were available for both boys and girls in Mexico, and the women enthusiastically supported the idea of schooling for their daughters. The NGOs made efforts to improve literacy among the adult women as well. They trained some of the already literate refugees to become educational promoters and to offer classes for adults, but the results were disappointing. Relatively few women satisfactorily completed literacy training, often pleading domestic duties as the reason for abandoning the courses. There were other problems. One of them lay in the inadequacies of the promoters, who were often barely literate themselves and, perhaps more significant for their female students, were predominantly male. The deeper reason for failure seems to have been the lack of confidence the women felt about their abilities. "I have a hard head," they sometimes commented to their teachers, or "at my age it is hard to make friends with the ABCs."[10]

With regard to healthcare, women reported having received basic women's health examinations for the first time while in refugee camps. When introduced to family planning, they at first were reluctant to consider it and feared discussing the matter with their partners, whom they expected to disapprove. Ultimately, however, many took advantage of the means provided. As in the case of education, the preponderance of male health professionals and promoters sometimes undercut women's willingness to seek medical attention. Yet they did make use of health clinics, and did so increasingly as women came to be trained as health promoters. Women also made use of opportunities to gain information about hygiene, nutrition, and child care. Neither men nor women among the refugees received counseling or other psychological assistance, even though this was recognized among the relief community as a serious need.

Refugees in settlements in Campeche and Quintana Roo were permitted to work up to a hundred days a year outside the settlements, and more than 40 percent of the women worked at intervals to supplement family income. It was fairly easy for women in these two settlements to find wage jobs in the tourist sector, and this first-time-ever income-earning opportunity contributed substantially to their self-esteem and independence. Potential jobs in Chiapas were fewer, residing mainly in agriculture and occasionally in work as maids. In Chiapas, however, women's organizations became most firmly rooted, and UNHCR gave financial support for gender and other forms of training.

A large number of NGOs, international and Mexican, worked with the refugees and especially the women in all three states, encouraging collective activities and organization. Much of the training was unstructured. The workers in camps and settlements sought to raise awareness among groups of women about concerns closest to their daily lives and about their inherent rights. When later asked what they had learned, the women in the interview sample most clearly recalled discussions about gender issues and women's rights to organize and participate.[11] Whereas in the Salvadoran case the agencies emphasized general capacity building, the agencies and organizations working with Guatemalan women engaged them in a more feminist discourse. Perhaps the most significant gain for women refugees was that virtually all became bilingual. Learning Spanish was a prerequisite to acquiring new skills and was essential to their interactions both with one another and with the support organizations that assisted them.

Women's organizations were the major vehicles for the incorporation of women into community life, especially in Chiapas. Slowly, the idea of organizing won acceptance from the women as well as from male family members who normally would have opposed their wives' and daughters' participation. By the 1990s, women's organizations had taken strong root among the refugee women in Mexico. The women saw that participating in the organizations would help them not only to meet their needs for food and health care, but also to preserve their indigenous culture. "We are now organized and we are learning. We have a voice . . . and we can speak."[12]

The most prominent of the organizations to mobilize refugee women was the Organización de Mujeres Guatemaltecas, Mama Maquín. Mama Maquín was established formally in 1990 in Chiapas. It was promoted, guided, and generously supported by Mexican and international NGOs, bilateral agencies, and by UNHCR to organize spaces in which women could meet and discuss issues of importance to them. Two additional organizations, Madre Tierra (Mother Earth) and Ixmucané, subsequently broke from Mama Maquín, and established themselves in Campeche and Quintana Roo respectively. The three promoted women's rights to be heard, to be educated, to organize, and to participate in the community. The organizations also promoted training in literacy, human rights, reproductive health, and leadership skills. For the women who participated in Mama Maquín and the other organizations, their world became larger and self-confidence grew. The formation of female leadership in the poor indigenous Guatemalan population was no longer an exceptional phenomenon. The leaders, moreover, intended to maintain their organization and ideals once back in their country.

Soon after women's organizations and female community participation gained wide acceptance, the refugee repatriation movement drew the women away from the women's issues that first brought them together. As one researcher familiar with the work of Mama Maquín put it, the women "had only about two years of feminization."[13] From 1992 on, Mama Maquín and the other women's organizations devoted their efforts fully to mobilizing on behalf of the return movement. Each of the collective returns that took place between 1992 and 1996 was a struggle, but for the women involved, these struggles were also empowering.[14]

The major organizational vehicle for the refugee return movement was the Permanent Commission (CCPP), established by the refugees with URNG involvement in 1987. The commission represented the refugee community in negotiations with Guatemalan government officials on land grants, rights for returnees in Guatemala, and other arrangements. The Directive Committee of the CCPP (symbolically) admitted women delegates in 1990.

The CCPP divided into three branches, each of which accompanied returning refugees to a different geographic area in Guatemala. The corresponding women's organization—Mama Maquín, Madre Tierra, or Ixmucané—went with them, but the three collaborated and shared objectives. With the first collective refugee return in 1992, the movement drew increasingly on the energies and organizational capacities of the women. When the refugee women who had so enthusiastically mobilized for this cause headed home themselves, however, the space for female political organization was drastically diminished.

∘ Return to Guatemala

Interviewed four or more years after their return to Guatemala, former refugee women expressed disappointment. Not only were their expectations of continued female participation, learning, and organized action in the return communities unfulfilled, but they faced new forms of insecurity, isolation, and want. Refugees who returned prior to the implementation of the peace accords were frequently harassed by military forces, despite having negotiated agreements that were supposed to protect them. The 1996 Peace Accords largely removed the military presence, but did not necessarily lower levels of violence. First, others sometimes contested areas of land the refugees claimed was theirs. Second, the government had given land formally claimed by the departed refugees to other people, often conditioned on loyalty to the military and service in the civilian patrols. As recounted by Clark Taylor and Paula Worby, many of the returning refugees faced the hostility of the new occupants, who found reasons not to leave.[15] Usually the rival claimants reached some agreement. Nevertheless, violence persisted in a number of communities whose residents resented the returnees from Mexico, not only because of the land they had acquired, but also due to the assistance they received from international and national humanitarian sources.[16]

Women experienced added difficulties. Overall, education, training, and organizational initiatives were interrupted during the process of resettling, reintegrating, and struggling to survive. While the Salvadoran returnees had settled together and maintained their organizations, the Guatemalans—outside of a few cooperatives—were largely dispersed. The refugee promoters for education and health were similarly scattered. The return movement separated women who had developed relations of trust by living in close proximity. Indeed, return brought many of the refugees to settlements far from their places of origin. Even those who returned to their places of origin reported finding strangers who had migrated there during the conflict. Thus the returnees often lived in communities where residents did not know each other, and their very different experiences fomented mutual distrust. In the absence of the catalyzing energy of the outside entities that mobilized, supported, and guided the women in exile, they found it difficult to build new relationships of confidence with their neighbors.

The obstacles to maintaining the gains made in Mexico seemed overwhelming. The women lived in extreme poverty; they felt isolated in new communities dispersed over a wide area; they lacked access to adequate education and health services; and they could not maintain proper nutrition levels for themselves and their children. Above all, the two seemingly insurmountable impediments were the renewed hostility of male family members to their continued community organization and participation, and the absence of support from NGOs, international agencies, and their own organizations.

While women had changed as a result of their experiences as refugees, men had changed little or not at all. As in El Salvador, the men no longer looked favorably on their wives or daughters engaging in activities outside the home. And, in some cases, the exclusion went further. Among the women who had been most active in mobilizing and negotiating in favor of the return movement, there was a strong sense of betrayal. The CCPP had negotiated land from the Guatemalan government for cooperative settlement by refugees who did not have their own land in the highlands to which they could return. One of the major issues for which women successfully argued concerned their rights to land ownership within the cooperative structures. They won agreement that titles should be jointly held by both husband and wife, and should revert to widows. They also expected to be accepted as full members of the new cooperatives. In practice—despite advocacy in favor of these measures from UNHCR in Guatemala—the male leadership ignored the legal principle of co-ownership affirmed in Mexico and sometimes threatened women who tried to insist on their rights to land. As for membership in cooperatives, only a few women were able to obtain land by this means. One woman who tried to do so recalled being warned by the cooperative leaders: "If we [women] were going to participate in an assembly or . . . give our opinions, then they could get the police to take us out."[17]

All of the women interviewed emphasized the essential role that outside organizations had played for them and affirmed their continued need for such support. Importantly the Guatemalan women leaders maintained Mama Maquín, Madre Tierra, and Ixmucané upon their return. All three organizations continue to operate, albeit with differing levels of success. Members have initiated income-generating projects and educational campaigns, but the resources and reach are clearly inadequate to the needs. The development agencies that do work in the returnee areas do not seem to have harnessed the potential contributions that returnee women could make.

Again the question: In this scenario, what in fact has changed? The women who reported having been transformed as a result of their experiences in Mexico have not reverted to their former attitudes of subordination and insignificance. They recognize themselves to have special needs and rights and defend these to the best of their abilities, though it is often difficult to do so. Like their Salvadoran counterparts, Guatemalan returnee women want education for their girl children; but when poverty precludes school for all family members, the girls are still more likely than the boys to be withdrawn from classes.

The healthcare learning that took place in Mexico has been retained with regard to hygiene, family planning, and nutrition, yet scarce resources limit application of what has been learned. Nutritional levels have declined. NGOs have provided services to some communities and a few government programs now also exist, but far more are needed. Health promoters trained in Mexico continue to render services to

Guatemalan communities, but not to the extent possible in Mexico. Moreover, most of the health promoters working in the communities are male. Women in the communities, who would be able to establish trust more easily, have not received training.

On a more positive note, the fact that the refugee women have mastered Spanish continues to open doors to the outside world for them. They can talk and learn from each other and follow events that take place outside their homes. Their Spanish language, more worldly views, and greater knowledge of their rights and capacities place them in a far stronger position to survive and even to succeed than their counterparts who never left the country.[18] As in the case of El Salvador, the transformation of Guatemalan women in Mexico may prove more visible in their children's future than in their own.

• Summary and Conclusions

Salvadoran and Guatemalan men and women who became refugees had difficult lives full of insecurity and hardships before, during, and after the conflicts. The women, however, were transformed in important ways by a paradoxical combination of tragedy and opportunity. Driven from their homelands, they were wrested from traditional settings of dependency and subordination to male family members. Forced to break their prewar isolation, they developed abilities they had not previously needed. The Salvadoran and Guatemalan female refugees and returnees recount strikingly parallel experiences with respect to origins of the conflicts, life in the camps, expanding opportunities for women, women's participation in organizing the return movements, and what happened once they were again in their countries of origin.[19]

In the refugee camps, international organizations, local and international nongovernment organizations, and volunteers provided humanitarian assistance, skills training, and professional attention for the refugees. Professional women as well as male staff members working for UNHCR and humanitarian nongovernmental agencies assisted them, encouraged them to grow individually, and helped them to expand their skills and self-confidence. The efforts of female professional staff members were especially focused on women for whom they served as guides and mentors. They were not instructed to do so, but acted from personal interest in serving this population. Refugee women learned a wide range of new skills, including literacy, Spanish language (in the case of the Guatemalans), and productive trades. They engaged for the first time in community activities, and worked collectively. They made political contributions that were valued by the community as a whole, and in the process became more self-confident, aware of their rights, and more assertive. In both groups, women participated especially actively in organizing highly visible collective return movements. Indeed, the most important aspect of learning that took place was in the realm of organizational skills.

Although they shared a strong desire to return, and expected to be able to maintain their gains and achievements once back in their home countries, both groups experienced dramatic declines in participation following their returns. As a result of international support for the basic needs of the refugee population, women in the refugee camps had more time for community activities and education. Returning later to communities that were as poor or poorer than when they had left, and still subject to violence, the returnees generally, and the women in particular, had to struggle simply to survive. Thus, women living in rural returnee communities have had little space for making use of newly acquired skills.

Equally if not more important than poverty-derived domestic burdens was male opposition and isolation. Male family members, by and large, considered the expansion in women's roles and activities to be a function of war and exile, and they expected their wives and partners to return to prewar roles once the crisis was over. Women's attitudes had changed, but not those of their husbands and partners. Although returning refugees did receive international assistance, few international support groups accompanied the returnees to their communities. Those that did either were unable to support women's organization and self-help, or had other priorities. The women's organizations born in the refugee camps did not survive well in isolation, and the catalytic energy from outside supporters was greatly missed.

Today, the lives of the women who experienced empowerment in exile have reverted largely to the conditions of the status quo ante, but with changed attitudes. In both El Salvador and Guatemala, there is evidence that the impacts of their experiences are likely to change the futures of their children. There are already indications in both cases that the younger returnees who came of age in the camps are seeking alternatives to traditional female roles.

• Policy Implications

International and national organizations working in conflict situations and looking to contribute to building a sustainable peace could learn from the parallel experiences of the Salvadoran and Guatemalan women. For one thing, as a fundamental principle, women should not be treated as passive recipients of humanitarian assistance but as active partners in managing life in exile. Refugee women's organizations should be fostered in the camps, as occurred in the cases reported here. In addition, just as the refugee women in these organizations were actively involved in planning returns, so too should they be represented in peace processes from the earliest stages, and be involved in postconflict planning for the rehabilitation and reconstruction of their communities. This will require improved coordination between and among national and international entities and across national boundaries to ensure that women are not discriminated against legally or in terms of access to resources.

Efforts to help women both in refugee camps and after return should be institutional policy rather than individual initiative. Female professionals who accompanied and mentored the Salvadoran and Guatemalan women in the camps did so as individuals since their organizations had no gender policies. Refugee assistance agencies could usefully model such gender policies on the basis of the practices in the Salvadoran and Guatemalan camps. In these two cases, the efforts to achieve female empowerment that took place in the camps were not far advanced when the refugees returned home. As a general principle, agencies working in refugee camps should try their utmost not to abandon such long-term processes solely because refugees have crossed the border to once again become citizens in their own countries.

Postconflict policies and programs affirm the importance of poverty alleviation. For their efforts to be effective, policymakers should give priority to income-generating activities that help rural communities in general, and women-headed households in particular, to reach a basic subsistence level. This will require governments and other entities to ensure women's access to land and credit. To sustain women's gains in education, health, and job skills acquired in the camps, governments, NGOs, and international organizations can support similar training programs in returnee communities. One important means of sustaining skills is to offer further training to health and education promoters and provide appropriate accreditation and salaries to those committed to working in rural communities. Governments thereby could utilize more effectively existing women's (and men's) skills for grass-roots development.

Supporting women's empowerment and rights requires the strengthening of women's groups and organizations. To achieve this objective outside of the unique context of refugee camps, women will need access to labor-saving devices and a better distribution of the family work load. A will to participate is insufficient unless women also have time to devote to organizing and engaging in community activities. Last, but certainly not least, women traumatized by war, flight, and exile need access to programs that can help them deal with their emotional scars.

If postconflict governments are to fulfill their often-stated pledges to construct cultures of peace and greater equality, a productive beginning would be to include women in the process and provide them with greater access to opportunities and resources. Refugee women returnees, like the Guatemalans and Salvadorans, can and should be critical actors in the process of building more open, equitable, and participatory societies in the aftermath of civil wars.

Sustaining the gains these women and women in similar situations have made requires men in general, and husbands and partners in particular, to accept the reality that migration, economic decline, and war constitute an irreversible set of experiences that permanently changes women's lives. Just as it is clear from the experiences of the Salvadoran and Guatemalan women that conflict and violence can open space and opportunities for gender relations to change, it is also clear that, when the wars are over, most women cannot return to the status quo ante. National governments, international agencies, NGOs, and women's organizations share a responsibility to raise the awareness and consciousness of men about the positive and negative impact of war on women.

• Notes

This chapter is based on the findings of a project of the Promoting Women in Development Program supported by the Women in Development Office of USAID through the International Center for Research on Women and the Center for Population and Development Activities.

1. In addition to the camps in Honduras and Mexico, UNHCR also operated camps for Central American refugees in Belize, Costa Rica, Guatemala, Nicaragua, and Panama. The governments of the United States, Canada, Australia, and several European countries granted refugee recognition to varying numbers of Guatemalans and Salvadorans.

2. Vázquez, "Refugees and Returnee Women," p. 10.

3. Among the women interviewed by Norma Vázquez, 90 percent said they had specific responsibilities in the camps; 50 percent of those who were in Mesa Grande and 67 percent from Colomoncagua participated to some extent in the formal workshops. See Catholic Relief Services, "Report of a CARITAS–CRS Mission to Honduras," pp. 11, 30.

4. Norma Vázquez reports that some 70 percent of the women interviewed reported engaging in political activities in the camps and, in some cases, military actions across the border. See Vázquez, "Refugees and Returnee Women," p. 12.

5. A February 1989 Catholic Relief Services report to UNHCR on this objective does not distinguish women's and men's participation. Evidence indicates that the women in the largest and most tightly organized of the camps, Colomoncagua, were the most interested in learning specific skills and had the strongest participation.

6. Vázquez, "Refugees and Returnee Women," p. 12.

7. The self-government also had its negative side: refugee organizations closely adhered to FMLN directives, were generally intolerant of dissent, and sometimes meted out harsh punishments to members of their community.

8. Among these, Mujeres por la Dignidad y la Vida (Las Dignas) has been especially important and influential. The organization is composed of former combatants, and has devoted considerable research to issues of gender and empowerment.

9. A Church-supported colonization during the 1960s and 1970s brought a number of indigenous families from the highlands to more fertile lands in Ixcan, where for a time they prospered. However, the same repression that destroyed social fabric in the highland areas drove the "colonists" out of Ixcan as well. See Yudelman, Calabia, and Myers, *We Have a Voice.*

10. Cabarrús Molina, Gómez Grijalva, and Gónzalez Martínez, "Guatemalan Women Refugees and Returnees," p. 18.

11. Ibid.

12. Yudelman, Calabia, and Myers, *We Have a Voice,* p. 23.

13. Comment of Ligia Gónzalez Martínez, presenting the reports at a conference in El Salvador, sponsored by PROWID and hosted by Las Dignas, 21 February 2000.

14. In Oslo, the Guatemalan government and URNG signed an agreement that pledged support to collective repatriations, respect for returnees' rights, and access to land. This agreement did not come into force until the final peace agreements were signed in 1996.

15. See Taylor, *Return of Guatemala's Refugees,* and Worby, *Lessons Learned.*

16. The tensions in one village in Ixcan where the old population, returnees, and newcomers were mixed are recounted in Taylor, *Return of Guatemala's Refugees.*

17. Cabarrús Molina, Gómez Grijalva, and Gónzalez Martínez, "Guatemalan Women Refugees and Returnees," p. 31.

18. Clark Taylor, in *Return of Guatemala's Refugees,* describes the differences in attitudes and activism between the returnee community and the families who never left. In fact, in some communities these differences led to open hostility. Nevertheless, the returnees' determination to improve their situation has produced political results.

19. Adapted from Sally Yudelman and Heidi Worley, "Similarities in Lessons Learned and Recommendations," internal project document, 4 March 2000.

3

Confronting the Aftermath of Conflict: Women's Organizations in Postgenocide Rwanda

Catharine Newbury and Hannah Baldwin

The war and genocide in Rwanda during the first half of the 1990s shattered the dense social ties upon which women, both rural and urban, had relied in the past. In particular, these conflicts had a devastating effect on women's organizations, destroying their physical infrastructure and decimating their human resources. Many members and leaders were killed, while others fled into exile. Those who survived were left destitute, fearful, and alone. Yet in the aftermath of the conflicts, women's organizations, both new and old, took a leading role in efforts to rebuild the country. Offering a range of services, these groups helped women reconstruct their lives through emergency material assistance, counseling, vocational training, and assistance with income-earning activities. In addition, many organizations provided a space where women could reestablish social ties, seek solace, and find support.

The rapid proliferation of Rwandan women's organizations during the second half of the 1990s seems nothing short of remarkable. How was this possible, in the shattered social terrain of postgenocide Rwanda? What explains the large number of groups? What is the nature of these groups, and how have the activities of women's organizations changed as a result of the conflicts?

This chapter examines the nature, roles, and impacts of women's organizations in postconflict Rwanda. Specifically, it discusses the various factors that contributed to their emergence in postgenocide Rwanda, the wide range of activities they have undertaken, and the factors affecting their performance. It also discusses the role of the international community in supporting these associations.

• The Reemergence of Women's Organizations

After the war and genocide of 1994, most women in Rwanda found themselves in desperate circumstances. Those who had survived the conflicts faced not only economic hardship but also social isolation. Their communities had been shattered and dispersed, and the men on whom they had depended were dead or had fled. Women still had to confront daily issues of survival—how to find housing when so many homes had been destroyed; how to feed and clothe themselves and their surviving children, as well as other relatives or orphans they had taken in; and how to deal with the debilitating traumas, both physical and psychological, of the horrors they had seen and experienced.

It was in this context of severe crisis, where the state lacked the means to meet critical needs, that women began to seek ways of cooperating to confront common problems. Groups of women formed in rural areas, building on previous rural organizations that had provided economic and social support to their members. In Rwanda after the genocide, many of these organizations grouped together women of one ethnic group—either Hutu or Tutsi. But in some areas, multiethnic associations involving both Hutu and Tutsi reemerged. Recognizing their need to live together again and to find ways of supporting themselves through collaborative activities, Hutu and Tutsi women sought to overcome the mistrust spawned by the war and genocide.

In Kigali, the capital, women who had participated in national women's organizations before 1994 started to meet. They talked and offered each other mutual support, while voicing their concerns about the desperate conditions facing so many women and children. They then began to seek ways to meet these needs. Joined by Rwandan women who had returned to the country from exile, they began to rebuild organizations grouped within Pro-Femmes/Twese Hamwe, a preexisting umbrella organization of women's organizations. At the end of 1994, they drafted the Campaign for Peace as a means of addressing Rwanda's postgenocide social and economic problems. This program, focusing particularly on the critical needs of women and children in Rwanda, proposed ways of involving women in efforts to promote overall reconstruction and reduce social tensions.

A second factor contributed to the growth of women's organizations at this time: Rwanda's tradition of vibrant organizational activity. In the early postcolonial period, official policies of Rwanda's First Republic had supported social centers *(foyers sociaux)* for women in each prefecture.[1] These *foyers sociaux,* focused mainly on the needs of rural women, also provided opportunities for leadership to the educated young women who staffed them.[2] Later, beginning in the late 1970s during Rwanda's Second Republic under Juvénal Habyarimana, grassroots organizations, cooperatives, and NGOs grew in number, assisted by church-related groups as well as by increased funding for rural development in Rwanda from international NGOs and other donors.[3] A study conducted in the mid-1980s showed that most of the rural groups surveyed devoted at least some of their activities to social services for women and children (health and nutrition) and that some groups provided training, education, and rural *animation* for women. Significantly, however, few groups gave much attention to women's agricultural work—the roles of women as producers.[4] A tally of 1,457 organizations in 1986 showed that 493 of them (or about one-third) were women's socioeconomic groups, and 143 were registered as women's NGOs. These groups sought to bring more attention to the conditions women faced and the need for women's involvement in development.[5] Such proliferation of organizations, growing out of earlier experiences with cooperatives, NGOs, and self-help groups, was fueled by the decline of state social services (linked with the economic crises of the period, which created a greater need for social safety nets); political liberalization; and increased external support for organizations.

A third factor in the reemergence of women's organizations in Rwanda after 1994 was support from the international community.[6] Rwanda received large quantities of emergency aid after the genocide, and this aid had a major impact, even if it was insufficient to meet all needs. Some bilateral and multilateral donors, influenced by the lobbying of Rwandan women's groups and leaders, by the postgenocide government, and by expatriates convinced of the importance of gender, paid special attention to the needs and roles of women. Donor resources established a supportive context for the renewed growth of women's organizations at the grass-roots level, and donor support was also essential to rebuilding initiatives of Rwandan women's organizations at the national level. Overall, the effects of these activities were positive and important to Rwanda's reconstruction. Aided by donors, some national organizations were able to undertake especially ambitious projects. However, they did not always have sufficient administrative capacity to implement these effectively.

Finally, the policies of Rwanda's postgenocide government constitute a fourth factor encouraging the reemergence of women's organizations after the genocide. The Ministry of Gender and Promotion of Women's Development (Migeprofe, formerly Migefaso)[7] supported

women's groups by establishing a ministry representative in each prefecture and commune; these officials (who were usually, but not always,
women) worked alongside and placed pressure on local government authorities to bring attention to women's concerns. The results were impressive. A 1997 study estimated that in each of Rwanda's 154 communes there were an average of about 100 women's associations—or a
total of more than 15,400 groups. The study attributed this growth to
both government policy and outside aid organizations that encouraged
women to form such associations.[8] An added impetus came from the
local level, where commune authorities often distributed garden plots in
drained marshes to groups (but not to individuals).

Thus, the urgency of women's needs, the tradition of past organizational activity in the country (which had given some women experience in leadership), and government and donor support were all important for the reemergence of women's organizations in Rwanda after
1994. Yet each of these supportive factors also entailed contradictions.
Emergency relief was not always well-planned; dependence of organizations on external support deepened, and some organizations became
overextended. Moreover, dovetailing the structures and personnel of
earlier organizations with the concerns and priorities of new groups established in Rwanda after the genocide created certain obstacles. Meanwhile, both the government and external donors exerted considerable influence over what women's organizations were able to do and how they
did it, particularly at the national level. Therefore, the agendas and access to resources of women's organizations were seldom autonomous.

• Nature of Women's Organizations

After the genocide, women's solidarity was important both among those
who stayed in the country and among those who fled to the camps.
Within Rwanda, these groups served as essential support and therapeutic
networks for women who had experienced trauma. Those who fled often
had suffered as well, and in the refugee camps they reestablished networks to provide mutual support—in helping with child care, in gaining
access to necessary resources, and in discussing the genesis of conflicts
and possible avenues to peace. In fact, throughout this period of turmoil,
women's groups provided the country one of its few enduring social con-
tinuities. However, despite substantial similarities in the characteristics
of women's organizations in post-1994 Rwanda, compared with those of
the period before, there were also important differences. Two of these

are discussed in this section: the noticeable increase in the number of these groups, both local organizations in rural and urban areas and national women's organizations, and the expanded range and scope of activities undertaken by them. A third area of difference, the contribution of such groups to women's political participation, will be discussed later.

Although precise information on the number of grass-roots women's organizations in postgenocide Rwanda is not available, it is clear that by 1999 there were many—an average of a hundred per commune—and that they were contributing not only to rural women's economic advancement but also to their empowerment.[9] In rural areas, the effectiveness of grass-roots organizations was often enhanced by their involvement in larger umbrella groups, which provided technical assistance and material support to the member associations.[10] At the national level, older organizations resumed their activities after the war and genocide, and new ones were created. As in the late 1980s and early 1990s, these groups proliferated in response to crisis conditions, although the situation after the genocide was much more severe. Again, as before, this growth occurred in a context where the state lacked the means to meet critical needs, while external donors provided resources to encourage the development of organizations.[11]

While grass-roots asociations in the country were numerous in 1999, Rwandan women's organizations operating at the national level were, understandably, more limited in number—an estimated fifty organizations. Of these, a majority were members of the Pro-Femmes/ Twese Hamwe collective. Expanding from a base of thirteen member NGOs in the early 1990s, Pro-Femmes had almost tripled in size to incorporate a total of thirty-five NGOs by the end of 1996.[12] With this growth came a greater diversity in the types of organizations. Included in Pro-Femmes since 1996 are older women's organizations that had existed in Rwanda before the genocide, such as Duterimbere, Association des Guides du Rwanda, and Haguruka; organizations that had been founded by women in exile from Rwanda, such as Amaliza, Benishyaka, and Benimpuhwe; and new organizations created to deal with the aftermath of the conflicts, such as Avega, Asoferwa, and Association des Femmes Chefs de Famille.

The member associations of Pro-Femmes can also be categorized in terms of their particular objectives. One type provides assistance to women of one or more particular categories—for example, widows, orphans, women caring for orphans, girls, and rural women. A second type emphasizes a particular form of activity or profession and makes its services available to women in general—often with an emphasis on the needy and vulnerable. Examples of the first type include Avega Aga-hozo, which assists widows of the genocide, and the Association des Femmes Chefs de Famille, which helps female heads of households. Examples of the second type include Haguruka, which provides legal aid for women, and Duterimbere, which makes microcredit available to women.

The literature on women's organizations in Africa notes a tendency for urban-based groups to mirror existing social cleavages between ed-ucated elite women and poor rural women. Indeed, for a number of cases elsewhere in Africa, studies have shown that national women's or-ganizations often do more to promote the social status and well-being of the urban women who staff them, than to address the most pressing con-cerns of the rural majority.[13] One might well ask, then, to what extent national women's groups in Rwanda serve simply as an arena for edu-cated elite women to promote their own interests. It is true that many Rwandan women's organizations, now as in the past, provide jobs and a platform for elite women. It is not uncommon for the leaders of these groups to have connections of some type with politically promi-nent people.

Clearly, these organizations serve as a training ground on which women can acquire leadership skills and build networks that position them for participation in other activities in the public sphere. Yet the stated goals of most groups are to assist vulnerable women and promote their empowerment. To what extent have these goals been achieved? That is a more complicated question, requiring information that goes be-yond the reports and evaluations produced by the organizations them-selves. An assessment of this sort would require a more in-depth study than was possible for the present analysis.[14] It is worth noting, though, that however much the actual achievement of their goals might fall short, most of these women's organizations are clearly meeting real, urgent needs. This is recognized by a broad spectrum of Rwandan officials and expatriates involved in reconstruction in Rwanda. Criticism, when heard, tends to focus on administrative shortcomings and accounting problems, on the heavy dependence of these groups on external aid, or on the seem-ing multiplication of (and possible competition among) national groups whose goals and projects sometimes appear to overlap.

It is notable that although most of the member associations of Pro-Femmes maintain an office in Kigali, many actually conduct a signifi-cant part of their activities in towns and rural areas outside the capital.[15] But there is significant variation in the size and capacity of these groups to reach out. Only a minority of the member associations of Pro-Femmes command sufficient resources to pursue truly ambitious projects. This variation in size, resources, and capacities among the member organizations can be attributed in part to longevity. For example, two of the oldest NGOs, Réseau des Femmes Oeuvrant pour le Développement Rural and Haguruka, are also among the strongest institutionally. Each of these organizations has its own building, is staffed with competent personnel, and carries out important programs. Both have attempted to extend their activities to rural areas. Duterimbere, a well-established organization focused on helping women obtain credit, had been one of Rwanda's most visible and respected women's organizations in the late 1980s and early 1990s. But in the period following the genocide, this group was plagued with financial mismanagement and lost credibility with donors. After conducting a critical self-study and instituting policies to address these problems, Duterimbere appeared by mid-1999 to have regained strength and purpose as a national women's NGO offering important programs to assist women in need of credit.[16]

Longevity, however, is not the only indicator of strength. One of the largest and most active women's organizations in Rwanda today is Avega Agahozo, founded in January 1995 to assist widows who survived the genocide. Aided by substantial funding from donors, the group had grown to about ten thousand members by 1999.[17] Another postgenocide organization with impressive resources is Association de Solidarité des Femmes Rwandaises (Asoferwa). Founded in September 1994 to assist widows, single mothers, and orphans, this group had grown to more than fifteen hundred members by 1999. With forty paid employees, many of them social workers, Asoferwa has been able to provide a variety of social services in different parts of the country, including psychosocial counseling for young people in prison. The organization is particularly proud of their model village at Ntarama, constructed with assistance from the United Nations High Commissioner for Refugees (UNHCR) and other donors.[18]

By contrast, Seruka is an example of an organization that despite its relative longevity, commands only limited resources. Established in 1991, with the late Agathe Uwilingiyimana as one of its founders, the group assists female heads of households, orphans, and other vulnerable groups. With its main emphasis on rural areas, Seruka has sponsored programs to help women achieve food security, work together in local organizations, and promote peace and national reconciliation. It has also provided microcredit assistance to urban and rural women to help them undertake income-generating activities. Like many other organizations, however, Seruka suffered severe setbacks during the genocide.[19] With help from donors, the group was able to rent office space and recommence its activities. But in 1999, this organization of more than two thousand members was struggling to continue its programs, with much more limited resources than groups such as Avega Agahozo or Asoferwa.[20]

The organizations grouped in Pro-Femmes are among the most visible advocating women's concerns. Other national organizations, not members of Pro-Femmes, are led by women and are working on women's issues. These groups may be fairly new (and thus have not yet joined Pro-Femmes), or they may have independent sources of external funding so that they do not need the support of Pro-Femmes. One such group is the Forum for African Women Educationalists/Rwanda (FAWE/ Rwanda), which sponsors programs that encourage girls to continue their education.[21] In addition to the many women's organizations in Rwanda, there are mixed organizations with women leaders and a gender component. The activities of such groups complement (and are complemented by) the work of women's organizations.[22]

• Activities of Women's Organizations

If the number of women's organizations in Rwanda grew significantly in the aftermath of the genocide and war in Rwanda, so did the scope of their activities. The most prominent example of this shift was the Campaign for Peace proposed by Pro-Femmes.[23] In promoting this program, Pro-Femmes contributed significantly to ongoing discussions among Rwandan organizations, the postgenocide government, and donors on the importance of targeting relief efforts to help women and on how these efforts could be carried out.[24] Putting forward a blueprint for "a process of reconstruction of the social fabric," the Pro-Femmes Campaign for Peace emphasized four main goals:

- Encourage a culture of peace
- Combat gender discrimination
- Promote socioeconomic reconstruction
- Reinforce the institutional capacity of Pro-Femmes and its member associations

To achieve these goals, Pro-Femmes and its member groups proposed programs that would promote respect for human life and emphasize tolerance, collaboration, and mediation and open discussion and negotiation to resolve conflicts, rather than the use of violence. The Campaign for

Peace also sought to increase the involvement of Rwandan women in resolving national problems, including those of refugees, returnees, and survivors, and to assist women in taking a more prominent role in income-earning activities so they could improve their socioeconomic status. Finally, the campaign called for greater participation by women in national, regional, and international efforts to promote peace. [25]

These and other activities of organizations in post-1994 Rwanda built on the past experience of women's organizations. But given the nature of the crises to be addressed, some activities were quite new. For example, much greater attention was paid to the problems of women and children heading households. Several groups focused specifically on the physical and emotional trauma of women survivors. And in contrast to the past, rural programs gave increased attention to the roles of women as agricultural producers and breadwinners for their families. Provision of shelter became a popular activity for many of the organizations, because of the need and because funds were available for building houses. Such projects were a significant departure from activities of the past. Also, in post-1994 Rwanda some women's organizations tended to be (in practice if not in their official objectives) ethnically homogeneous. But this is a politically sensitive issue—not something people would speak about openly.

◦ Confronting Rural Poverty: Shelter, Livestock, and Agriculture

Assisting female heads of households and other vulnerable groups to repair damaged houses or build new ones became an important activity for several national Rwandan women's NGOs, as well as for some local women's NGOs (such as Duhozanye in Butare) and for mixed groups of men and women promoting rural development initiatives. The emphasis on shelter was promoted by the government and supported by significant funding from multilateral donors (such as UNHCR) and several international NGOs. The women's organizations involved in such projects saw housing as an important first step for women in rebuilding their lives. A woman with no place to live can hardly be expected to support herself and care for her children—much less have the confidence and wherewithal to participate in community activities.

Shelter projects were also meant to reduce social tensions by providing lodging for former exiles who, having returned to Rwanda after the genocide, were occupying other people's homes. Such considerations were important for donor projects and for the postgenocide government.

They were confronted with the overwhelming tasks of rehabilitating and reintegrating eight hundred thousand exiles ("old caseload refugees," mostly Tutsi) who had returned from outside Rwanda in 1994 and 1995, as well as accommodating more than a million "new caseload refugees" (mostly Hutu) who returned from the refugee camps in the Congo and Tanzania at the end of 1996 and in the early months of 1997.

In addition to these considerations, the government had another agenda—a policy of attempting to transform rural settlement patterns.[26] According to this policy, all new housing construction is to be sited in village settlements called *imidugudu*.[27] This controversial policy was not open to discussion, as far as the government was concerned. Despite reservations based on experience with "villagization" elsewhere in Africa (programs that in virtually every case have entailed substantial coercion), many donors went along with this policy. Given the urgency of the postgenocide situation and the nature of emergency relief aid, the villagization policy did not receive the careful scrutiny and study that such a massive program for social engineering would normally undergo.[28]

By 1996, villagization had come to be accepted government policy for all new construction.[29] Thus, Rwandan women's NGOs and international NGOs involved in building houses had to work within the limits of the *imidugudu* policy. However, the projects organized by Rwandan women's NGOs were often able to avoid some of the problems associated with the villages constructed by international NGOs and other donors. In some cases, the organizations were able to negotiate with local authorities to build houses on individual sites near a road, rather than in rigidly defined conglomerations.[30]

In addition to shelter, women's NGOs also sponsored programs to distribute small livestock (pigs or goats, in particular) to women and vulnerable groups and to aid grass-roots organizations to improve agricultural production.[31] Programs to distribute goats carried out by Women in Transition (WIT) and by Rwandan women's NGOs (some of them with assistance from the Rwandan Women's Initiative of UNHCR) contributed to women's and children's well-being by increasing agricultural yields and improving women's social standing. "A person who has a goat is *someone* in the local community" was a common refrain heard during the fieldwork.

◦ **Microcredit Lending, Community Development,**
   and Promotion of Income-Earning Activities

The most visible national women's organization working in the area of microcredit is Duterimbere. In addition to granting small loans and guaranteeing larger loans, Duterimbere holds training programs for loan applicants and organizes workshops on management of small business endeavors. To enhance its credit activities, the organization established a savings and loan cooperative, the Coopérative d'Épargne et Crédit Duterimbere.

Seruka is another Pro-Femmes member that provides microcredit to rural and urban women. The organization has had good success in repayment by rural women, but it has encountered difficulties in obtaining repayment from urban loan recipients, an indication of the difficult economic conditions that poor women in the capital face. Seruka, Réseau des Femmes, and other organizations also sponsor training for rural women's groups, and they provide advice, technical assistance, and resources to help promote income-earning activities.

WIT's programs of assistance in agriculture and petty trade require recipients to repay loans, but without interest. In WIT's early phase, recipients initially were expected to repay 80 percent of what they had received. The repayments were then put into a fund the commune used to assist orphans. Later recipients repaid 100 percent.

From April 1999, WIT–funded organizations made repayments to the women's communal fund that each commune had been encouraged to establish, as part of a program by Migeprofe to encourage microcredit for women. These funds charge a below-market interest rate (usually 6–8 percent) for their loans—a situation that some observers fear may create problems for future sustainability of the program.[32]

° ## Advocacy: Legal Aid and Workers' Rights

Several organizations that emerged in Rwanda after the genocide seek to promote women's rights.[33] The oldest and most visible of these is Haguruka, which means "stand up" in Kinyarwanda. Haguruka tries to educate women and children about their rights and help them plead for redress in the legal system. Jurists the organization employs provide legal aid at Haguruka's center in Kigali, helping women claim their rights in court. To extend the reach of its activities, Haguruka obtained funding from the Rwanda Women's Initiative of UNHCR to train thirty-six paralegal trainers. Working within the framework of Haguruka's Mobile Legal Clinic, the paralegals are providing legal aid in prefectures outside Kigali and training others to do this type of work.

Haguruka also lobbied for revision of the inheritance laws, which discriminate against women. The new law, to which Haguruka provided input, will give daughters the right to inherit land and property from parents, and widows the right to inherit from deceased husbands. This legislation is urgently needed, given the large number of female-headed households and the lack of secure access to land or property these women face under current law. In 1998, for example, by far the largest proportion of cases that Haguruka dealt with concerned rights to property and inheritance.[34] Yet passage of the new inheritance law was painfully slow. In mid-1999, the bill had still not received legislative approval, despite significant pressure from groups in Pro-Femmes;[35] the law was finally promulgated the following year.

Women's rights as workers are another important advocacy area. Though wage earners constitute only a small minority of the Rwandan population, labor issues are nevertheless of concern. Often a single employee supports a large extended family. This is especially true for women wage earners, and since 1994 the needs are even greater. Many women feed, clothe, and house significant numbers of children (their own and orphans they have taken in) on meager salaries.

The Conseil National des Organisations Syndicales Libres au Rwanda (COSYLI), a trade union organization with both men and women members, includes women among its leading officers and has attempted to raise public awareness about the problems women employees face in the public and private sectors. To promote this objective, in 1998 COSYLI organized four informational seminars—two in Kigali and two in Gikongoro—that brought together government officials, employers, and women leaders and employees to discuss the conditions and obstacles women workers face.[36]

In 1999, COSYLI leaders were particularly concerned about the dismissals of workers from government service in connection with austerity policies agreed on by the Rwandan government and multilateral financial institutions. Anecdotal evidence suggested that the dismissals may have targeted older women, although by mid-1999, COSYLI had not been able to obtain systematic data on this. Concerned about the economic repercussions for older women laid off from work (especially since such women often provide support to many children), COSYLI was pushing for transparency and public discussion about the criteria to be used in dismissing public service employees.

○ Promoting Girls' Education

Amid concern over the rising illiteracy rate among women in Rwanda since 1994, several Rwandan women's organizations have centered their efforts on educating girls. In March 1999, FAWE, Pro-Femmes, and Migeprofe organized a series of workshops and media programs to raise awareness about the importance of girls' education. In another initiative in 1999, Réseau des Femmes and FAWE, working with the newly created Association of Women Students at the National University of Rwanda, launched a research program to determine why girls drop out of school and to develop an action program to sensitize girls and their parents about the importance of girls' continuing their studies.

◦ Vocational Training and Civic Education

Among the thirty-five member organizations of Pro-Femmes, at least eighteen carry out some sort of training program. Both older and newer organizations engage in such activities, which vary depending on the particular concerns of each organization. Réseau des Femmes, for example, has organized gender-sensitization programs for government authorities in rural areas and civic-education programs and workshops on how to run viable organizations for women at the grass-roots level. Haguruka has organized workshops on women's legal rights and how to defend them.

Many Rwandan organizations support vocational training, an activity that has increased substantially since 1994.[37] Imparting useful skills to disadvantaged women is a major emphasis for Umushumba Mwiza/ Le Bon Pasteur. This residential center, established on the outskirts of Kigali in 1985 by a Catholic prayer group, provides yearlong vocational training and psychological support to women in distress. The center staff is proud that they achieve a 70 percent success rate in finding employment for their trainees.

Umushumba is well established, but because it lacks adequate resources it cannot expand to meet critical needs. Another, newer organization founded since the genocide, the Association des Femmes Chefs de Famille (AFCF) has very limited resources and yet still provides useful services for women and children heads of families.[38] In 1999, AFCF was struggling to launch an ambitious training program in computer skills to assist young women whose studies were interrupted by the conflicts.[39] While waiting for additional donor support, AFCF has set up a typing service and school-supply store to generate revenues to keep the organization afloat.

◦ Health Services, Trauma Counseling, and HIV/AIDS Awareness

As in vocational training, the activities of women's organizations in the area of health have helped meet an important need. At the national level, two of the member NGOs of Pro-Femmes primarily address health concerns, while at least eight others give some attention to health. Such initiatives are important in a context where government programs are woefully inadequate. Moreover, while helping women with physical ailments and trauma counseling, these organizations also provide spaces where women can meet to overcome loneliness and attempt to rebuild a sense of community.[40] Even these useful programs, however, fall short of meeting the huge need. Moreover, urban women are generally more likely than rural women to find access to assistance.

One particularly successful urban-based initiative is the Kigali-based Polyclinic of Hope, which helps widows and women victims of sexual violence. Jointly established just after the war and genocide by Rwandan women returning from outside the country and women who had been living in the country, this effort offered medical treatment and solace to women who had been brutalized in the conflicts. Initially funded by Church World Service, the polyclinic later received funding from the WIT program of USAID, and from other donors. By 1999, the Polyclinic of Hope had broadened its activities to provide the services of a doctor and a pharmacy for women and to support two groups that meet weekly. One of these groups brings together Tutsi survivors of the genocide. The other consists of Hutu women who have lost husbands or other family members in the conflict and who are economically vulnerable. The weekly meetings impart great solace and support to members of each polyclinic group. As one woman explained, "Before we came here, most of us were confused and disoriented. We would sit in our own place and cry. When we came together, we began to smile again. . . . this is because of the group; when one comes here, it's like going to visit one's family. We are happy to be together and share friendship."

In addition to helping women with health needs, the polyclinic has launched programs to provide housing to members[41] and (with assistance from WIT) to make small loans available to women engaged in petty trade. Thus, although the polyclinic originally emerged to address one critical problem (health and trauma issues), the organization later enlarged the scope of its activities in response to the broader concerns of its members. Many women's organizations in contemporary Rwanda experienced a similar pattern of growth.

∘ Resolving Conflict, Empowering Women, and Fostering Peace

Like many other efforts centered on women and gender in postconflict Rwanda, the Pro-Femmes Campaign for Peace was responding to and building on initiatives at the grass roots, where women were coming together to help each other and work out ways of living together again. In concrete terms, the Pro-Femmes program provided encouragement and assistance to women attempting to form organizations, counseling services for women and children traumatized by the conflicts, public education campaigns in the media, and training programs to promote tolerance and reduce conflict. In November 1996, the United Nations Economic and Social Council recognized these activities by honoring Pro-Femmes with the Mandajeet Singh Prize for Tolerance and Nonviolence.

• Factors Affecting Performance and Impact of Women's Organizations

We have seen that a varied, growing array of Rwandan organizations have participated actively in the reconstruction of the country after the genocide. Women are well represented and visible—not only in organizations that exclusively or mainly target women but also in many organizations that include both sexes. At the national and local levels, such associations can claim impressive achievements. Their activities respond to a broad spectrum of important needs: support and solace for widows and orphans; aid for women's income-earning initiatives; vocational training and adult education; assistance with small livestock, improved seeds, and agricultural programs to increase yields; health services and trauma counseling; advocacy for women's rights; and promotion of girls' education. These efforts cannot be expected to overcome poverty. Structural change is needed to achieve that. Nevertheless, strong, independent, and outspoken women's groups can draw attention to specific problems that affect women and children, while providing resources that help individual women and groups confront these problems.

Alleviating suffering and assisting women in a postconflict context to get back on their feet economically can be seen seen as a path to broader goals—a means to support women's political participation and to promote reconciliation. Here also, women's organizations in Rwanda have done a great deal. By the end of the 1990s, more women were participating in the public arena at the local level than ever before, thanks in part to organizations that fostered such participation. At the same time, some women's organizations were helping women whose trust had been shattered to live and work together with others again—part of an incremental process of reconciliation. Nevertheless, significant challenges remain in efforts both to empower women and to improve their economic situation. In trying to meet such challenges, Rwanda's women's organizations have faced a number of obstacles, briefly described here.

◦ **Social and Cultural Factors**

Women's associations still have to contend with "traditional assumptions" about the place of women in society and cultural values that perpetuate social inequality.[42] For example, in the colonial period and still today, women have found it difficult to own land and property in their own right because of societal and legal constraints.[43] Historically, a woman's knowledge and abilities in Rwanda often went unrecognized, and her access to resources was usually controlled by men—her father, brothers, husband, or husband's brothers—or, if she was a widow, by her sons. A corollary was that, in general, a woman's status derived from the status of her husband or brothers, although some upper-class women could still achieve public visibility and leadership.[44] Today, though women's dependence on men persists in different ways, it is still true that proximity to powerful men is an important political asset for women who wish to exercise leadership.[45]

In the past, Rwandan women normally remained silent in the presence of men and acted as if they knew little. Yet behind the scenes, sisters, wives, and mothers often had a good deal to say, and they were sometimes listened to. Moreover, collaboration and cooperation among women in Rwanda have deep historical roots.[46] The public reticence of women was changing by the 1980s,[47] with their organizational activities taking a more assertive public stance. These changes, especially visible in the 1980s and early 1990s, were spurred by the economic needs of women at the grass roots in rural areas, by educated urban women in the expanding political space opened by political liberalization, and by the changing role of women in religious organizations (such as Catholic prayer groups, which served other purposes as well).[48]

Thus, Rwandan women's organizations during the 1990s have built on previous collaboration among women. However, while attempting to combat and redress the subordination of women in Rwandan society, some organizations still (perhaps unconsciously) reflect cultural values that tend to perpetuate social inequality and invidious distinctions among women.

One such cultural value suggests that if a family member steals or harms another person, the family as a whole is responsible for restitution.

This attitude resonates today in the treatment of women whose husbands died in the Congo or whose husbands are in prison. Some people assume that if a man was involved (or suspected of involvement) in the genocide, his wife shares blame. In rural areas, such women are sometimes shunned and marginalized by local government authorities—and even by local women's organizations. But in some areas of Rwanda, women's organizations have attempted to combat this by including wives of prisoners among their members.

Another example is the emphasis in Rwandan cultural values on wearing proper clothing, an important marker of social distinctions. A woman who lacks "decent" clean clothes might hesitate to go out in public, much less speak out on community issues.

A greater diversity of backgrounds and varied life experiences among women in Rwanda is noticeable after 1994. The return from exile of many women born outside Rwanda or who had left when they were young has energized women's organizations, bringing new ideas and dynamism to their activities. But this cultural mix has also spawned competition, exacerbated by distrust resulting from the violence of the civil war and the genocide. As one woman leader commented, "If only there hadn't been the genocide." Some women who returned from exile have more advanced educational qualifications than women who completed their studies within Rwanda—yet another potential source of friction.

◦ Political Factors

The power context in postgenocide Rwanda shapes not only how women participate in politics but also the impact of such participation. Women are participating more in the public sphere, but men still control the state and make key policy decisions. With this in mind, it is useful to consider four political factors that affect women's organizations in contemporary Rwanda in diverse and sometimes contradictory ways. First, an important consequence of the war and genocide is that ethnicity has become more important in Rwanda, despite the announced intentions of the government to abolish ethnic distinctions.[49] Few Rwandans will talk about ethnicity openly (at least not with outsiders). Yet in Rwandan politics today it matters what a person's (presumed) ethnic background is, where that person lived in Rwanda, and where that person came from if he or she is an exile who came home after the genocide. Understanding these distinctions can be critical to understanding the dynamics within and among women's organizations. Although

Rwandan women have displayed a remarkable capacity to transcend differences and work together, distinctions based on ethnicity, class, region, place of origin, and life experiences remain salient.[50]

Second, the Rwandan state is now, as it was in the past, strongly hierarchical, with a tradition of top-down decisionmaking and little tolerance for people or groups who challenge the hegemonic discourse of those in power. Although the people holding power in Rwanda have changed since the war and genocide, these features have not.

Third, "clientelism" permeates Rwandan politics—both internally and between the Rwandan government and external donors. Having a well-placed patron is often critical to political survival and to the ability of a person, agency, or group to obtain resources. This is not, of course, unique to Rwanda, but it has been an enduring (and especially powerful) element of the political landscape. There is a perception among some of the smaller (and less well-funded) NGOs that leaders of groups connected to politically well-placed individuals (often men) are more likely to succeed in obtaining funding or other resources.[51] The research team was unable to study this in depth; more data would be needed before drawing firm conclusions on the subject.

Finally, the nature of public discourse also influences the activities of women's organizations. The postgenocide regime in Rwanda prides itself on encouraging open discussion of issues. Government officials point to the elections in 1999 for local councils at the *cellule* and *secteur* levels as evidence of a commitment to popular participation in governance. There are many topics, however, on which people do not feel free to express themselves.

∘ Dependence on International Donor Support

Most Rwandan women's associations are still heavily dependent on international funding, with little likelihood that they can become completely self-sustaining soon. External support is critically important if the gains that have been made are to be sustained, but donor funding is already beginning to decline. Aid as "income" is not what most donors have in mind, nor is aid that promotes class divisions over gender solidarity.

Women's organizations in Rwanda receive criticism for their heavy dependence on donors for funding.[52] It is true that the need for donor support influences how groups set priorities, implement projects, and evaluate their activities. This dependence should be placed in context, however. Some organizations have tried to raise funds locally to support their activities, but few of the national women's organizations would be able to survive on such income alone.[53] For most national women's organizations in Rwanda, and many at the local level as well, dependence on international funding is an unavoidable reality.

The almost total dependence of women's organizations on international funding has obvious adverse consequences. International donors' tendency to shift their priorities from year to year makes it difficult for women's organizations to undertake long-term planning. Even when they carefully design a long-term initiative, they are under constant threat that it may abruptly close. Moreover, as the resources for humanitarian and development assistance diminish, donors are withdrawing from funding and ongoing programs, creating problems for women's organizations. This has created a feeling of vulnerability among women leaders.

◦ Problems of Cooperation and Coordination

The rapid growth of national associations has tended to foster fragmentation. Despite efforts to achieve greater coordination and unity, there is in fact considerable dispersion of energies among women's associations, as well as some duplication of programs and competition to obtain donor resources.

Pro-Femmes/Twese Hamwe was founded in 1992 as an umbrella organization in an attempt to coordinate women's organizations and avoid unnecessary duplication of activities. The initiative came from several Rwandan women leaders who saw benefits from collaboration and coordination. Donors also favored such an arrangement because it facilitated their efforts to assist women's organizations without having to deal individually with many separate groups. After the genocide, Pro-Femmes reemerged and has continued to serve as an important nexus for communication and collaboration—as exemplified in the collective action of member groups in support of the legislation to give women inheritance rights.

In addition, as an umbrella group for distributing funding from donors, Pro-Femmes has attempted to coordinate the activities of its member organizations. This coordination is loose and not always effective; considerable duplication of activities occurs.[54] Though some duplication is understandable and probably even necessary, it tends to perpetuate distinctions.[55] Problems arise when there is competition over resources, often shaped significantly by the play for power within the postgenocide regime.

• Women and Political Empowerment

Donors, the Rwandan government, and women's groups have put considerable emphasis in their public statements on the need for women to transcend divisions and work together to reconstruct Rwanda. Such a viewpoint is reflected in a 1997 United Nations International Children's Emergency Fund (UNICEF) assessment: "The associative movement is an exceptional opportunity to reinforce women's role both in general and in the specific framework of reconstruction, development, and the promotion of peace."[56] Overall the results of the fieldwork support this assessment. Working together in groups has enabled a significant number of women to take on formal political roles at the local level. Organizations have provided opportunities for women to gain experience in leadership and to express their concerns in public arenas. Incremental steps also have been made toward reconciliation in some areas because participation in the common activities of their organizations has helped women find ways to live and work together again. An overview of such efforts is provided in this section, which concludes with a discussion of some uncomfortable realities about power and policy in postgenocide Rwanda—realities that present obstacles to efforts to promote women's empowerment and societal reconciliation.

The 1997 UNICEF report issued a strong critique of women's underrepresentation in local government structures:

> Female representation at a peripheral level is practically nonexistent. Yet it is at the local level that the promotion of women must be concretely realised. A change is thus urgently needed at the communal level and beyond. The government's decentralisation projects that aim to reinforce local bodies (at prefectoral and communal levels) will have to improve female representation.[57]

In 1998, as if in response to this critique (but also spurred by women's initiatives in Gitarama Prefecture), the Rwandan government began a process of electing women's councils at the local level.[58] These ten-person councils, each elected at the level of the *cellule, secteur,* commune, and prefecture, are supposed to provide an opportunity for local women to have a say in issues that affect their communities—such as health, education, and development. The local women's councils also are to manage the newly introduced women's communal funds and serve as local representatives of Migeprofe. Moreover, women are also well represented in the separate structure of local government councils elected during March–May 1999. On many councils, women councilors constitute 50 percent of those elected.[59]

Although women have apparently made gains in obtaining formal participation in decisionmaking at the local level, it is unclear which issues these councils will be allowed to address and how much autonomy they will have from local government officials. Also important will be the leeway for council members to raise concerns emanating from the local community. For the present analysis, it is notable that many of the women elected to these councils had had previous experience as leaders or members of women's organizations or mixed organizations.[60] Clearly, the activism of women at the grass-roots level, as well as government and donor encouragement for women's organizations, has opened political space for women's participation in public arenas.

It is encouraging that women have such opportunities to participate in local decisionmaking through the seats reserved for women on local government councils and in the structures of women's councils. The proliferation of government councils, however, presents some difficulties for organizations. Specifically, by co-opting much leadership talent into formal government structures, government is in danger of taking over space that could (or should) be occupied by civil-society groups. What effect will this drain of leadership have on attempts by Rwandan organizations to strengthen civil society? We know from studies elsewhere in Africa that women active in ostensibly nonpolitical organizations can wield important political influence at the local level.[61] Women need to be well represented in formal positions in government structures. But strong women's organizations are also necessary to serve as an alternative to state power, especially in the Rwandan context where legitimacy for the government at the local level appears problematic.

The question of autonomy for women's organizations is timely. Despite recent moves toward granting more responsibility to communes and prefectures, the Rwandan government is still highly centralized. A few men at the center make most important decisions. As of 1999, even though the number of women in key decisionmaking positions was greater than it was during the Second Republic,[62] women were still seriously underrepresented in this area. At a seminar held in Kigali in 1999 on "Gender and the Legal Status of Women in Rwanda," the government drew criticism for this situation:

> The key question at present is that of participation of men and women on an equal footing in decision-making positions. It is in this area that

the most tenacious inequalities persist. In Rwanda the distribution
of power in public life and in private enterprise shows an underrepresentation of women . . . [indicating that] the participation of
Rwandan women in decision-making power and national planning is
still short of what is desirable.[63]

• Challenges for the Future

The literature on state and society in the Third World posits a synergistic
relationship between state and society; an effective, legitimate state is,
ideally, based on strong civil-society institutions that can counterbalance
state power.[64] This type of relationship for women's organizations does
not currently exist in Rwanda. Whether it can develop depends on several
factors. Especially important are the degree of unity among women's
groups and the attitude of influential government officials. In this regard,
two concerns merit particular attention. The first involves the broad role
of the postgenocide Rwandan government in supporting women's organizations and women's initiatives. The second involves questions about
which policies are open to public discussion and influence.

Support from the Rwandan government (especially Migeprofe) has
been essential for the success of many of the initiatives supporting
women's organizations.[65] Moreover, the relationship between Migeprofe and donors such as WIT has been positive overall. Yet support can
be double-edged. It may also entail, or augment, control. It can make
women's groups vulnerable to withdrawal of support if a group or individual happens to displease those in power. Also, while Migeprofe may
work well with outside groups at present, a government ministry (especially one with significant external support) is susceptible to changes in
leadership. How such changes will affect organizations cannot be pre-
dicted. Thus it is not desirable that government structures expand to ab-
sorb all of the existing political space. If women's organizations are to
grow stronger and if civil society is to be strengthened, then not all
donor aid to women's initiatives should be funneled through government channels.

A second major challenge facing advocates of gender equity and
women's advancement in Rwanda lies in the realm of policymaking.
Ordinary citizens or even leaders perceive that certain issues are so sensitive that they dare not address them openly through public discussion
in civil society.[66] Will the expanded political space that allows for

women's participation in some spheres (such as local government concerns) permit debate and real input by women on other issues that could greatly affect their livelihoods and opportunities for economic security? Will these be viewed as political concerns, open to debate, or will they be defined as "technical" questions, which only particular (primarily male) government decisionmakers may decide? Whether Rwandan women of diverse social strata are able to voice their concerns and be heard will affect not only their lives, but also the legitimacy of the government and possibilities for peace and reconciliation.

• Notes

1. Staffed by educated young women trained as social workers, these centers encouraged rural women to meet and discuss common concerns. Despite a patronizing emphasis on helping women be better homemakers, the social centers did promote collaborative interaction between rural women while providing opportunities to grow vegetables and engage in income-earning activities such as raising small livestock. Moreover, the *foyers* also served as an arena where women could share their experiences and develop their own initiatives.

2. School ties linked these women together, as most of the social assistants working in the *foyers sociaux* had been trained at the Karubanda social-work school in Butare. At the same time, these women had their horizons broadened by the experience of traveling far from home to work in rural areas in different parts of the country. They felt a strong esprit de corps and acquired valuable experience and leadership skills that positioned them for employment in other domains later—whether in government service, local NGOs, or international NGOs.

3. Adding to their traditional social services of medical work, education, and social services, during this time the Catholic, Protestant, and Adventist Churches also encouraged community organization and rural development. This was supplemented during the 1980s by increased foreign assistance, including contributions from youthful expatriate volunteers wishing to promote rural concerns.

4. INADES Formation Rwanda, "Inventaire O.N.G. 1985," pp. 17–18. This report, based on a 1985 survey of 133 groups, expressed concern over "the relative lack of attention to the agricultural activities to assist women, given the [important] role of women in agricultural production in Rwanda." Many of the earlier efforts to support rural women tended to reinforce women's subordinate role in society; there was an emphasis on domestic responsibilities rather than agrarian, commercial, intellectual, or political activities. The report also found that although most of the Rwandan NGOs surveyed were linked with churches, the number of secular organizations was increasing. Noting a continued heavy dependence on financial resources from outside the country, despite some progress in raising resources locally, the report recommended increased efforts to expand self-financing. It also deplored the fact that Rwandans headed only about 36 percent of the NGOs surveyed.

5. De Keersmaeker and Peart, *Children and Women of Rwanda,* p. 109.

6. De Keersmaeker and Peart mention the first two of these factors. The researchers believe that external funding and support were also important. See *Children and Women of Rwanda,* p. 109.

7. The name of the ministry has undergone several changes since 1994. Then in early 1999, a reorganization and ministerial shuffle led to the former Ministry of Gender, the Family, and Social Affairs (Migefaso) being divided into two ministries: the Ministry of Social Affairs, and the (current) Ministry of Gender and Promotion of Women's Development (Migeprofe). This discussion will use the appellation that was current in 1999 (Migeprofe).

8. Most of these groups were small, with fewer than twenty members, and informal. Others were formally registered with the government. Groups of both types provided important services for women at the grass roots—assistance in income-earning projects, mutual support, and an arena where women could lobby for more attention to women's concerns. Some groups also played a role in reintegrating refugees. Observing that such groups were often involved in agricultural production and mutual aid in times of sickness, birth, or death, the report suggested that generating income was not the main focus for most of these organizations. See de Keersmaeker and Peart, *Children and Women of Rwanda,* p. 110.

9. De Keersmaeker and Peart, *Children and Women of Rwanda,* p. 110. The Women in Transition program funded by USAID since 1996 played an important role in supporting such associations.

10. One example of such a collective is the Conseil Constitutif des Femmes (COCOF) in Gitarama Prefecture, begun in 1994 to help widows and women whose husbands were in prison to establish organizations. In 1999, COCOF's 2,055 members were grouped in 97 organizations. Many of the member organizations were engaged in agriculture and small livestock projects; others produced handicrafts such as baskets, and some formed rotating credit groups. The intergroup has promoted cultivation of peanuts and soya, to improve soil fertility and family nutrition, and maintains a store for members where they can obtain tools and agricultural inputs. In 1999 the organization had plans to expand its range of merchandise, but lack of resources has hampered this initiative.

11. USAID took the lead on this issue, with the introduction of its Women in Transition (WIT) program at the end of 1996. Later programs for assisting women, such as the Rwanda Women's Initiative (RWI) of UNHCR, appear to have been influenced by the WIT approach. Both WIT and RWI worked closely with Migeprof. See Baldwin and Newbury, "Evaluation of USAID/ OTI's Women."

12. Pro-Femmes/Twese Hamwe, "Mieux connaître le collectif."

13. The classic discussion of this is found in Wipper, "Maendeleo ya Wanawake Organization."

14. A recent study of one of Rwanda's most active and effective groups, Réseau des Femmes, shows that this organization has successfully reached into the rural areas through a network of staff and volunteers. See Burnet and Mukandamage, "Réseau des Femmes."

15. Indeed, Pro-Femmes is proud of being a truly national organization: "The organizations [that] compose it work in all areas of socioeconomic activity

and in all the prefectures of the country, serving the population at the grass roots." Pro-Femmes/Twese Hamwe, "Campagne action."

16. Having lost much of its personnel during the genocide, Duterimbere was under new, less experienced leadership in the immediate postconflict period. Flush with large donor inputs, the NGO shifted from its earlier emphasis on helping people of modest means, and approved large loans to urban elites. When many of these loan recipients defaulted, Duterimbere's financial viability and credibility with donors plummeted. To save the NGO from imminent collapse, several board members joined with organization members to demand changes in personnel, a reorganization of the governance structures, and more stringent financial procedures to ensure proper use of funds. These reforms and the self-study, which called for a return to Duterimbere's foundational ideals, have strengthened the organization.

17. Avega Agahozo conducts activities of both an emergency and a long-term character, including healthcare and trauma counseling, repair and construction of housing, encouragement for income-earning activities, aid to grassroots organizations, training for development, and advocacy for justice and commemoration of victims of the genocide.

18. In addition to houses, Asoferwa's Village de Paix Nelson Mandela includes a primary school, a health clinic, a grinding mill, a workshop for tailors, a center for literacy training, a market, and a reservoir. The organization had ambitious plans for further expansion at Ntarama, with additions for a dairy, a tannery, a health center, and a guest house. As of 1999, however, a lack of funds had delayed implementation of these projects.

19. Seruka lost several of its leaders in the massacres, and some fled the country. The organization's offices were destroyed and its office equipment looted.

20. For example, lacking a vehicle, Seruka's staff members use public transportation to reach the rural sites where their projects are located. This is in distinct contrast to a group such as Asoferwa, which in 1999 employed four chauffeurs to drive its vehicles. Members' dues and interest income from microcredit initiatives provide some income for Seruka, but this is insufficient to cover the core needs of the organization. Despite such constraints, from 1995 (with the help of modest assistance from donors) Seruka carried out a variety of projects—such as provision of small loans to women for petty commerce or agricultural production; a model house-building project in Kigali Rural Prefecture; the establishment of mutual savings funds in three prefectures (Gikongoro, Gitarama, and Byumba); and help with school fees and school materials for orphans of the war and genocide. Like many of the organizations that responded to a survey conducted during our fieldwork, Seruka had drafted plans for additional projects it wished to undertake, but lack of funding prevented the organization from implementing them. One of the projects donors did not fund was to provide assistance to returnees from the refugee camps in Congo and Tanzania.

21. In 1999, in collaboration with several other women's NGOs, FAWE/Rwanda was conducting research on why girls drop out of school at a higher rate than boys. To highlight the importance of girls' education, in 1999 FAWE/Rwanda championed single-sex secondary schools for girls. The first of these opened in Kigali in 1999, and FAWE plans to establish at least one such school in each of Rwanda's other eleven prefectures. In 1999, FAWE/Rwanda's

projected budget was US$70,000, an increase from about US$10,500 in the previous year. See "70,000 USD Earmarked for FAWE–Rwanda Chapter," *The New Times* (Kigali), 3 May 1999.

22. Of many such organizations, two—Iwacu and RISD—are noted here as illustrative examples. Iwacu, founded in 1981, with legal recognition obtained in 1984, is dedicated to supporting and expanding the cooperative movement in Rwanda. Its operations were suspended during the genocide but resumed in 1996. Iwacu provides technical support and loans to cooperatives and runs a well-organized center in Kigali that gives training sessions and seminars for people involved in the cooperative movement. The Iwacu director in mid-1999 was a woman, as were several of its administrative cadre. Included in the goals of the organization is a commitment to providing training to women and girls involved in groups or organizations. See Iwacu, "Do You Know Iwacu?" The Rwandese Initiative for Sustainable Development (RISD), founded after the genocide, aims to ensure that women's concerns are taken into account in planning for development. Although RISD's concerns are not limited to women's issues, the organization includes women among its high-level staff. In 1999, RISD was monitoring and attempting to shape the ongoing debate over government plans to introduce land reform in Rwanda. RISD wanted to ensure that women's needs and rights would be addressed in the legislation and policies to emerge from this process.

23. This was not, however, the first time women in Rwanda had spoken out for peace. In 1992, Rwandan women, regardless of class, ethnic status, or political affiliation, joined together in the Women's March for Peace to protest a violent attack against Agathe Uwilingiyimana, who was at that time minister of primary and secondary education. (Uwilingiyimana, a Hutu, was later to become prime minister; on 7 April 1994, she was one of the first officials killed during the genocide.) Participants in the Women's March for Peace also demanded that the government bring an end to the war that had ravaged Rwanda since October 1990, with its severe effects on women's circumstances and family livelihoods.

24. The program was formally adopted by the member associations of Pro-Femmes in 1995, in discussions that formed part of the preparation for the Beijing conference in August of that year. The project was revised and elaborated on during the subsequent three years.

25. Pro-Femmes/Twese Hamwe, "Mieux connaître le collectif," pp. 7–8.

26. Most rural dwellers in Rwanda live in scattered homesteads, with their houses surrounded by the intensively cultivated gardens in which they grow food and other crops for family subsistence and sale. Household waste and manure from small livestock and cattle (for those fortunate enough to have cattle) are used to fertilize crops, particularly the banana groves that shade homesteads in most areas of the country. Traditional Rwandan belief holds that the "smoke from the cooking fire of the house" keeps banana groves healthy. Bananas are important both for food and for making banana beer, a source of income for rural households and an essential part of everyday social relations and rituals accompanying occasions such as marriage, birth, and death.

27. The singular (one village) is *umudugudu*.

28. See Hilhorst and van Leeuwen, "Imidugudu: Villagisation in Rwanda."

29. From the viewpoint of the postgenocide government and survivors of the genocide, concern for security is an essential consideration driving the villagization policy. Grouping the population into villages is seen as necessary to protect people from the violent incursions of guerrillas (*génocidaires* and opponents of the current regime), who in the years after the genocide attempted to topple the fragile new government. Critics accept that villagization was perhaps justifiable in the eastern prefectures. There, large numbers of exiles from the Tutsi diaspora (the "old caseload refugees") had returned to settle after the genocide. Then, at the end of 1996, hundreds of thousands of returnees from the refugee camps in Zaire and Tanzania flowed back into Rwanda. There was an undeniable need to find ways to provide housing and arrange for field sharing. In the late 1990s, however, this policy was extended to the northwest (Gisenyi and Ruhengeri), where conditions were different.

30. A shelter project sponsored by WIT in Rusumo Commune encountered such flexibility on the part of the *bourgmestre,* as did a WIT–funded housebuilding project in Rukara. Giribambwe, one of the member NGOs of Pro-Femmes, built houses in Gitarama with funding assistance from WIT. For other examples of villages constructed by Rwandan women's NGOs, see Pro-Femmes/Twese Hamwe "Mieux connaître le collectif," p. 10.

31. Programs to distribute goats usually involve a grant of funds to an organization to cover purchasing half the number of goats as there are members of the group. Later, when the goats produce offspring, each organization member who received a goat in the first round is required to give a female offspring to another member who has not yet received a goat.

32. Baldwin and Newbury, "Evaluation of USAID/OTI's Women," pp. 17, 23.

33. Other member associations of Pro-Femmes that list legal advocacy or legal assistance to women among their activities include the Association Rwandaise des Femmes des Médias, Benishyaka, Dukanguke, Fondation Tumerere, and Icyuzuzo. In addition, as part of an effort to inform women of their rights, Asoferwa has undertaken research on the roots of conflict in Rwanda, and Avega Agahoza has sponsored research on violence against women during the genocide.

34. Haguruka, "Rapport Annuel 1998."

35. Haguruka and other members of Pro-Femmes lobbied in favor of the legislation, which the minister of Migeprofe presented before the Parliament in March 1999. Although officials said the legislation would soon be voted into law, as of mid-1999 the bill was still under consideration.

36. COSYLI, "Rapport du séminaires."

37. Without more sustained study, one cannot adequately ascertain the full extent of such activities. However, many organizations include vocational or other training among their stated activities; in most cases, such training is carried out in combination with other activities.

38. AFCF was founded in 1994 by twenty women survivors of the genocide. An average of three women a day come to the AFCF requesting assistance; AFCF helps those it can and refers others to health clinics and other programs where help can be obtained.

39. With help from Pro-Femmes, the United Kingdom, and several other donors, AFCF set up a modest office in the commercial center of Kigali and by

mid-1999 had obtained seven computers. Before beginning its training program, the organization still needed funds to rent classroom space and acquire furniture. It also required additional computers to train twenty students at a time. To obtain this additional funding, AFCF had applied for a loan from the Survivors' Fund, an institution set up by the government to provide assistance to survivors of the genocide and massacres of 1994.

40. Examples of such activities include the following: The Association Rwandaise pour le Bien-être Familial aims to promote family health by supporting family planning, sexual and reproductive health, and the health needs of women and children. The association organizes educational programs for adults and youths on responsible parenthood and balanced family life. It also collaborates with the government, NGOs, and other donors to increase public awareness about family health issues. Another member organization of Pro-Femmes, SWAA/Ihumure, promotes awareness about AIDS among women and sponsors AIDS–prevention programs. Benishyaka includes among its programs psychosocial counseling for victims of sexual violence and for traumatized children. It also sponsors campaigns to encourage family planning. Several other groups, such as Avega Agahozo and Rwandese Women Helping Orphans, also provide women victims of sexual violence with trauma counseling, health services, or both.

41. Once the polyclinic had obtained registration as an NGO, it was able to obtain funding to provide houses for some members; others were still waiting as of mid-1999. The group had been promised assistance from the U.S. government for construction of eighty houses for its members, and once the prefect of Kigali allocated plots, building was to begin. In the meantime, those without a house were renting small rooms.

42. The analysis in this chapter has portrayed contemporary women's associations in Rwanda as a tool helping women overcome traditional constraints to their participation in productive work and in public decisionmaking. We recognize that such a portrayal is somewhat misleading because the term "tradition" implies a kind of homogeneity and unchanging character to women's situation. In fact, political and economic changes during the colonial and postcolonial periods reshaped women's work, gender relations at the household level, and the position of women in the larger society. For a discussion of such transformations elsewhere in Africa, see Bujra, "Urging Women," pp. 117–140; and Amadiume, *Male Daughters, Female Husbands.* It should be emphasized, therefore, that women's associations emerged in response both to legacies from the past and to the changes occurring during the twentieth century, and in mobilizing women these associations often built on earlier patterns of women's cooperation.

43. A good example of this is the fact that in colonial and postcolonial Rwanda, agricultural extension agents (who were almost all men) ignored the broad, deep knowledge women possessed about soil conditions, different types of seeds for food crops, and optimal cultivation techniques. Additionally, although women do most of the work in coffee production, coffee has been seen as a men's crop. An excellent analysis of the situation of rural women in postcolonial Rwanda is found in de Lame, *Une colline entre mille ou le calme avant la tempête.* On the tendency of government agricultural officials and development

programs to ignore the knowledge of women farmers, see Pottier, "'Three's a Crowd,'" and Voss, "L'Amélioration de la culture du haricot."

44. Thus, in precolonial Rwanda, upper-class women (for example, royal wives and wives of chiefs, large landowners, or cattle owners) often presided over their own coterie of subordinates (clients), to whom they would distribute cattle to create ties of loyalty and service. One of the most famous of such women was Kanjogera, a wife of the notorious King Kigeri Rwabugiri, who reigned during the last quarter of the nineteenth century. After Rwabugiri's death in 1895, Rutarindwa (son of one of Rwabugiri's other wives) took the throne as the legitimately installed heir. Kanjogera and her brothers Ruhinankiko and Kabare, however, staged a coup d'état in 1896, killing Rutarindwa and his supporters and then installing Kanjogera's young son Musinga on the throne. Kanjogera's ruthless wielding of power has entered into the lore of Rwandan political discourse. During the Second Republic in Rwanda, the politically active wife of Juvénal Habyarimana, the military president who himself had taken power by a coup d'état in 1973, was often referred to in popular parlance as "Kanjogera."

45. This is hardly unique to Rwanda. But it is a consideration for (informal) qualifications for obtaining and maintaining leadership in women's organizations in contemporary Rwanda. It is also relevant in a society with a high percentage of female-headed households and an assertive administrative penetration at the local level.

46. In the past, girls forged close ties as adolescents when they engaged in all-female meetings in which they learned about proper sexual behavior of adult women. The young people involved in these groups often remained close friends and confidantes well into adulthood. Sometimes this was extended to religious participation as well, within both traditional and Christian religious practices.

47. C. Newbury, "Rwanda."

48. This activist trend was brought to a head in 1989, when a former woman member of the Mouvement Révolutionnaire National pour le Développement Political Bureau was killed in a suspicious automobile accident. It was widely believed that she had been killed because of her outspoken critiques of government policies—especially on issues important to women (e.g., government corruption). Many women took notice and commented on her death. Given the nature of the conditions under which she died, few in Rwanda believed this was an accident; most saw it as a political assassination.

49. The main distinction is between Hutu and Tutsi, but these are not corporate groups, and there are often significant differences within each. For example, among Tutsi, there are differences between those who have always lived within the country and those who returned from exile after the genocide. Among those who returned from exile, it matters whether one formerly lived in Burundi, Congo, Tanzania, Uganda, or elsewhere. Among Hutu, there remain important historical and political differences between Hutu from northern Rwanda and Hutu from south-central Rwanda.

50. Such divisions are not always easily visible to outsiders; nonetheless, they can affect the internal structure and functioning of women's organizations as well as the extent of cooperation and coordination among them. There is

anecdotal evidence of some organizations dismissing one or another employee or leader who was less politically well connected than a rival. Such rivalries sometimes take on an ethnic character or involve competition between women who returned to Rwanda from exile and women who had lived all their lives in Rwanda. This type of competition is not surprising, but it can undermine efforts to achieve unity and solidarity, and it affects how organizations are perceived by ordinary people.

51. Political considerations may also influence an organization's access to resources in circumstances where a government ministry is able to control who will benefit from external aid.

52. De Keersmaeker and Peart, *Children and Women of Rwanda*, p. 110.

53. Many of the women's organizations at the national and local levels obtain income from dues paid by their members. In addition, some organizations sponsor income-earning activities, such as selling clothes tailored by trainers and trainees in a vocational program for seamstresses, renting meeting space owned by the organization, obtaining interest from loans made to women's groups, and taking donations of consultant fees from consultants volunteering their time to the organization.

54. For example, the fact that there exist several organizations to assist widows in postconflict Rwanda could be seen as a duplication of efforts, but, as explained in an AFCF document, there is a convincing rationale for this: "[AFCF] was created by the initiative of 20 widows, survivors of the Genocide and the Massacres of 1994. We wanted to get out of our isolation and work together to fight the poverty of our families, poverty due to the loss of our husbands and our children and the pillaging of our belongings during the genocide. Other groups that existed at the time had their objectives. In Rwanda after the genocide, there were 500,000 widows [*sic*], and it was practically impossible to resolve their problems through a single organization." AFCF, "Renseignements concernant notre association," 8 August 1998, typescript.

55. There are several reasons for overlapping activities. First, as noted, Pro-Femmes grew from thirteen member associations in 1992 to thirty-five member associations after the war and genocide. The rapid proliferation of associations made coordination difficult and duplication of some activities inevitable. Second, many of Pro-Femmes' member associations obtain separate funding from donors apart from the funding funneled through Pro-Femmes. Third, the crisis conditions in postconflict Rwanda led some associations to expand into new activities to meet critical needs. A corollary to this was that to obtain project funds associations found it necessary to reshape their activities to fit what donors were willing to support. Finally, different associations that engage in similar activities tend to serve different constituencies—women of different backgrounds, ethnic categories, and experiences during the war and genocide.

56. De Keersmaeker and Peart, *Children and Women of Rwanda*, p. 110.

57. Ibid.

58. Elected women's councils were first introduced in Gitarama Prefecture in September and October 1998 (see Rugiriza, "Démocratie"). The councils were then extended to the rest of the country through elections held during the second quarter of 1999. The queue system of voting used for the women's

council elections and other local council elections in spring 1999 involved voters lining up (in public) behind the candidate of their choice. Although the Rwandan government and some expatriates have praised this form of voting as democratic, the lack of a secret ballot has been sharply criticized by some observers both inside and outside the country.

59. On each local government council, four of ten seats were reserved for women candidates. In addition, women were elected in significant numbers to council seats that were open to both men and women.

60. For example, the rural umbrella group COCOF, in Gitarama Prefecture, estimated that two-thirds to three-fourths of the women elected to local councils in communes COCOF served were members of women's organizations connected to COCOF. Co-optation into government service of talented leaders in the NGO sector is also an issue at the level of central government institutions. In May 1999, the executive director of Haguruka was elected to serve on the new Human Rights Commission established by the central government; her predecessor had left Haguruka after being named secretary general in Migefaso (later, Migeprofe). Mixed organizations also face this issue. Leaders of Imbaraga, a national organization for farmers, were pleased that numerous Imbaraga leaders were elected to the new government. This created something of a leadership crisis in local branches of Imbaraga, however, because the bylaws of the organization prohibited combining leadership in Imbaraga with government service.

61. See, for example, Tripp, "Expanding 'Civil Society.'"

62. For example, whereas women constituted about 11 percent of the National Development Council (parliament) of the Second Republic, in 1999 women held 20 percent of the seats in the transitional parliament of the postgenocide government. Whereas in the past there had been one woman minister, in 1999 there were two. Also in 1999, there were more women secretaries general (the position just below the minister) in the ministries than there had been before.

63. Kibiriti, "Stratégies facilitant l'application," p. 12.

64. Migdal, Kohli, and Shue, eds., *State Power and Social Forces.*

65. Both the former and the current minister of Migeprofe have strongly encouraged other parts of the government and international donors to address women's concerns. At the commune and prefecture levels, representatives of Migeprofe and its predecessor have demonstrated a commitment to improve the economic situation of women and promote their equality. They have often served as crucial intermediaries in directing assistance to vulnerable groups. For example, the WIT program has benefited significantly from a synergistic relationship with Migeprofe.

66. A partial list of such issues includes the following:

• Villagization policies *(imidugudu).* By 1999 villagization had been generalized in eastern Rwanda and was being extended to the northwest (Ruhengeri and Gisenyi). Government plans envisaged further expansion of the villagization program in all areas of the country.

• A draft land-reform policy is in preparation, to encourage privatization of land with freehold tenure. How can Rwandan women influence such an important reshaping of the rural landscape?

• The war in Congo, which began in August 1998 (an extension of the 1996–1997 war), was still ongoing in mid-2000, entailing great loss of life on all sides. Pervasive militarization of state and society in Rwanda, a legacy of the war of the early 1990s and the genocide, has been prolonged and intensified by the war in Congo.

• The provisions of structural adjustment policies promoted by the World Bank and the International Monetary Fund tend to restrict government employment and funding for social services, and thus may undermine efforts to alleviate social and economic distress among vulnerable groups in Rwanda. Will women, especially women at the grass roots, have any input in these policies?

4

Women's Organizations in Postconflict Cambodia

Krishna Kumar and Hannah Baldwin

The Cambodian Profile (p. 39) examined the effects of conflict on women, their status, roles, and social and economic activities. It identified some of the gender issues and problems facing contemporary Cambodian society. This chapter looks at women's organizations that have emerged to deal with these issues and problems. It describes their nature, the factors that contributed to their emergence, and the activities they undertake. It also examines the contributions of these organizations to the empowerment of women. Finally it examines their relationship with the international community.

• Emergence of Women's Organizations

The emergence of independent women's organizations has been a postconflict phenomenon. True, a body called the Women's Association of Cambodia existed during the Vietnamese occupation of 1979–1989. It had the mandate and authority to promote the advancement of women—which it did. But the association was sponsored and controlled by the state. It was not autonomous and independent, the defining characteristics of civil-society organizations.

Several factors have contributed to the growth of independent women's organizations in postconflict Cambodia. The first was the political opening created by the democratic transition. After an interruption of more than two decades of totalitarian and authoritarian regimes, the country enjoyed a semblance of democracy in the early 1990s. Its constitution guaranteed essential civil and political rights and provided a legal framework for forming voluntary organizations. This political opening, limited though it was, has been an essential, though not a sufficient, condition for the growth of all kinds of civil-society organizations, including women's organizations.

Another factor was the presence of a large number of international nongovernmental organizations (NGOs) involved in both humanitarian assistance and sustainable development. As the international donor community was generally reluctant to channel funds to the government, it has depended on NGOs to administer the programs. The international NGOs were philosophically committed to the growth of indigenous voluntary organizations, which would gradually replace them and carry on their activities. The international organizations were also under pressure from the government as well as donor agencies to reduce visibility. Consequently, many NGOs working on gender issues supported the formation of indigenous women's organizations.

A third factor has been the generous availability of resources for women's organizations. The international community viewed the growth of civil-society organizations as an essential component of its efforts to promote democracy. These organizations stand as a buffer between the state and the citizen, curtailing the totalitarian impulses of the government. Consequently, the international community provided generous financial and technical resources to fledgling indigenous organizations, including women's organizations. Practically all existing women's organizations received support from multilateral and bilateral donors for both programs and organizational development. Funds were no problem in the early 1990s; the real hurdles were organizational capacity and the vision of women's organizations. In recent years, however, international funds have become scarce, creating problems for many organizations.

A fourth contributing factor has been what we might call the growth of "gender sensitivity" among national policymakers in the early 1990s. This sensitivity resulted from the growing recognition that the sustainable development of Cambodian society is not possible without the involvement and participation of women. The presence of women expatriates and returnees working with multilateral and bilateral agencies, with the NGO community, and even with the government contributed to this awareness. Moreover, influential women leaders realized that women's organizations, led and managed by women and working for their welfare, are essential for promoting gender equality and addressing social ills in Cambodia. Gender provided the philosophical and practical justification for establishing women's organizations, particularly those engaged in advocacy functions.

Finally, the return of Cambodian women who had gained leadership experience or education outside the country was another contributing factor. Many were visionaries possessing leadership qualities, and a few took the lead in establishing women's organizations in the early 1990s. Examples of such women include Mu Sochua Leiper, a founder of Khemera and now minister of women's and veterans' affairs; Thida C. Khus, founder of Silaka; and Nanda Pok, who started Women for Prosperity. All are expatriates or refugees who returned to Cambodia during or after the peace process. Having lived in Western democracies, they were aware of the contributions that civil-society organizations can make to the articulation of interests of different cross sections of the populations.

Table 4.1 lists most registered organizations presently active. It also lists a few as-yet unregistered organizations engaged in interesting work. General characteristics of these organizations are mentioned below. It does not include grass-roots, religious, or village-based organizations, which are not required to register as formal organizations.

• Nature of Women's Organizations

Table 4.1 shows that thirteen of eighteen women's organizations are located in the capital city and only five in the provinces. Given that all international NGOs and donor agencies are based in Phnom Penh, this is hardly unexpected. However, while located in the capital, many work in the countryside or support programs benefiting people throughout the country.

The table also shows that seven of the eighteen organizations were established in 1993, and another three in 1994. Thus during 1993–1994, more than half were founded. One explanation is that during these years there was a surge of optimism and hope—or perhaps simply an opening up of political space—as the democratic transition occurred. Moreover, generous international assistance was available to establish civil-society organizations.

Broadly speaking, these organizations can be classified into three categories. One consists of the social-service organizations that provide a set of services to women and children, particularly those affected by the conflict. Khemera, Cambodian Women's Crisis Center, and Cambodian Women's Development Agency and Homelands illustrate this category. Over time, such organizations have also begun to undertake advocacy activities. Another category consists of those whose primary work is economic. Help the Widows is a good example. It is engaged in microcredit and has established informal women's groups to channel credit to women. Finally, the advocacy and democracy-promoting organizations are involved in lobbying and public education efforts to improve women's

Table 4.1   Women's Organizations in Cambodia

Name	Location	Activities	Established
Arun Reah	P	Vocational training, microcredit	1994
Association Lumière des Femmes Rural	P	Vocational training	1997
Battambang Women's AIDS Project	P	HIV/AIDS education and research	1993
Cambodia Community Building	C	Microcredit, health	1995
Cambodia Migration and Development Committee	C	Vocational training, women trafficking, prostitution, human rights	1997
Cambodian Women's Crisis Center	C	Domestic violence, women trafficking, prostitution	1997
Cambodian Women's Development Agency and Homelands	C	Literacy, human rights, HIV/AIDS, women trafficking, prostitution	1993
Help the Widows	C	Microcredit	
Indradevi Association	C	Human rights, HIV/AIDS, women advocacy	1993
International Friendship Organization for Development	C	Vocational training	1996
Khemera	C	Community development, vocational training, microcredit, domestic violence	1991
Khmer Women's Voice Centre	C	Democracy, women advocacy, human rights	1993
Kompong Thom Cambodian Association for the Support of Women	P	Microcredit, domestic violence, economic development	1993
Project Against Domestic Violence	C	Domestic violence	1995
Silaka	P	Management training	
Women for Prosperity	C	Political participation, women advocacy	1994
Women Organization for Modern Economy and Nursing (WOMEN)	C	HIV/AIDS	1993
Women's Media Center of Cambodia	C	Women advocacy, mass media	1993

Sources: Directory of Cambodian NGOs; Cooperation Committee for Cambodia.
Notes: A few organizations that were listed but not active were eliminated; a few that were not listed but operational were added. P = province, C = capital city (Phnom Penh).

status in society and increase their participation in the political arena. This category includes organizations such as Women for Prosperity, Women's Media Centre of Cambodia, and Khmer Women's Voice Centre.

The top leadership of women's organizations initially came from four groups of women. First were Western-educated Cambodian expatriates. The second consisted of women who had lived in refugee camps on the

Thai border, many of whom received education, gained organizing experience, or assumed leadership roles in the camps. The third included female employees of international NGOs in Cambodia who acquired practical experience in running voluntary organizations. The last group was those women who lived in the country during the conflict but worked for the Revolutionary Cambodian Women's Association, a mass organization under the Vietnamese-supported communist regime.

Why the preponderance of expatriate and refugee women in leadership positions? The obvious explanation is that overseas exposure gave them new skills and expertise. It widened their social and political horizons. The foreign sojourn also weakened the shackles of traditional society, giving them a new vision and new perspectives. They often learned English, which helped them to communicate effectively with the international community.

The top leaders of these organizations show considerable vision, commitment, and capabilities. However, a vast gulf lies between top leadership and mid-level managers and fieldworkers. This is partly due to the general low educational level of women who can successfully assume those positions. But it also reflects the reluctance of leaders to delegate authority and invest in human resource development.

- **Women's Organizations:
  Serving a Medley of Causes**

Khemera is not just the first Cambodian women's NGO—it is the first *Cambodian* NGO. Founded in 1991 by a group of Cambodian women, it was formed and grew under the direction of Mu Sochua Leiper, now a cabinet minister. The organization targets poor women through community-based development programs. Khemera's activities fall into five main program areas: literacy, childcare, healthcare, family support, and women in business.

The Cambodian Women's Development Agency (CWDA) was founded at the end of the communist Vietnamese occupation as an independent NGO. Director Kien Serey Phal is one of the few women who remained in Cambodia throughout the conflict and now directs a woman's organization. CWDA is recognized as one of the best-managed organizations in Cambodia. Its activities include health programs, community development, promoting basic literacy, and HIV/AIDS education. The organization seeks to empower grass-roots organizations and village communities. CWDA also supports initiatives against trafficking in and violence against women.

Help the Widows is one of the few economic associations run by a woman. Sareth Soun founded the group and directs it. Help the Widows provides microloans to women to help them expand their economic activities in agriculture and petty trading.

Indradevi Association was founded in 1993 by Dy Ratha. Operating in one of the poorest neighborhoods of Phnom Penh, the group carries out education, information, awareness, and counseling on HIV/AIDS and other sexually transmitted diseases. It also advocates for women's rights.

Established in 1997, the Cambodian Women's Crisis Center (CWCC) addresses violence against women. It seeks to stop forced prostitution, domestic violence, and the trafficking of women and children. CWCC was founded and is directed by Chanthol Oung, a human rights lawyer. The organization opened a shelter for abused women after several women escaped from a brothel and had no place to stay.

• Focus of the Activities of Women's Organizations

Women's organizations have been active in economic, social, and political spheres and have carried out a vast array of projects and programs. Microcredit lending has been one of the most important activities of these organizations. One-third of the women's organizations listed in Table 4.1 administer credit programs for women to initiate and operate microbusinesses. Loans are provided to a group of three to seven members who are collectively responsible for ensuring repayment. In the absence of access to formal lending and banking institutions, such programs have been popular with women. For example, Help the Widows (which now serves all women) started with 50 to 60 women; it had more than 2,700 members in 1998. International NGOs have established local partners to channel funds for group loans. Although most of the local partners cannot be designated as women's organizations, women are well represented in them and have begun assuming leadership positions. Almost 95 percent of the participants in group-lending programs are women.

Vocational training is another important area of concern for women's organizations. Six of eighteen organizations provide some vocational training to women. Such training typically focuses on food catering, sewing, and hospitality. A few organizations have also organized agricultural extension training programs for women farmers. A major limitation of such training programs has been that they are often undertaken with little regard to the market and the individual needs of the trainee. Some organizations have established handicraft outlets to sell products made by the trainees. The sustainability of such outlets, which are geared to international, not local markets, remains questionable. As international funding for vocational training has diminished, women's organizations are phasing out such activities.

Women's organizations have been active in social fields, particularly domestic violence, prostitution and trafficking, and HIV/AIDS. Four women's organizations seek to create public awareness about and provide help for victims of domestic violence. Reacting to the gravity of the problem as demonstrated by a 1994 USAID–funded survey, fifteen local NGOs launched the Project Against Domestic Violence (PADV). One of the most successful activities of the newly founded organization was street-theater performances on domestic violence. The troupe held thirty-nine popular performances in five provinces and reached an audience of approximately 250,000.

Women's organizations also provide services to victims of domestic violence. Khemera provides housing, vocational training, and small loans. Its shelter accommodates three hundred women from throughout the country. The CWCC also runs a counseling program for abused women and arranges for legal assistance. If deemed appropriate, it contacts the family of the victim and explores the possibility of reconciliation.

Women's organizations were the first to raise awareness of the issue of forced prostitution and the trafficking of women and children. The organizations provide shelter, counseling, vocational training, and legal assistance to women who want to leave the profession. For example, the CWCC manages a shelter, arranges for counseling, and conducts classes on literacy, sewing, hairdressing, and women's rights. It also works with selected garment factory managers to arrange job opportunities. CWCC also supports educational media initiatives. It has produced videos on the exploitation of commercial sex workers, which have attracted some government officials' attention. This has led to more effective enforcement of laws against trafficking and forced prostitution.

As far as HIV/AIDS is concerned, women's organizations are mostly engaged in research and public education. The Battambang Women's AIDS Project, in collaboration with Population Services International, regularly carries out surveys on knowledge, attitude, and practices, holding focus-group discussions with the population at risk. Its findings are used for scientific research and policy formulation. The Cambodian Women's Development Agency conducts annual surveys among commercial sex workers to assess the effects of AIDS–awareness initiatives.

Women's organizations also expend considerable effort on educating vulnerable populations. The Battambang Women's AIDS Project produces AIDS–prevention videos and a television program that is both popular and instructive. It also produces educational material and posters for use by other organizations. Indradevi Association carries out education, information, awareness, and counseling programs on HIV/AIDS and other sexually transmitted diseases among vulnerable groups. In 1997, its educational outreach program provided information to 4,398 sex workers and 712 brothel owners.

Several women's organizations support democracy and human rights. The Khmer Women's Voice Centre was among the first women's organizations to undertake voter-education programs for the 1993 elections. It organized meetings and workshops and printed literature to encourage both men and women to vote. Women for Prosperity seeks to enhance the political participation of women. With a grant from USAID, it organized leadership workshops in the capital and in eleven provincial towns for women candidates for the 1998 elections. Attended by 698 female leaders, the workshop covered such topics as public speaking, interviewing skills, and writing press releases. The organization also published a report profiling women candidates from all political parties, presenting each party's platform on women's issues. The organization holds leadership training courses for mid-level decision-makers such as commune and district chiefs in the provinces.

Finally, many women's organizations are doing pioneering work in raising public awareness of gender issues in Cambodian society. They have successfully used radio and television, print media, and meetings and workshops to articulate various issues and promote gender equality. The Women's Media Center produces radio, television, and video programs in cooperation with other voluntary organizations, reaching a large audience. It has a successful weekly television program that highlights gender issues in culturally appropriate ways. Another group, the Women's Voice Centre, uses print media. It has published several illustrated booklets and posters highlighting women's issues.

• Overall Impact of Women's Organizations

Despite their small number and limited economic and technical resources, women's organizations contribute to the empowerment of women in a variety of ways. First, they work directly for women's economic empowerment by assisting vulnerable women through vocational training and microcredit programs. The interviews and focus groups conducted by the CDIE team indicate that credit programs are particularly effective and help women initiate small income-generating activities such as farming, poultry raising, and petty trade. Access to credit has improved their economic position, enabling them to meet the minimum necessities of life. More important, it has given them new confidence and identity. Some income-producing women experience better treatment by their husbands and other members of the family. In other words, economic empowerment seems to contribute to social and cultural empowerment in Cambodia.

As mentioned earlier, women's organizations are addressing critical social problems facing women in Cambodian society, such as HIV/ AIDS, domestic violence, and trafficking and forced prostitution. Although only a small fraction of the needy women receive help, the assistance makes an important difference in their lives. The real contribution of these organizations lies in generating public awareness of these problems: they have put the problem of domestic violence on the public agenda. Traveling from province to province, the Project Against Domestic Violence confronted men and women with the issue. Pioneering efforts of many organizations have helped to center public attention on the plight of commercial sex workers and the victims of forced prostitution. Their activities have led to the arrests of many brothel owners and the rescue of young girls enslaved as prostitutes. Radio and television programs sponsored by women's organizations have pressured law enforcement to intervene. Women's organizations have also been pioneers in educating people about the growing problem of AIDS.

Women's organizations have begun to influence the political landscape. During the 1998 elections, a few women's organizations participated in voter-education programs for women. Women for Prosperity trained women candidates, raising public awareness of gender issues by publishing information on each party's platform for women. The organization has now begun to address leadership training for increasing women's participation in politics. By promoting participation, the group is also highlighting the issue of gender equality. As a mid-level trainee told the CDIE team members: "After our training we are aware of what government does [and] also knowledgeable about equality. Men cannot abuse women if women know their rights. Now we understand how to work together for justice."

More important, women's organizations have been raising awareness of gender issues through the mass media. The Women's Media Center of

Cambodia, for example, produces a TV series, in the style of opera and drama, that explores gender-related subjects in inventive, entertaining, appropriate ways. These comedic shows are "particularly effective because they challenge traditional gender roles in the family and in society in ways that permit men and women to see the reality of discrimination and ways to ameliorate it without much loss of face or indignity to the family's reputation."[1] The series is popular. Such programs are influencing middle- and upper-middle-class women in particular, who have more access to radio and television than do poorer women. The programs have started making women aware of their rights and responsibilities. They also are causing women to rethink their traditional role and status in the family and society.

Impacts of Women's Organizations

"It is too early to tell about the effects of women's organizations. I would call their contributions modest, . . . but they are doing some good work."

—*Academic scholar*

"During the past five years, women's organizations have come a long way. They are helping raise a consciousness about gender issues. I am very much impressed by the use of radio and television by women's organizations."

—*International PVO official*

"There is no doubt that their [women's organizations] activities have helped a segment of Cambodian women."

—*Prominent Cambodian human rights leader*

Thus women's organizations are redefining and expanding the limited social, cultural, and economic roles available to women in Cambodian society. Empowerment remains a critical issue for women, whose social status and respect in society have been altered by loss of family, demographic shifts, changing kinship and marriage patterns, and a woman's increasingly burdensome role as sole supporter of her children. Leaders of women's organizations provide important role models. Those models contrast sharply with the sexualized and objectified image of women common in the imported movies and television series that dominate the media in Cambodia, as well as local advertising that often demeans or brutalizes women.

Women's organizations bring unique benefits to the women who administer them as well as to their beneficiaries. First, the leaders experience opportunities and a climate of respect that contrasts sharply with the status they tend to be accorded in mixed groups. Second, the nature of power relationships experienced by women in women's organizations is qualitatively different. Here women manage the organizations, providing opportunities and access to power they do not experience in society at large. Third, women are emboldened to speak openly in female-run meetings, whereas in mixed meetings social norms often prevent women from taking a proactive role. Finally, women's organizations provide a training ground for broader leadership roles. The experience women gain in managing can serve as a springboard for future national leadership. Witness the rise to power of Mu Sochua Leiper, founder of Cambodia's first NGO and currently minister of women's and veterans affairs. Others are sure to follow.

• Factors Affecting Performance and Impact

Women's organizations face many social and cultural obstacles. Cambodia has no tradition of civil-society organizations. Although there once was a community network surrounding the Buddhist temple, it bore little semblance to present-day organizations. Consequently, all civil-society organizations, including women's organizations, face difficulties in gaining legitimacy and in obtaining broader social participation.

The low social status of women compounds the problem of women's organizations. Women employees of organizations do not usually receive the respectful treatment accorded their male counterparts, and encounter difficulties in working with government officials and local community leaders. Even in mixed organizations, male officials dominate their female co-workers, lowering women's morale and self-confidence. Finally, women's organizations suffer from the depletion of social capital. There is a widespread shortage of trained and educated women who possess technical and managerial skills. The shortage is likely to persist because of the low enrollment of girls at all educational levels.

Cambodia's political environment *inhibits* the effective functioning of voluntary organizations. However the government lacks the capacity to deliver services to its citizens, and thus tolerates and occasionally supports service-oriented organizations. These groups provide assistance to needy segments of the population, relieving the pressure on government to provide services. There has been tension and apparent competition for resources between government and women's organizations, particularly at the province and district levels. The Battambang Women's AIDS Project is a case in point. The organization encountered initial resistance from local health officials, who saw its activities as competition and were jealous of its access to donor resources. The organization was able to overcome the resistance with tact and persistence, and now works effectively with the officials.

The government is more seriously threatened by the activities of advocacy groups and organizations that promote democracy. An experience of Women for Prosperity provides a not-uncommon example. That group ran into a government stone wall on a USAID–funded project for the 1998 legislative elections. The group had planned to produce debates on women's issues for airing on national television. However, the Ministry of Information feared that the debates (by representatives of the various political parties) might demonstrate government foot-dragging on gender issues. It withheld cooperation. The organization got the message and dropped the project. It did, however, find an amenable radio station, which agreed to air some of the debates.[2]

Women's organizations depend totally on international funding. As most of these funds are short-term grants, the organizations are unable to engage in long-term planning and capacity development. The yearly funding cycle emphasizes the capture of next year's funds, not development of a long-term vision or assessing lessons learned and comparing results with other organizations in order to improve programming. The existence of some women's organizations with a clear vision, targeted programming, and a degree of expertise in a specific sector may seem to contradict this observation. However, closer examination reveals that these are organizations whose activities mirror current donor interest. It is conceivable that these same organizations will diversify their programs—or falter—when donor priorities shift.

Because of this dependence, women's organizations are under constant pressure to change their agendas to reflect the apparent funding priorities of the international community. Several women's organizations have responded to recent reductions in donor funding by developing "flavor of the month" programming, with little apparent attention to the development of expertise in a given area.

There has been little effort by women's organizations to coordinate their activities. Instead, there is intense competition for scarce funds and duplication of popular programs. The tendency to copy successful activities without sharing information and coordinating efforts reduces the overall effectiveness of women's organizations. Organizations need to specialize in a specific area, developing expertise and sharing their lessons learned in order to increase the effectiveness of their work.

Finally, women's organizations suffer from serious organizational and managerial limitations. The organizations reflect the Cambodian model of social organization: a hierarchical structure with a charismatic leader and a tendency for patron–client relationships. Charismatic leaders monopolize power and authority. They are reluctant to delegate decisionmaking to mid-level management. Consequently, there is little division of labor. The result is that the participatory approach—with teams and mentoring—is generally absent. This limits the organizations' ability to respond to new challenges and opportunities. It also minimizes the diversity of ideas necessary for innovation and development, and leaders are overwhelmed and operating with high levels of stress.

Few organizations nurture a second-generation staff that could gradually assume the role of leaders. The training programs for mid- and junior-level staff, sponsored by the international community, are generally inadequate, as they do not focus on the specific needs of the trainees. Moreover, because of low English levels, in which these courses are conducted, many participants fail to get the full benefit of the training. Often organizations are reluctant to send their staff for long-term training out of the fear they might not return after completing it. Women leaders themselves participate in most training, rather than sending lower-level staff. That serves only to widen the gap between leadership and the rest of the staff. The general reluctance to nurture mid-level staff for leadership positions is a serious impediment to the sustainability of these organizations.

Many organizations also lack the capacity to plan strategically. Many are unable to articulate their organizational goals and develop long-term strategies. This problem is accentuated by the short funding cycles of donors, but other factors, such as the charismatic nature of the leadership, shortage of trained manpower, and preoccupation with ongoing activities, are contributing factors. The absence of strategic thinking accounts for the absence of any systematic monitoring of their ongoing programs, evaluation of their effectiveness, and drawing of lessons-learned for the future.

• The International Community: A Critical Role

Although the initiative for the establishment of NGOs came from enterprising Cambodian women visionaries, these organizations could probably not have survived without the assistance of international agencies. The international community has provided three kinds of assistance to women's organizations: financial, technical, and political.

First, international organizations have provided financial assistance. Virtually all the organizations the CDIE team interviewed had received their entire funding from the international community. They depend on the donor community for program as well as core budgets. Cambodian organizations, like civil-society groups worldwide, have found it extremely difficult to develop sources of independent funding. Unlike voluntary organizations in the West, civil-society organizations in the Third World cannot rely on donations of labor or money. While organizations providing vocational training in handicrafts might appear to be an alternate source of income, these groups usually lack entrepreneurial skills and know-how, markets, and a reliable marketing system. Only organizations that provide microcredit have some alternative sources of funding, getting a share of interest paid by clients.

Second, the international community has provided technical assistance to women's organizations in various ways. Several international NGOs have established fostering relationships or partnerships with local NGOs to develop and strengthen their capacities and capabilities. PACT, an international NGO, for example, initiated a "local NGO incubator" approach to provide training, technical support, and direct grants to the first generation of voluntary organizations in Cambodia. Silaka, the woman's management training organization, was an early recipient of its assistance, but now provides management training to other organizations. PACT continues to provide funds to local organizations for staff training. The Asia Foundation, through its partnership with a number of political and human rights–oriented women's organizations, supports and fosters their development.

Other international NGOs developed the competency of their own staff in order to eventually "spin off" or convert the local chapter of the international organization into a national NGO. In other cases, international NGOs encouraged their employees to found organizations in order to continue the programs they were managing. In still other cases, international NGOs themselves were behind the establishment of an organization. The Project Against Domestic Violence provides a good example of how USAID, through the Asia Foundation, has helped found an organization.

There has also been support for training and participation at international conferences by local NGO leaders so they can gain skills and knowledge, and benefit from the experiences of NGO leaders facing similar problems worldwide. In addition, the international community supports training programs for the staff of women's organizations. Increasingly, many organizations are questioning the utility and relevance of training programs funded and managed by international NGOs. The training does not necessarily build on the knowledge or needs of trainees or their sponsoring organizations. Sponsors make little attempt to conduct a regular, systematic assessment of organizational capacity and rarely develop training plans for individual staffers and the organization as a whole. Training is also conducted haphazardly and often in English, making it difficult for many trainees to comprehend the content. Therefore, many training programs have not been useful to women's organizations.

International NGOs have also promoted the integration of gender issues in development programs. Donors support the Gender and Development Program for Cambodia, a semiautonomous organization, which will become a full-fledged local organization in 2001. With its emphasis on training and internship, advocacy and network building, and research and resource development, the Gender and Development Program serves an important need of women's organizations.

Finally, the political support of the international community has been critical to organizations promoting democracy and human rights. A female leader of a prominent organization told the CDIE team that "more important than economic and technical assistance was the feeling that you [USAID] were with us." The moral support of the international community may also serve to protect women's organizations.

Despite the good intentions of the international community, there are a number of limitations to these approaches. Many international NGOs lack requisite skills and patience to mentor indigenous organizations. Often they are in a hurry and seek to transfer skills with little understanding of the hurdles facing the partnering organization. Second, while they mentor, they also serve as models for indigenous organizations. But, in Cambodia, their model is not always appropriate. International NGOs operate with a large support staff, air-conditioners, and four-wheel-drive vehicles. The problem is that many women's organizations follow their examples despite the high costs.

Technical assistance may also be inappropriate, and may not meet the needs of the organization. For example, the international community often provides short- and medium-term advisers to women's organizations. Such expatriate experts usually work in an organization for up to one year. Organizations as diverse as Project Against Domestic Violence, Khmer Women's Voice Centre, and Cambodian Women's Development Agency all continue to make use of foreign advisers. Many organizations have benefited from the services of such consultants. But even the presence of a long-term expatriate consultant, who might work in-country for as long as three years, might prove ineffectual given the linguistic and cultural barriers, as well as internal organizational constraints.

• Areas of Tension Between Women's Organizations and the International Community

Cambodia has an excellent record of cooperation between women's organizations and the international community. Both work closely together and share mutual trust and understanding. However, as expected in any complex institutional relationship, there are tensions, which arise largely out of differences in their mutual expectations.

One major source of tension lies in funding. In the past, the international community has provided generous financial support for both programs and organizational development. That situation is changing. Women's organizations complain that the donor community is increasingly cutting core funding. Moreover, funding for programming is usually provided annually, creating uncertainty among staff and beneficiaries. While such criticisms are justified, the funding agencies have their own constraints. After a political crisis in 1997, the volume of development assistance to Cambodia has declined significantly; the funding agencies have no alternative but to reduce their financial support to women's organizations. It is logical that they expect that recipient organizations tighten their budgets and explore alternative sources of funds. Donor agencies feel uncomfortable with the present dependence of women's organizations on their funding.

Another area of tension is the issue of accountability. Many funding agencies, on the one hand, increasingly demand detailed financial records and program accountability. Some also require performance and impact data for their own reporting purposes. While most organizations can provide financial records, they have difficulty in monitoring and evaluation. Often they have no institutional capacity to collect the necessary data, and they see no justification for expending time and effort on gathering such information. Funding agencies can solve this problem by doing two things: (1) providing technical assistance to organizations to help them develop appropriate forms and procedures, and (2) lowering information requirements to a minimum.

Women's organizations, on the other hand, resent what they regard as the short-term vision of donors and international NGOs. They see the latter as constantly changing direction. One woman leader told the team, "The donor has objectives; we must fit their program." The pattern becomes apparent as one examines the evolving donor missions over time. These changed from relief to community development to healthcare and literacy and then to advocacy, political rights, and participation. For women's organizations that see the deep poverty and continuing need for social welfare activities that are apparently falling out of vogue, the result can be devastating.

Still another source of tension is the management style and organizational culture of women's organizations. These organizations usually suffer from a lack of division of labor, absence of written rules and procedures, the dominant personality of the founder, and the Cambodian tendency toward hierarchical organizations. Moreover, they lack the capacity to plan strategically. Many international donors are uncomfortable with the situation and press them to initiate reform. NGO leaders resist such pressure, viewing it as an unwarranted intrusion into their affairs.

Finally, tensions also arise because of barriers of language and culture, heightened by Cambodia's long isolation from the world. The vast disparities between the salaries of the staff of the international community and of women's organizations, and the apparent superiority of the educational background of the former, create resentment and mistrust. That serves to reinforce traditional models of hierarchy and the roles of leaders and followers. International organizations have done little to build bridges outside office hours, and the two communities remain worlds apart. Women's organizations note that even with medium-term technical consultants who work for up to a year, it takes months before they are able to communicate in meaningful ways. The director of an organization underscored the profound cultural gap in the following words: "These consultants come from a different culture. They see different solutions. We can't follow their recommendations. They are too pushy."

• Sustainability of Women's Organizations

As Cambodian women's organizations are totally dependent on external funding, a question is generally asked about their sustainability without international assistance. Perhaps, at this time, the answer is in the negative. Cambodia is impoverished, and its government faces enormous fiscal problems and therefore is not in a position to help these organizations in a substantial manner. Nor is the nascent private sector affluent enough to fund voluntary organizations. Thus, the dependence on external funding is likely to continue. As a leader of an organization stated during an interview, "Donors are always talking about sustainability, but there will be sustainability only if the country is better off."

The international community recognizes this reality. It is concerned, though, that women's organizations harbor unrealistic expectations and are not making sufficient efforts to become economically more self-reliant. But women's organizations model their programs and choice of expenditures on international NGOs, which is their only example of what such an organization should be. A well-educated Cambodian expatriate manager of an organization can earn as much as US$24,000 a year. Top local employees have a lower salary that can nonetheless reach $600 a month—still vastly different from the local teacher who may officially earn $10 a month, $15 at most. Often women's organizations own several vehicles, and these are viewed with great envy even by top government officials. The consensus is broad in the donor community that women's organizations should learn to live frugally and raise some resources, however small they might be.

To many in the international community, sustainability is intertwined with human resource development and efficient management. They suggest that with the improvement in technical and managerial staff, problems of cost effectiveness, efficiency, and sources of alternate funding will become clearer and the concerned organizations will be in a better position to face them. Some derive hope from the fact that management of the organizations has improved over time and there is a greater awareness of these problems. Many organizations have been gradually acquiring "critical consciousness," which is enabling them to project their vision for the future and assert their independence from the donor community.

Some experts have suggested that women's organizations transform themselves into membership-based institutions to become more vibrant and sustainable. Such a change would help them develop deeper roots in the community and mobilize available local resources. More important, it would improve their bargaining position with the government and the international community. So far, leaders of women's organizations have shown a marked resistance to the idea. A few international donors suggest this is because officials of membership organizations are elected and the leaders are concerned about a challenge to their authority. But it is the reality of Cambodia's poverty that probably underlies this problem. To function, membership organizations require dues. In addition, many U.S. organizations use volunteer labor for much of their work. But Cambodians have neither the funds to contribute to membership organizations nor

---

On Sustainability: A Clash of Views

"For local organizations to be sustainable, there is a need to go to the grass roots. Advocacy organizations are by and for elites. When an organization operates effectively at the grass roots, it gets the support of the community. Donor support to elite groups doesn't encourage a self-reliant system."

—Local NGO leader

"All this talk about sustainability is not relevant in the present conditions. We are not in a position to raise resources locally. Who has the money to give these organizations. You [USAID] should support them."

—Cambodian researcher

"They have to face the fact that our resources are limited. We cannot fund them indefinitely. Our budget has been drastically cut this year."

—USAID official

---

the luxury of volunteering. Women leaders are struggling to support their families. They depend on their salaries to ensure an education and future for themselves and their children.

• Conclusion

Cambodian women's organizations are true pioneers in the Cambodian context. Working in a postgenocide, postconflict, postcommunist setting, in a culture where social values and the position of women have been seriously eroded, they face enormous obstacles. Comparing women's NGOs in Cambodia with their sister organizations in other countries, one is struck not only by their recent formation and limited numbers, but also by the clarity of their vision, the strength of their commitment, and their unwavering determination. Women face enormous hurdles as they work to overcome their own trauma, and the impact of that trauma on their society, which has led to trafficking, abuse, and women's loss of social status. Despite these problems, women leaders are forging ahead, seeking social justice and economic development for themselves and their country. Cambodian women are providing leadership to identify and address critical social problems. They are responding to the population's unmet needs where government has failed. The continued international support for this fledgling women's movement is essential for the future of Cambodia, and the hope for a peaceful, democratic future.

• Notes

1. Frieson, "Role of Women's Organizations."
2. Ibid.

5

Georgia in Transition:
Women's Organizations and Empowerment

*Alice L. Morton, Susan Allen Nan, Thomas Buck,
and Feride Zurikashvili*

This chapter explores the role that Georgian women's organizations play in channeling assistance to women and in helping them meet the challenges of the postconflict situation economically, socially, and politically. It emphasizes the extent to which participation in such organizations holds promise for women's empowerment and the democratization of the postconflict polity.[1] The chapter is divided into four main sections. The first section examines the evolution of women's organizations in Georgia in the postconflict era, the main activities of Georgian women's organizations, and the main constraints inhibiting their performances. The next section analyzes the main impacts women's organizations have had on their beneficiaries, on leadership roles for women, and on government policy toward women. The last two sections explore the influence that the international community has had and outline general findings and conclusions about women's organizations in Georgia.

The findings presented in this chapter are based on the field research conducted by a four-person USAID field team in the fall of 1999. The team held extensive interviews with leaders and beneficiaries of women's organizations along with USAID and other donor staff. Much of the data is based on a survey distributed to 105 direct and indirect beneficiaries of women's organizations.

• Georgian Women's Organizations

Conflict in Georgia began virtually as soon as the USSR collapsed and independence was declared in 1991. Thus, in determining how the third sector—civil society, including the staggering growth of women's organizations—emerged, it is important to distinguish between the factors created by the conflict and those that grew out of the overall economic and institutional collapse. These factors, in turn, should be viewed as distinct from, though linked to, the subsequent shift from centrally planned communist economics to market-oriented reforms and democratic political models.

Women's organizations began to be established from the first days of independence, although the growth in absolute numbers increased most markedly between 1995, when the economy and polity improved, and 2000. This is when the third sector began to open up. This tendency was particularly marked in Tbilisi, Georgia's capital city, although organizations oriented toward internally displaced persons (IDPs) also began to proliferate in regions where the internally displaced were resettled.[2] Even at the beginning, donors stimulated this rapid growth—for example, the joint UN–Government of Georgia "Women in the Development Process Project" organized national and regional women's forums.[3] Both with help and on their own, Georgian women began to identify common problems and create new organizations to respond to them. Over time, the priorities of these organizations changed. That reflected an evolution not only in the problems themselves but also in the responsiveness of leaders of women's groups to donor signals. Table 5.1 shows how the concerns of women's organizations have evolved since independence.

The ground swell of interest among women in addressing the first problems identified in Table 5.1 appears to have been quickly reoriented toward additional topics because of the Abkhazian and Ossetian conflicts and, later, because of the reorientation of donor programs away from humanitarian assistance. In 1999 all the 1997 and 1998 priorities remained valid, but because of the election, further emphasis was given to injecting gendered content into political-party platforms, encouraging women candidates to take part in parliamentary elections, strengthening women's participation in local governance, and transitioning from humanitarian assistance, through self-reliance, to development approaches.

Since the first grants given by the Soros Foundation, it seems that donors have identified the problems and set the overarching agenda for women's organizations in Georgia. Yet individual groups have, to a large extent, started out with their own agendas and sought to meet perceived needs of their respective target populations. As time has passed, donors have had a significant effect on their development, capacity, strategic thinking, and communications, as well as on the fundamental issues addressed and funding mechanisms.

Table 5.1 The Evolving Concerns of Women's Organizations

1991	Protection of human rights; protection of women's rights (disclosure of facts of violence, rights of women prisoners); charity (vulnerable population groups).
1992	Charity (vulnerable population groups, widows and orphans, people deprived as a result of the conflict); elevating women's status.
1993	Charity (internally displaced persons, families of soldiers and families with many children); psychological rehabilitation of the victims of violence; medical assistance to women; assistance to professional women for participation in business.
1994	Charity (internally displaced persons, families of soldiers and families with many children, homeless children, disabled persons); psychological rehabilitation of the victims of violence; medical assistance to women; rights of certain population groups (ethnic minorities, women in confinement, newborns, professionals); assistance to professional women to raise professionalism; cultural–educational measures; assistance for women's employment.
1995	Charity retains all above orientations; rights of certain population groups (ethnic minorities, professionals, orphans and homeless children, disabled children); assistance for employment; prevention of conflicts; legal education for women; familiarization with women's international movement experiences; improvement of women's socioeconomic conditions. (This was the year of the Beijing Women's Conference.)
1996	Charity retains all above orientations; rights of certain population groups (disabled, internally displaced persons, ethnic minorities, professionals, orphaned and homeless children); employment of the disabled; prevention of conflicts; women's legal education; familiarization with women's international movement experiences; improvement of women's socioeconomic conditions.
1997	Elevation of women's roles and status in social, economic, and political life; active involvement in the management process; extensive participation in the distribution of natural, material, and financial resources; facilitation of participation in the conflict resolution process; design of development programs; employment assistance.
1998	All priorities of 1997 remain valid; additional priorities: elevation of the level of civic culture of women; assistance to women in the process of self-actualization; eradication of the gender imbalance in political and economic life; elaboration of the strategy of the women's movement; development of recommendations for state gender policy.

Although the official number of registered women's organizations is one thousand, one organization claims there were only between fifty and sixty truly active women's groups as of late 1999.[4] Many of these organizations are small, underfunded, lacking in capacity, and probably ultimately unsustainable. Nevertheless, they have two advantages. First, their leaders are members of the intelligentsia and thus have access to those with influence and money in the Georgian elite. Second, because the array of topics relevant to women is broad, there is more than enough scope for start-up organizations to make a bid for funding from either local or international donors. Those that are already established have a good chance of receiving more funding once they have accounted for their first grant.

◦ Activities of Women's Organizations

Women's organizations in Georgia carry out a fairly wide range of activities. Although some specialize in lobbying the government on particular women's issues, the majority are multipurpose, which means that there is a great deal of overlap among them.

Because of the many social, economic, and political changes associated with the transition from a centralized state structure to a market-based economy and a democratic political system, all Georgians have been undergoing stress for the past nine years. Various studies indicate that stress-related illnesses are common among all segments of the population, but perhaps are most common among women.[5] The Association of Internally Displaced Women, which has been functioning since 1995, aims to restore the psychosocial well-being of women and implement educational programs. International NGOs such as the International Foundation of Conflictology and Negotiations Strategy and the Foundation for Human Resources have carried out various activities with the association, including psychotherapy and psycho-correction groups.

Many NGOs, both local and international, are beginning to recognize that men aged thirty-five to fifty are particularly vulnerable both psychologically and economically. Almost all internally displaced persons interviewed, both men and women, indicated that men are doubly traumatized because they are unable to support their families and because they have lost the war. Many are further shamed by the fact that their wives are bringing in whatever nonpension income they consume through low-status activities such as petty trading. These men are in such denial that they tend to shun income-generating or employment activities and retraining opportunities. Programs for men (and women) are largely in the self-reliance category, which usually refers to small and medium-sized enterprises or vocational training.

Many donors are sponsoring microcredit schemes and training programs in small and medium-sized enterprises for both men and women. There are also some vocational training programs, although probably fewer. The Foundation for International Community Assistance, funded by USAID, is the only nongovernmental organization with a micro-lending program that does not require collateral. It targets women and makes many loans to the internally displaced on the basis of their apparent creditworthiness, since this is a group-lending operation and solidarity among displaced people (particularly women) is high. Most other programs operate or are designed to begin operating with highly subsidized interest rates. The Norwegian Refugee Council, for example, has had good luck with its other programs with the organization Women in Business.

Because internally displaced women have become increasingly involved in small-scale trading in markets and bazaars throughout the country, donors and women's organizations have begun partnering together on microcredit lending to women traders. The Norwegian Refugee Council has united with Women in Business to create a small-business revolving fund for up to a thousand clients, with the ultimate goal of transforming it into a self-sustaining credit union. Beginning with 100 lari (US$50) loans at 3 percent interest with six-month terms, the loans will increase in number and volume as they are repaid. Although still in its first stages, the Norwegian Refugee Council/Women in Business partnership has had an almost total repayment rate. Similarly, the international NGO Save the Children works with the women's organization Constanta, whose primary role is to provide low-interest loans to groups of internally displaced women traders. By the spring of 1999, Constanta's loan portfolio consisted of nearly 220,000 lari and 2,480 clients, with a loan default rate under 2 percent.

Almost all the women's NGOs surveyed had some training or education-related activity. Educational levels of women in Georgia have traditionally been quite high. Among internally displaced persons, many women with university and graduate degrees have gravitated to the third sector in order to help others help themselves. They are involved in providing education (including English courses) for orphans and young people, as well as peace education for youths. One concern is that the level of educational attainment of all internally displaced youth is declining. Many are unable to go to school because they do not have money for books and appropriate clothes or they need to help make money for their families.

After the Abkhazian conflict, the Zugdidi representation of the Abkhaz Women's Council created the NGO Hope. Because Hope is typical of small, multiservice NGOs that are starting out, several of its educational activities are profiled below.

Some women's organizations are primarily or exclusively advocacy organizations, working closely with members of Parliament and others to ensure that Georgia implements the Convention on the Elimination of All Forms of Discrimination Against Women, which the government signed in September 1994. With the support of USAID and other donors, the Young Lawyer's Association, while not a women's organization as such, has done considerable work to define and guarantee women's legal, human, and civil rights.

Two Women's Organizations

Sokhumi

Three displaced women, two engineer–economists, and one teacher started Sokhumi, a humanitarian–cultural foundation, in September 1997. It was registered two years later. The president's husband, an industrialist, has sponsored this foundation. It has fifty women members who volunteer their time. Sokhumi has carried out fourteen programs, of which three help the elderly and three rehabilitate children. The foundation has established five centers: (1) a women's business development center, (2) an information center, (3) a youth center, (4) a social rehabilitation center, and (5) a cultural and educational center. It has received support from private-sector, government, and international NGOs.

Hope

Despite its "dependent" status as representative of the Women's Council, Hope has carried out five projects since its inception in May 1996. The first project, sponsored by Oxfam and the Prince and Princess Ammata Foundation, was a social program to help refugee children and women. Hope has cooperated with and received funding from Consent, an association of IDP women that conducts workshops, training, and consultation. Hope also has run three programs for young orphans. Under one of those programs, it ran a camp for thirteen- and fourteen-year-old orphans. The organization has since developed two other projects that it has submitted for funding. UNHCR is interested in funding one of the projects but is faced with budget constraints. The First Bank of Abkhazia, which serves internally displaced persons, has also promised to fund some activities, but Hope has yet to receive funding. In the interim, Hope is running a Sunday school at the director's home.

In January 2000, the Georgian women's group Women's Initiative for Equality began spearheading efforts to create an umbrella group of women's organizations. The Women's Initiative seeks to force implementation of various policies, including Presidential Decree 551, which is designed to enhance women's participation in political activity. (As of press time, the decree had yet to be signed.)

○ Constraints on Performance

A variety of factors prevent Georgian NGOs—and perhaps particularly women's organizations—from enhancing their performance. A majority are not unique to Georgia and are characteristic of most developing countries. Examples include the lack of a history of voluntarism, problems of corruption and inadequate codes of ethics, blurred distinctions between the third sector and the private sector (or in the Georgian case, the public sector), overlapping board memberships, and hijacking of the nongovernmental sector by interlocking elites.

A second group of factors, once again common to the nongovernmental sector in other countries, has to do with funding, financial management, and financial planning for sustainability. Most donors are relatively strict about bookkeeping and accounting for funds. USAID, though, is generally considered to be the strictest in its accounting requirements. That Horizonti has passed a Section 195 USAID audit after only one year of operation is a singular success. Few donors, however, have been prepared to invest in helping private voluntary and nongovernmental organizations plan for sustainability over even the medium term. Even in countries where NGO block grants have been in existence for a long time or where NGO umbrella projects have been put in place to enhance the capacity of local NGOs, disaster frequently strikes when the donor departs or when the local NGO is supposed to "graduate" to self-suffieciency.

Many Georgian NGOs are in comparatively better positions than their non–former Soviet Union counterparts because their founders, members, and even many of their beneficiaries are literate and highly educated. The idea of public accountability may not be widespread, but the fundamentals of keeping accounts are. Competent bookkeepers and accountants—especially women—are among the categories of the newly unemployed. But strategic planning for sustainability is a skill probably as poorly represented in Georgia as in most transitioning countries. Nonetheless, some of the organizations encountered are already established as foundations and will likely be able to devise ways to obtain additional capital. Several of these and others, such as the Abkhaz Women's Council, have started reaching out to local private-sector firms for event or special-appeal funding.

• Impact of Women's Organizations

∘ Beneficiaries

Clearly, women's organizations are having a significant impact on a variety of beneficiaries. Largely service-oriented organizations are delivering programs ranging from psychosocial rehabilitation to credit and business-planning training. Among the women's organizations working on women's rights and advocating women's empowerment in the political, economic, and social spheres, capacity is increasing and progress is being made through legislation. The major problems are now considered to be information dissemination and training in all societal sectors rather than legislative reform as such.

Government- and donor-sponsored women's organizations are also contributing significantly to knowledge building, research, networking, leadership training, and direct service provision to a wide range of beneficiaries, including internally displaced persons. The most reputable government-organized women's organization is the Abkhaz Women's Council, which—even though it is an independent, nonpartisan, nonpolitical NGO—still receives in-kind support from the Abkhaz government-in-exile and the Georgian government. The most notable donor-organized NGO is Horizonti, which evolved from an earlier group and was quickly certified as an eligible private voluntary organization for USAID funding. Horizonti provides grant funding for a variety of purposes to other Georgian NGOs, including women's and internally displaced women's organizations.

It is difficult to provide hard data on the numbers and varieties of beneficiaries served by local NGOs. Many women's organizations have a small membership and the numbers of beneficiaries they help directly may be limited. This is the case for many women's organizations dealing with internally displaced persons, in part because they are new and in part because they have yet to be considered for larger funding. This may soon change with the advent of the proposed UN–World Bank–Government of Georgia program for self-reliance, including a proposed self-reliance fund.

◦ Women Leaders

Given the number of highly educated women in Georgia, combined with the disastrous posttransition economic slump, many qualified women have suddenly been economically and professionally displaced. As one informant expressed it, "Before, women were less visible because they were inside buildings, working in offices. Now, they have lost those jobs and have to seek other kinds of employment literally in the street, often below their former status, and well below their qualifications." This also applies to internally displaced women, both those who provide assistance and those whom they assist. They are trading in the bazaars, on roadsides, in subway underpasses, and in local communities. Some, usually the elderly, are begging. Others are working in the service sector as, for example, manicurists or kiosk keepers and shop clerks. Once in leadership positions and with experience in high-level occupations, both displaced and other Georgian women professionals are being disempowered.

One way for these women to recoup their lost status is to found or participate in nongovernmental organizations. This in part explains the recent proliferation of NGOs of all kinds, especially those pertaining to women. Although women from the intelligentsia do not monopolize power and authority, they do constitute a barrier to women who are less highly trained and skilled who might otherwise create or manage NGOs or other types of groups. There is a sense in which these women leaders—even though they too suffered deprivation in income, social status, and physical comfort—are still at the top of the social hierarchy, just below the former *nomenklatura*. For example, one founder of a women's organization is a senior academician whose husband was a city mayor in Abkhazia. Another is a former deputy in the Supreme Council in Abkhazia. Yet another is the wife of a prominent industrialist who herself was a highly skilled professional until she became internally displaced.

The situation is similar for women who are in leadership positions of non–IDP women's organizations. Not surprisingly, as Georgia continues its transition to a democratic state with a free-market economy, new leadership positions open up. But in many instances, the same people fill them or influence who fills them. Socioeconomic and political status, personal or family wealth, and current influence—whether legitimate or based on corrupt alliances—all tend to meld together a series of interlocking elite groups.

Few women's organization leaders have attempted to make the jump from the third sector to politics. The most prominent exception is Lika Nadaraia, head of the Feminist Club, who ran unsuccessfully for Parliament in 1999 on an independent ticket. Many women's organization leaders shun the political limelight and disagree strongly with leaders such as Ms. Nadaraia who are trying to enter politics. Several leaders interviewed pointed out that NGOs need to improve before they can forge direct links with political parties.[6]

There is a strong and perhaps growing divide between political-party activity and women's NGOs. As the UN Development Program noted in a focus-group survey on the conditions of women in Georgia, women increasingly have joined women's organizations in lieu of political parties because they perceive that political parties are not sensitive to their needs.[7] Moreover, to be effective, the organizations themselves needed to remain or appear to remain independent of political links. Several organizational leaders repeated the widely held belief that the political system was ineffective at promoting needed reform and that parties and political figures were often too compromised or corrupt to take action to improve the lot of women throughout the country.[8]

The few women who have made it into the upper reaches of political life have openly eschewed women's organizations and many of their concerns, much to the regret of women organizational leaders. Established female politicians fear being marginalized and isolated in the eyes of the overall Georgian electorate as "women's leaders" and hence are openly antagonistic toward "feminist" ideas and the legal promotion of women's rights in general. Irina Sarishvili-Chanturia, the most prominent women in politics and leader of the opposition National Democratic Party, openly derided feminism as "worse than homosexuality."

∘ Government and Public Policy

Although the Georgian government has cooperated with women's organizations and recently promoted gender issues, it has done so largely under pressure from international agencies and increasingly well organized women's organizations. The Georgian leadership and Parliament legally enabled the growth of civil society in general and women's groups in particular by passing the Civil Code in 1995. But the government has not made gender issues a high priority in its struggle to establish and strengthen Georgia's democratic governance and economy. Both the women's leaders interviewed and the existing literature indicate that many of the most pressing discrimination issues (the right of inheritance, equal employment opportunities, decisionmaking within the household) have deep roots in Georgian cultural traditions. The government itself has done little to challenge or even monitor traditional discrimination. There are, in fact, no current laws or policy statements defining and regulating discrimination against women.[9]

The government waited nearly five years to submit its first full report on discrimination in Georgia to the UN's Committee on the Elimination of Discrimination Against Women. Not surprisingly, many of its findings were perfunctory and overly optimistic. In response to the government's report, three women's organizations (the Women's Rights Study Group of the Georgian Young Lawyers Association, the Feminist Club, and the Center of Strategic Research and Development of Georgia) wrote a "shadow report" drawing on the research and findings of a large number of Georgian women's groups. The shadow report was deeply critical of both the paucity of women's rights in Georgia and the government's efforts in promoting them.

Both the government and the shadow report were submitted separately to the Committee on the Elimination of Discrimination Against Women, which in turn judged them, drew lessons from each, and presented a list of recommendations. These recommendations were then delivered to the Georgian government. In a surprising move, President Shevardnadze prepared a draft decree (Presidential Decree 511) in the summer of 1999 based on the committee's recommendations. Many women's organizations were understandably enthusiastic about this development, taking it as a positive step in the evolution of women's organizational strength. Since its drafting, though, the decree has languished on the floor of Parliament.

Most women's organization leaders interviewed for this study characterized the government's positions toward women's organizations, women's rights, and gender issues as largely indifferent. Many were disillusioned with the leadership's inability and unwillingness to implement laws and decrees designed to promote women's rights. Others remained exasperated with the government's acceptance of traditional gender roles.

• Women's Organizations
and the International Community

The international community and official aid donors have been the primary source of funding for women's organizations since the first wave of registration in 1994. Indeed, while analysts and scholars have pointed to the recent explosive growth of organizational life in Georgia as a highlight of post-Soviet reform and societal change, they also stress that this explosion would not have occurred without a healthy infusion of international assistance. Today, nearly all major international assistance institutions active in the country provide financial support to women's organizations. Conversely, most women's organizations remain wholly or mostly dependent on some form of international assistance for survival.

Donors have recognized that women's organizations are particularly effective partners in assessing the needs of vulnerable communities, particularly internally displaced persons. Many international organizations are aware that war and displacement have uniquely affected women, many of whom have increasingly carried the burden of providing for their families. Women have thus been singled out for a variety of programs, ranging from emergency humanitarian assistance to small-business development. The nature of international assistance has changed radically in recent years. The transformation is particularly true of aid designed to help the displaced and more vulnerable segments of Georgian society. Before 1998, donors concentrated on two broad types of assistance. On a macro level, much effort was directed at helping a battered and unstable government shore up tottering economic and political institutions in the wake of its near collapse in 1993.

At the same time, international assistance organizations targeted the internally displaced and other intensely vulnerable populations by providing food, clothing, and rehabilitated shelter—aid, in other words, targeted to satisfy the most immediate needs of the more drastically affected. Within several years, however, many donors concluded that local populations were not being sufficiently helped through their programs. Some feared that a culture of dependency on emergency assistance had been created within the community of displaced persons, while little had been done to alleviate the suffering of the majority of Georgians, 43 percent of whom lived below the poverty line.[10]

Beginning in 1998, donor agencies and international NGOs—including USAID, the Norwegian Refugee Council, the International Rescue Committee, Save the Children, and CARE—began shifting their programs from emergency humanitarian assistance activities to sustainable-development programs designed to help vulnerable communities and individuals help themselves. Donors began looking toward enhancing the self-reliance of displaced persons through professional and agricultural training activities and microcredit programs. The strategy was to provide a bridge from emergency to development programs for displaced and in-place communities alike. Local people now were not just being targeted for relief; in some instances, they were involved in carrying out and sometimes even designing novel programs.

Through its Community Participation Program begun in 1999, for example, the International Rescue Committee took the bold step of grouping internally displaced persons with local residents in ten western Georgian communities to address broader community needs and problems. Similarly, Save the Children's US$6 million Georgian Assistance Initiative, funded by USAID, sought to address the difficulties faced by broader war-damaged communities, including but not exclusive to displaced persons, through grants to local and international NGOs with innovative ideas in the fields of health, housing, and agriculture.

In their desire to target local populations more effectively, donors have emphasized newfound relationships with Georgia's nascent NGOs—in particular, women's organizations. Donors have provided women's groups with funding for a wide range of projects covering the full spectrum of their operational activities. Groups such as the Abkhaz Women's Council and the Association of Internally Displaced Abkhaz Women have been increasingly important conduits for distributing humanitarian aid and providing basic health services. More broadly, donors acknowledge the quiet but growing role women play as decisionmakers and leaders within their nuclear families and communities, particularly in collective centers for internally displaced persons. USAID, for example, has funded a series of leadership training programs organized by the Academy for Educational Development for heads of women's organizations.

As donors move away from humanitarian assistance and cooperate more fully with women's organizations, some difficulties have been encountered. Women's organizations, like all NGOs in Georgia, are generally donor-dependent. Their programs and even their very existence are often tied to donor funding and the grants available to them. To attract needed funding, dynamic organizations such as the International Medical Women's Fund do not specialize in a sector in which they might have a comparative advantage, such as health. Instead, they broaden their scope to include issues such as women's legal rights education. Other groups, such as Constanta, are literally donor-organized women's organizations. These organizations are created for the simple reason that international assistance organizations conclude that no existing women's organizations could be effective partners. Other women's organizations are government organized, created by government individuals or offices to attract funding designed for NGOs. Although much of the work done by such organizations has been and continues to be productive, the existence of successful government-organized nongovernmentals and donor-organized nongovernmentals reflects the fact that few mature and fully independent women's organizations exist in Georgia. Alternatively, where a local women's organization has preassistance capacity, it may find donor management styles difficult to accept, as was the case for the Foundation for the Development of Human Resources. Although not a women's organization, the foundation has reached a stage that several women's organizations will soon attain.

• General Findings and Conclusions

○ Limited Participation

The fieldwork confirms earlier findings that membership in women's organizations tends to be limited, even for organizations with regional branches. A survey of internally displaced women conducted by the team indicated that only 17 percent of respondents belong to any organization, including NGOs and political parties. Women's leaders and experts stressed that women do not necessarily want to collaborate any more than men do. One possible explanation is that ordinary women, particularly those who are internally displaced, are too preoccupied with the struggle for survival, thereby having little time to give to organizations.

○ Upper-Socioeconomic-Strata Leadership

Leaders of women's organizations come almost exclusively from the intelligentsia, although some are wives of businessmen or politicians. With one exception, all the leaders the team met had at least an undergraduate degree, and many had been professors or researchers. Most also had previous political and social visibility. However, they were not operating in their fields of expertise and in most instances admitted that they had had little management experience or organizational know-how.

○ Duplication of Activities

Most of the organizations studied are carrying out similar activities. They are not specializing but instead are replicating other organizations' activities, often in the same location. Since many are operating outside their main areas of expertise, they would benefit from the help of outside specialists but apparently do not call on other women and organizations to meet this need. Interviews indicated that one potential consortium intended to include sixteen women's organizations but was not yet formally established because no one could agree on a leader.

○ Perceptions About Donor Impartiality

Everywhere the team traveled, including Tbilisi, there was a conviction that only an in-group of NGOs receive donor funding and that this group does not grow much. It is perceived that once a particular NGO becomes a given donor's "darling," it continues to receive funding from that donor to the exclusion of others. Members of donors' local staffs— or their relatives and friends—create some of these favorites. Moreover, the spouses or family members of Georgian government officials tend to create or work for NGOs that receive donor funding, or they receive scarce positions at international NGOs that have grant funds.

∘ Sustainability of Women's Organizations

As mentioned earlier, most estimates concur that women's NGOs worth counting number no more than sixty or so, although a thousand are registered. These so-called best-placed women's organizations either have managed donor funds effectively more than once or have participated in enough donor-funded capacity building to be seen as worthy of funding. Sixty women's NGOs for a population of 5.4 million, of whom more than half are women, seems at first glance to be relatively few. On closer inspection, though, we find there are more nascent women's regional organizations not yet counted among this group. These are likely to receive direct grants from at least one donor in the next three years. In addition, local councils and municipalities will probably begin to receive direct funding (for example, from the World Bank and USAID)—a development that in some cases may diminish available funding for NGOs.

The next few years are an ideal time for donors and NGOs to work on partnerships, consortia, and endowments so that sustainability becomes more likely beyond even the sixty "best" NGOs. Not all organizations, no matter how worthy their aims or how gifted and sincere their founders, can ultimately be sustained unless the Georgian economy improves dramatically and a new tradition of voluntarism is developed. To survive without significant external funding, membership-based organizations will need to become bigger and require membership dues. Whether this kind of organizational structure lends itself to life in post-Soviet Georgia remains to be seen.

• Notes

1. The USAID mission to the Republic of Georgia cleared the study's scope of work and assisted the study team in making contact with key informants in the Georgian and international nongovernmental organization (NGO) communities. However, the mission wished that it be made clear that this report is not an evaluation of its programs.

2. One relatively reliable source for the number and respective scopes of local NGOs in Georgia oriented toward internally displaced persons is a directory put together by CHCH in 1999 in the context of the European Union delegation's program, Development of IDP–Oriented NGOs in Georgia, with assistance from the International Rescue Committee, the UN High Commissioner for Refugees, and UNOCHA. This directory lists fifty organizations, with separate listings for local branches of some. Of these, the team visited or spoke with representatives of about one-third, both in Tbilisi and in the regions. This list includes both women's organizations and those whose members or leaders

are both women and men. ATINATI, for example, was founded by a couple, as was the cultural–humanitarian foundation Sokhumi.

Regarding women's organizations, the Horizonti Foundation's 1998 *Caucasus Women's NGOs Needs Assessment* is a better source. The Georgia portion of that study included forty organizations, thirty-two from Tbilisi and eight from the regions. The selection criteria were similar to those used for this study: (1) organizations for which women's problems represent either the main or an additional sphere of activity; (2) organizations represented in the Women's Leadership Training Program financed by USAID and implemented by the Academy for Educational Development; (3) recently established and Soviet-era organizations; and (4) geographic location. The database for this study was made up of the Horizonti Foundation's own lists, the Georgian NGOs Database published by ITIC, and other data sources, including the Ministry of Justice, with which organizations must register.

3. Gender Development Association, *Conditions of Women in Georgia*, pp. 79–82.

4. Lela Gaprindashili, email correspondence, 19 November 1999; Nina Tsihinstavi, interview, 11 October 1999; Marina Meskhi, interview, 20 October 1999.

5. See Kharashvili, *Psychosocial Examination of IDP Children and Women*, and Dourglishvili, *Social Change and the Georgian Family*.

6. Georgian Young Lawyers' Association et al., *Report of Non-Governmental Organizations on the Status of Women*; Tsihinstavi, interview, 11 October 1999; Meskhi, interview, 20 October 1999.

7. United Nations Development Program, *Human Development Report: Georgia 1998*.

8. Tsihinstavi, interview, 11 October 1999; Meskhi, interview, 20 October 1999.

9. See Georgian Young Lawyers' Association et al., *Report of Non-Governmental Organizations on the Status of Women*.

10. World Bank, *Georgia: A Poverty Report*.

6

Women's Organizations in Postconflict Bosnia and Herzegovina

Martha Walsh

This chapter examines women's organizations in postconflict Bosnia and Herzegovina. It describes their emergence, activities, and programs and the changes in their activities over time. It then assesses the impact of these organizations in addressing gender issues associated with the conflict. Finally, it discusses the nature of assistance provided to them by the international community and the areas of tension between them. The chapter is based largely on the information obtained during interviews conducted by the author with the leaders and staff of women's organizations, staffs of international organizations, representatives of the donor agencies that support women's organizations, and a cross section of Bosnian women. Five organizations were selected as case studies to illustrate different activities and the types of development and expansion that have taken place in the past few years.

- ### Emergence of Women's Organizations in Bosnia and Herzegovina

Before the conflict, NGOs did not exist as such in Bosnia and Herzegovina, though there were some clubs organized around leisure activities (for example, hunting and fishing clubs) and associations of disabled persons. The absence of NGOs may be explained by two factors. First, the services that NGOs now provide had been provided by the government. Second, there was no political space or climate for the development of civil-society institutions. Although there was a mass women's association linked to the Communist Party of Yugoslavia, it was not as active as those found in other countries that had mass party-based movements such as Cambodia and Vietnam. Moreover, its close ties with the party deprived it of autonomy.[1] Although feminist organizations emerged in Croatia, Serbia, and Slovenia in the late 1980s and early 1990s, none appeared in Bosnia and Herzegovina.

The humanitarian disaster created by the war exceeded the capacity of the government to meet the overwhelming and diverse needs of its people. This vacuum was largely filled by women. Both beneficiaries and service providers were mostly women, since the vast majority of able-bodied men were in the army. The first women's organizations consisted of volunteers who provided emergency food, clothing, and shelter for refugees, the elderly, and other vulnerable groups. Psychosocial counseling and medical care for rape victims was also one of the immediate needs addressed by women's organizations.

A number of these organizations became implementing partners of the UN High Commissioner for Refugees (UNHCR), which served as lead agency coordinating humanitarian relief during the war and in its immediate aftermath. Most groups that started during this era are still present, but the number of organizations run by and for women has mushroomed in correspondence with the general surge in local NGO activity. Some local and international observers suggest that the dramatic increase in women's organizations may reflect their exclusion from representative- and executive-level politics, and in that sense, women's organizations represent a parallel political structure. This may be true for some, but as will be discussed, few women's organizations have fully grasped the notion of civil society.

In the postconflict era, the development of women's organizations had a variety of roots. Some, such as Bospo and Bosfam, were spin-offs of international agencies (the Danish Refugee Council and Oxfam, respectively). Others were formed to address specific needs arising in the postconflict era, including income generation (Vidra) and legal rights (the Center for Legal Aid for Women). Others, such as Zena Zenama (Women to Women) and Udruzene Zene (United Women), were founded specifically to challenge and improve the position and status of women in society.

• Nature and Activities of Women's Organizations

The difficulty in defining "women's organizations" is exemplified in the current NGO community in Bosnia and Herzegovina. According to the 1999 International Council for Voluntary Organizations directory, there are 284 indigenous NGOs in Bosnia. Of these, 112 include "women" in the sectoral areas in which they work, although only 56 mention women's issues in their mission statement. Other lists put the number of women's organizations at about 90. Yet women head up almost half of all local NGOs; thus, organizations headed by women do not necessarily target women exclusively. This is one of the problems in labeling an organization a "women's organization." For example, women head many of the disabled-persons associations, whose collective lobbying efforts have been extremely effective in producing visible results, such as disabled parking spaces and wheelchair paths on sidewalks in Sarajevo.

Some groups simply refuse to be identified as women's organizations. Bospo in Tuzla shuns the label even though it runs one of the largest microcredit schemes targeted exclusively to women. Others, such as Vidra in Banja Luka, identify themselves as women's organizations but reject any connections with a feminist agenda. Moreover, there are other groups that tackle "gender issues." One example is the overtly feminist organization Zena Zenama. It is working on a campaign to support conscientious objectors, the vast majority of whom are male.

This is not to say that all women's groups have such a flexible structure, as clearly some are as hierarchical and bureaucratic as male-dominated NGOs. In fact, many of the key women's organizations are characterized by having one charismatic leader, without whom the organization would cease to function. As one person put it, the name of the NGO is often synonymous with its president's name. This trend, however, appears to be changing. International staff who work closely with women's organizations have noticed an effort to cultivate a second tier of leadership, particularly among young women staff members. In some cases this has happened by default when leaders are ill, burn out, or travel too much, and in other cases the process has been by design. Still, the leaders of women's organizations are almost exclusively from the social elite. This positioning does not necessarily impinge on their efficacy in serving their beneficiaries, and in some ways allows them more access to resources. However, it may cloud their ability to identify beneficiaries' vulnerabilities and capabilities. For example, a staff person at a women's NGO in Banja Luka stated that microcredit loans would be inappropriate for their beneficiaries because they were uneducated.

This section focuses on organizations run by women for women beneficiaries. However, care must be taken not to exclude or discount the activities of women engaged in other sectors, as such leadership facilitates the mainstreaming of women and gender into other sectors and thus deserves recognition and support.

The activities of women's organizations fall into the broad categories of democracy and human rights, microcredit and income generation, education and training, and psychosocial support and health. Despite common assumptions that women's organizations are more likely to be welfarist/humanitarian, more organizations in Bosnia and Herzegovina were found to have an exclusive emphasis on democracy/human rights (eleven) than on a humanitarian mandate (eight, including those within the psychosocial and microcredit categories). Most, however, are a mixture of these components, reflecting the specific donor objectives and demands of emerging civil society.

◦ Democracy and Human Rights

It is generally perceived by local observers that the increase in the number of NGOs addressing democracy and human rights is almost entirely donor-driven. This may be less true among women's organizations, particularly those in the Republika Srpska (RS). Of the women's organizations that emphasize democracy and human rights, commitment to these issues began before donors started providing significant funding for such work. Organizations that identify themselves as feminist see feminism and democracy as inextricably linked. As the cofounder of Zena Zenama put it, "Feminism and democracy are dealing with the idea of equality and they are resisting the power of despotism. . . . The ideal of equality incorporates them, so it is very important for me to explore experiences in relationships between these two traditions."[2] The activities undertaken by women's groups in this area include roundtable discussions, advocacy campaigns, media spots, free legal aid to women, and the production of educational materials on rights issues.

◦ Microcredit

Women's organizations are also providing microcredit to women borrowers, among whom displaced women and female-headed households are the primary target groups. Loans range between 1,000 and 5,000 deutsche marks and are provided on a solidarity-group basis whereby each group member is jointly and severally liable for the repayment of each loan in the group. This arrangement thus serves as collateral. The repayment rates are exceptionally high. Although a popular activity, microcredit is complicated in Bosnia as it is technically illegal for nongovernmental institutions to provide credit. Some NGOs have been able to circumvent the rules, but the larger programs work through Local

Initiatives Departments (LIDs) in the Employment and Training Foundations of the governments in each entity. The LIDs then provide the capital to the lending agencies. The bureaucracy and administration involved prevents small organizations from participating as lenders. With a view to establishing sustainable microfinance institutions (MFIs), the World Bank has now identified seven organizations (mostly local) to serve as MFIs. Among them is Bospo, whose clientele consists entirely of women.

∘ Education and Training

Although education and training programs are not as popular now as they were two years ago, they are still considered important, particularly for women without formal education who want to acquire marketable skills. The skills training offered includes sewing and knitting as well as computer, foreign language, and secretarial skills. There are concerns about whether this type of training gender-types women, and whether these skills are marketable to begin with. A secretarial school for women run by the International Catholic Migration Commission, initially targeted at demobilized female soldiers, has a 64 percent job placement rate. That high rate can be accounted for in part because the training is accompanied by an aggressive effort to identify job vacancies. By contrast, a computer course run by a women's organization in Banja Luka has not led to employment for any of its participants. Other forms of training are nevertheless being offered by women's NGOs, such as NGO development training and instruction of trainers and facilitators. These skills can prove useful in a growing development culture where meetings and conferences, led by facilitators, occur regularly. Organizations such as Medica Zenica, however, charge only larger NGOs for their services and provide their services free to smaller groups. Facilitation skills also can be a means of strengthening cooperation between local women's organizations.

∘ Psychosocial Support and Health

Few women's organizations are addressing general health issues. While some continue to provide psychosocial counseling, the number doing so has declined noticeably since the immediate aftermath of the war. One of the first women's NGOs in RS that provided psychosocial services is now in danger of closing altogether. The programs that continue to function in this area are those that have built a reputation in this field and widened their networks to secure funding.

◦ Change in Focus and Activities

During and immediately following the conflict, in 1996, the activities of women's organizations were almost exclusively humanitarian, with a concentration on psychosocial support. Some have suggested that at first these activities were identified and pursued by local women. There is at least one case in which a women's organization intended to begin an income-generating program after conducting a survey of beneficiary needs. But international donors told this group that it would not receive funds unless a psychosocial component was added to its proposal. The negative effect of such a directive is twofold: it denied women's organizations the right to determine their own needs, and it imposed a "victim" identity that did not exist.

By 1997, the situation had changed. Funds for psychosocial programs began to dry up, and the emphasis switched to income generation. Most international and local observers agree that this transition was largely donor-driven and corresponded with strategies to revitalize the economy and reduce overall dependence on international aid.

The Bosnian Women's Initiative was cited as the primary catalyst for the switch in focus among women's organizations. While the projects first supported were very traditional, the fields into which women are currently expanding include production of paper bags and toilet paper, coffee bean roasting, and a taxi service. It has been suggested that this change reflects two interlinked processes. In the beginning, women worked in the areas that were familiar and comfortable (i.e., women knew how to knit, even though it was not usually for commercial purposes). It took some time for women to move out of this comfort zone and undertake activities that they were not familiar with. Second, there was also an increasing awareness of the market, particularly with regard to goods that were imported but could be simply and cheaply produced locally (e.g., toilet paper). These factors combined to bring about a transition from sympathy projects to those with potential commercial viability.

Democracy, return of minorities, and legal information centers are other areas into which women's organizations are moving. As noted earlier, democracy projects within some women's organizations were initiated before heavy donor emphasis in this area, and increased international support has clearly turned these into growth areas. As most aid projects now are tied to the return of displaced persons to their home of origin, a number of women's organizations also have taken on this initiative. Again, this appears to be a response to international agendas rather than an organic initiative. Linkages with minority return have become a decisive factor for funding projects under the Bosnian Women's Initiative. Also associated with return is an increase in organizations providing legal aid.

• Impact of Women's Organizations

Before considering the impact of women's organizations, one must remember that these organizations have existed in Bosnia and Herzegovina only for a maximum of six years. The society has experienced massive upheaval, resulting in socioeconomic and political chaos—and opportunity.

One can view the impact of women's organizations at the micro and macro levels. The most significant and tangible impacts are perhaps at the micro level, where differences are made to individual lives. Microcredit projects have saved women beneficiaries and their families from destitution, replacing coping strategies with a livelihood. Activities at the micro level have instilled confidence in many of the beneficiaries, putting them in a better position to pursue other economic and personal endeavors.

In the area of psychosocial rehabilitation, too, the results can be dramatic. Receiving psychosocial support as well as help with vocational studies and other matters, many women have been able to return to their communities with new skills and confidence.

Women's organizations also may play a part in raising consciousness among individual women. Among feminist organizations such as Medica Zenica, Udruzene Zene, and Zena Zenama, involvement in a women's organization with a feminist agenda has refined and altered individual notions of feminism and contributed to personal growth. For some women, the experience of working at or with these organizations has enabled them to articulate educated arguments for feminist ideals that they understood intuitively but could not express.

Despite these successes, one must recognize that while effective women's organizations have reached out to some vulnerable groups of women, others have been missed. Few, if any, organizations are addressing the situation of "Roma" (gypsy) women, who were among the most vulnerable populations before the war. Although much assistance is targeted at female-headed households, it appears to be directed primarily at war widows or those with missing husbands. Anecdotal evidence suggests that divorcées are not among this target population, despite the fact that they may be as vulnerable as, if not more so than, women with dead or missing husbands. Alimony laws exist but are seldom enforced. Thus, divorced women may find themselves without housing or the means to feed their children.

At the community level, the impact of women's organizations is especially evident in income-generation projects. First, with an income, female beneficiaries do not drain community resources. Second, a number of the projects started by women's organizations respond to diverse needs within the community. For example, a women's group in Bihac used microcredit to start a minibus service to bring people from outlying villages to town to visit relatives in the hospital. In Mostar, a group of mothers with mentally disabled children started a workshop for mentally disabled persons seventeen and older who had completed school for children with special needs, filling a gap in the provision of services for mentally disabled young adults.

In addition, women are working individually and collectively within local community associations. The Center for Civic Initiatives in Banja Luka encouraged the development of a community group, including both men and women, to dispose of an unsanitary and unsightly garbage dump in their area. Men and women worked together to persuade a contracting company to remove the garbage, and then lobbied the municipality to provide fuel for the removal trucks.

At the macro level, women report that women's issues are being discussed more openly and regularly. However, structural barriers to women's equality remain. This may be explained by the lack of a cohesive women's movement in Bosnia that is able and willing to speak out on mainstream political issues in addition to gender-specific issues. Even among vocal women's groups, some observers have noted a lack of "gender awareness" or sensitivity in their being able to define gender issues. For example, the president of a women's organization in Banja Luka expressed discomfort with "feminist ideas" and the implicit emphasis placed on opposition between women and men. Although the organization took part in the preparation of the Women's Human Rights report, she felt that women's rights were secondary to broader human rights issues. There may be an absence of comprehensive gender training provided to women's organizations, because it may be assumed that women's organizations do not need such training. Such responses indicate that many clearly do. A glance at the gender breakdown of the heads of international organizations and embassies shows that the international community is not setting a positive example. All but one of the primary political and diplomatic personnel are men.

In addition, local observers note a general unwillingness to cooperate with women politicians. On the one hand, the government has been unresponsive to advocacy initiatives by women's organizations, leading to a sense of futility. On the other hand, given a deep cynicism and distrust of the government, some groups feel that involvement at any level with politicians may compromise the goals of their organizations. Such organizations are not yet confident of having established sufficient independence to engage with the government. It will take time and perhaps the identification of issues of mutual concern before links can be improved. Still, there are some women who, recognizing the potential pitfalls, bridge the gap by serving in both the political and NGO worlds.

From a gender perspective, it appears that women's organizations have succeeded in addressing some "practical gender interests" and have begun to move on to "strategic gender interests." However, for the

---

Bridging the Gap

In the aftermath of the war, Gordona Vidovic and others recognized that those who fought the war and those for whom the war was fought were not adequately represented by the political parties. They then established the opposition (Serb) Peasant Party to represent the interests of "peasants"—mainly agricultural workers.

As an opposition party in the small town of Modrica in Republika Srpska, the party had its work cut out for it. Through informal contacts, Vidovic met with women's organizations in Banja Luka and in Bosnia–Herzegovina, but the nongovernmental organization phenomenon had not yet arrived in the more remote parts of the Republika Srpska. She decided to found a women's organization—which would start by providing legal aid, since she is a lawyer—as a way of raising the political consciousness of women. Through her clients she learned about the day-to-day problems of women, and she began to speak out about them. She also monitored the activities of the Parliament. She struggles to maintain the independence of the NGO but also recognizes that there must be links between political parties and NGOs to promote the advancement of women.

Buducnost has received support and assistance from Delphi International/Star, and the Peasant Party participates in training sponsored by the National Democratic Institute. The assistance has come free. The aid has been critical, particularly in NGO development and media. Vidovic has noted that given her dual role, some donors have been wary to put up funds—and the NGO particularly has suffered as a consequence.

effective sustainable empowerment of women, practical and strategic gender issues need to be substantively linked. One woman suggested that through microcredit programs, women should be made more aware of the general economic situation and the laws that discriminate against them as women and small entrepreneurs.

• International Assistance to Women's Organizations

International assistance to Bosnian women's organizations has taken a variety of forms, including direct cash grants, microcredit, and training. In general, most cash grants have been accompanied by management, fund-raising, proposal writing, advocacy, and microcredit training.

◦ Types of Assistance

Most of the cash grants provided to women's organizations are for specific projects. Few cover general operating costs. The largest funding institution devoted to women's projects is the Bosnian Women's Initiative, which provides grants for, among other things, a partial salary subsidy. These grants are largely geared toward covering equipment or production costs. Kvinna till Kvinna (KtK), however, supports a small number of women's organizations with the general aim of increasing women's voices in society and their awareness of women's rights. Similarly, the Delphi International/Star Project provided direct grants of between 5,000 and 60,000 deutsche marks to advocacy-related organizations while also supporting broader projects, such as workshops, conferences, and training sessions. Some groups have received funding from the European Union's Phare project and other European donors. USAID's Office of Transition Initiatives (OTI) provides onetime grants to projects for specific items. According to the Office of Transition Initiatives, women's organizations constitute 13 percent of recipient organizations and account for 9 percent of total funds distributed. As the Delphi Project has wound up, the OTI funds are the only current source of USAID funding for women's organizations.

Microcredit programs targeting women beneficiaries are almost exclusively at the low end of the loan market, dispersing only between 1,000 and 5,000 deutsche marks per loan. Moreover, the largest credits do not emphasize gender as a significant component. A study conducted by the Delphi International/MEET Project found that women receive less than 26 percent of all microcredit grants (save Bospo) and the average loan size is 20 percent higher for male borrowers.[3]

Training at the organizational level concentrates on NGO development, capacity building, fund-raising, and advocacy. Several different agencies provided these sessions, and women's organizations that had taken part in them noted the importance of the support. Given that the whole concept of NGOs was new to Bosnia–Herzegovina, the training was vital if organizations were to survive and grow in the postconflict era. Advocacy training was particularly well received; there is no word in the local language for "advocacy." Delphi International/Star provided resources that enabled women from Bosnia, Croatia, and Macedonia to put together a workbook on advocacy that has been widely distributed. Those who have used it consider it valuable in their everyday work. Training also has served as a way to develop leadership among the individuals within an organization.

∘ Areas of Tension and Cooperation Between Women's Organizations and International Donors

Many women noted the vital role that international agencies have played in building links between international women's organizations. First, the links have released women's organizations from the isolation created by the war. Being part of a global women's network is important, ideologically and financially, for the work of those groups.

Cooperation with donors has been best where the donors were responsive to the needs and issues identified by the women's organizations themselves. Both KtK and Delphi International/Star were cited as primary examples of this kind of partnership. It allowed the organizations to develop organically, which many felt was the key to a successful and sustainable organization. Delphi in particular played a key role as facilitator of a women's network, organizing conferences and workshops requested by the members of the network.

Political support, where it has been given, has also been essential. The women's voter-education project was again mentioned as an example as the Organization for Security and Cooperation in Europe (OSCE) gave its full political backing to the project. This has also been a source of tension, however.

Despite the enthusiasm with which women acknowledged support of the international community, most were able to identify a number of difficulties they had had with donors. First, there was reported to be a lack of coordination between the donors. This, some noted, has resulted in wasted funds and ineffectual programming. As a result of some women's organizations confronting international staff with this problem, a Gender Coordinating Group was established under the auspices of the Office of the High Representative's (OHR) Human Rights Task Force. It includes UNDP, UNICEF, OSCE, the Council of Europe, the International Human Rights Law Group, Oxfam, Kvinna till Kvinna, UN Mission in BiH (UNMIBH), OHR, the International Organization for Migration (IOM), and the National Democratic Institute.

A second but related issue is the problem with the donor agendas. Some of the stronger women's NGOs have been able to reject donors, including USAID, which have approached the NGOs with projects outside their intended scope of work. Smaller and less financially secure groups are more likely to succumb to such pressure. For example, a small women's legal aid center in the RS has recently taken on a UNHCR project to provide cattle to people returning to the area. In addition to a perceived arrogance on the part of donors, the pace at which the agendas change prevents continuity and development of proficiency in a particular area. This indeed both fuels competition for funds and restricts the ability of organizations to specialize in a particular area, thus restricting the development of a broad range of services that could be provided by NGOs in general.

Related to this is the attempt to develop the third sector, or civil society. Although most NGOs, including women's organizations, address "civil society" somewhere in their mission statements or sectoral areas, it is not clear that all groups share the same understanding of the term. Some women's organizations feel they are not capable of effecting change because they are not connected to a political party. This phenomenon may have resulted from international agencies using local NGOs as service providers during the war, without committing resources at the time to develop their potential as civil-society institutions.[4]

Some organizations also commented on the use of inappropriate development models. Some agencies have attempted to apply in Bosnia project designs developed elsewhere in the world without duly considering contextual and cultural differences. To a certain extent, these comments also applied to staff of international agencies. A few organizations indicated that some donor staff have been poorly prepared to work in Bosnia. They further noted that the staff of women's organizations found this level of ignorance tiresome because they needed to provide history lessons before explaining the content of their project. This is

said to have led, in some cases, to a careless selection of local implementing partners.

In the same vein, some organizations commented that donors and
international agencies tend to give attention to only a small number of
larger organizations concentrated in the major cities, neglecting and
marginalizing budding groups in more remote areas. In particular, there
was notable frustration at the selection of "favorites" that receive the
bulk of attention and funding regardless of their areas of expertise or
absorptive capacity. At the same time, international staff have commented that some of the larger women's NGOs are unwilling to pass up
projects or funding that could otherwise go to smaller groups.

The emphasis on donor visibility, noted during the war in Bosnia,
disturbed some women's organizations that found the only evidence of
the donor's presence in certain areas to be agency emblems posted on
fences or buildings.

Although political support given in the context of the women's
voter-education project was vital to its success, women's organizations
also have commented on the lack of support given at other times, which
in some cases obstructed their work. Bosnian women's organizations
also have been disappointed by the lack of vocal public support from
senior USAID officials on the contributions that women's organizations
have made in promoting democracy.

Table 6.1   Summary of Points of Cooperation and Tension

Cooperation	Tension
Response to needs identified by local women's organizations	Lack of coordination between donors/international organizations
Links with regional and international women's organizations	Donor directives
Facilitation of local networking activities	Lack of continuity
Leadership/advocacy/media staff training	Imposition of inappropriate models
Political support	Lack of political support/obstruction Lack of vocal support from senior USAID officials
Training in capacity building	Uninformed staff
Study tours abroad	Careless selection of local partners

◦ Levels, Timing, and Duration of Funding

One lesson that appears to emerge from international assistance to Bosnia is that large-scale, high-profile, and well-funded projects may be less successful than smaller initiatives. The Bosnian Women's Initiative is an example. When it was launched as a US$5 million fund for women, the ensuing chaos in establishing operational strategy and selection criteria resulted in fierce competition between women's organizations and weak, ill-conceived projects, because the motive seemed to be to engage as many women as possible under the grant. Since then, the approach has been to scale back and decentralize. The maximum number of beneficiaries per project is now about twenty-five, which appears to better promote long-term sustainability.

Meanwhile, smaller-scale funding umbrellas, such as Delphi International/Star and Kvinna till Kvinna, appear to have achieved more with less. Funding has been concentrated on a few key groups, but general funds also have been available to support the wider network. It appears that the flexibility of the funding has been more significant than the amount. Moreover, the lack of funding available to women's groups in the Republika Srpska meant that they learned they could make something from nothing. This, however, is not to say that women's organizations do not need funding. Operating costs and staff salaries quickly drain resources. Because local organizations are rarely allowed overheads, funds must be siphoned off general project funds, restricting the amount available for implementation. Here donor coordination could be essential in limiting duplication and concentrating resources on specific targets.

Compounding restrictions on budgets is the general short-termism of funding periods. The longest funding cycle is one year, reflecting the donor community's holding pattern in an emergency phase without a longer-term plan. For most women's organizations, this short-term approach has not been problematic because funding was virtually ensured from one of a number of sources. Some organizations have begun to think in terms of five-year plans, while others confess to being wholly unprepared.

The time delay between acceptance of proposals and disbursal of funds was noted as a particular problem for projects funded by the European Union, where the lag can be up to a year. This affects both international and local organizations, although international organizations are more likely to have access to funds from headquarters to tide them over during the lag. In addition, in some cases, the proposal application is particularly complex, and the funding stipulations are inflexible.

Attempts to identify impacts and emphases on output within strict time limits also have hindered the performance of women's organizations. One example of the consequences of time constraints and outputs is Knitting Together Nations, a World Bank initiative. Knitting Together Nations is modeled after a project in Bangladesh that created a low-income women's sewing enterprise that now competes in international markets. Donor enthusiasm for Knitting Together Nations created unrealistic expectations, culminating in a disastrous Paris fashion show nine months after the project started. Most donors pulled out of the project.

• Sustainability of Women's Organizations

Donors have been raising the sustainability issue with local partners since 1997, but because money has always been available—in some cases, increasing amounts of it—sustainability has not been taken seriously. This year (1999), however, marks the end of the four-year funding program for Bosnia and Herzegovina. In addition, the Kosovo crisis has diverted both funds and personnel away from Bosnia. Still, the state of the economy and the legal infrastructure do not bode well for most organizations. Income-generating activities are under particular threat, given the requirement to register as a business and thus become subject to stiff tax liabilities—such as the 80 percent employer contribution on staff salaries to social-security benefits. Most donors recognize the difficulty in achieving sustainability, despite an increased emphasis on it.

Given the enormous growth of the NGO sector since the end of the war and the increasing diversion of aid, the process of "developmental Darwinism" is likely to begin soon. That is, the strongest NGOs will survive, while the weaker organizations will either fade away or join other groups. Because a number of women's organizations have established links with international women's groups and developed supporters outside the donor community in Bosnia, they may be more likely to withstand the inevitable withdrawal of funds.

Local fund-raising is still difficult but not impossible. The Center for Civic Initiatives in Banja Luka reported that some of the smaller community groups have succeeded in securing both in-kind contributions and cash donations from local businesses. Some of the larger women's organizations also are finding ways to support at least part of their activities. When Delphi International/Star required its grantees to come up with 15 percent of their budgets in other funds or in-kind contributions, the organizations were able to meet this requirement—although with some difficulty. Medica Zenica, for example, rents out one of its schoolhouses while the students are away in summer. The funds they receive to use this facility as a conference center enable them to pay for the girls' schooling. Although ingenuity makes up for some project costs, the operating costs of the larger organizations will remain dependent on external funding of some sort.

• Conclusions

There is no doubt that international assistance has been critical in improving and even saving the lives of many women during and after the war in Bosnia. It has also contributed to an increased awareness of gender issues through the funding of studies and advocacy campaigns, particularly those seeking increased political participation for women. However, as illustrated here, there were a number of missed opportunities and many lessons to be learned from the experience of providing assistance to women's organizations in postconflict Bosnia.

A key lesson follows from the truism that assistance that targets women is largely channeled through women's organizations. This stems from the war effort in which women constituted the majority of beneficiaries and ran many of the assistance delivery organizations. It also reflects the tendency of women-run organizations to reach out to women. In that sense, it has enabled the inclusion of a greater number of female beneficiaries.

Women-run organizations, however, have in some cases been pigeonholed into providing humanitarian or other "soft aid." In the postconflict era, the impact of humanitarian assistance is overshadowed by more lucrative infrastructure and other construction-related projects operated primarily by men. Simultaneously, making women's organizations wholly responsible for women's needs relinquishes male-run and international organizations from the responsibility of including women or considering gender issues. Such a division makes the introduction of gender awareness more difficult. In addition, channeling aid to women through women's organizations does not necessarily result in the empowerment of women at the grass-roots level.

Few women's organizations in Bosnia were able to make the link between aid and empowerment. Those that did emphasized concepts of "ownership" and self-help. Aid alone is not sufficient to induce empowerment. A holistic approach is needed to address institutional and societal as well as economic constraints to the advancement of women.

• Notes

1. Cockburn, *Space Between Us,* p. 157.
2. Zena Zenama, "Annual Report."
3. Delphi International/MEET, *Special Report on Women's Participation Levels.*
4. Smillie, "Service Delivery or Civil Society?"

7

Women's Organizations in El Salvador: History, Accomplishments, and International Support

Kelley Ready, Lynn Stephen, and Serena Cosgrove

Women's organizations in El Salvador have undergone a unique evolution, first in relation to the conditions of war that permeated El Salvador from 1980 to 1992 and then in response to economic restructuring and the challenges of democratization following the war. The conditions of El Salvador's civil war, along with the fact that many women's organizations became stronger during the war, have resulted in a unique set of organizations that are marked by their autonomy at the beginning of the twenty-first century. Early-conflict women's organizations (1980 to 1985) were characterized by their attachment to a wide range of popular grass-roots organizations and attempts to incorporate women into these groups. Many of these organizations mobilized women around economic issues, survival in the war, and human rights. A few formed in this period began to work with battered women and to question women's legal, political, and domestic subordination. Few, however, were willing to embrace the concept of feminism. Late-conflict and postconflict women's organizations (1986 to 2001) are characterized by women challenging gender hierarchies within mixed grass-roots organizations and putting forth a gendered discourse on specific women's rights, ranging from violence against women to inequities in the labor force. Feminism also became more prevalent during this time.

In this chapter we look at the particular changes found in women's organizations and link them to specific historical, social, and economic circumstances. We then evaluate what the impact of women's organizations has been in terms of empowering Salvadoran women and make recommendations for international donor organizations so that they can better serve Salvadoran women's organizations.

• The 1980–1992 Civil War

From 1980 to 1992, a civil war raged throughout Salvadoran society, leaving no one on neutral ground. The war is best understood as one in a long series of protests by those who had been systematically excluded from economic and political influence in El Salvador.[1] The primary protagonists in the war were the Farabundo Martí National Liberation Front (FMLN) and the army, police, and security forces of the Salvadoran government. (The FMLN, formed in 1980, traces its heritage to its namesake, Farabundo Martí, who was killed by a firing squad in the 1932 Matanza, or "massacre.")

It is estimated that one of every hundred Salvadorans was murdered or "disappeared" during the war. As of late 1991, eighty thousand had died and seven thousand more had disappeared. Human rights organizations such as Amnesty International have linked the Salvadoran military to tens of thousands of cases of assassination, torture, rape, and imprisonment of peasants, union leaders, students, and others.[2] Although the vast majority of human rights abuses, assassinations, and massacres were conducted by national security forces, the FMLN also engaged in violence, including kidnappings, bombings, and extortion in the countryside.

Prior to the war, during the late 1960s and 1970s, a broad range of grass-roots movements flourished among peasants, urban workers, students, teachers, professionals, and the urban poor.[3] People participating in these mass organizations, and the guerrilla movements they spawned between 1970 and 1979, were responding to increasingly severe economic conditions and political repression.[4] The spread of liberation theology by Christian-based communities was also prevalent in the 1970s. These communities became increasingly involved in making economic and political demands for the poor.

The government's response to an increasingly militant civil population was increased repression. By 1974, death squads and various branches of the national security forces were operating with impunity. People were attacked while engaging in civil protests, and some were targeted for assassination, capture, and torture.

• The War's Impact on Women

All women in El Salvador were affected by the war, whether or not they were part of an organized constituency. As those responsible for generating household income (during the war, up to 51 percent of households were female-headed), providing child care, and securing medical assistance, food, and shelter for the family, women were profoundly affected by living in an unstable social, political, and economic environment. One of the most profound effects of the war on women was the need to leave their children in the care of others or even to send them abroad for their safety. Indeed, many women were separated from some or all of their children during the war. Thousands of women were killed during the conflict as well, most as civilian victims. Hundreds of thousands more were driven from their homes, lost multiple family members, and suffered rape, abuse, torture, and imprisonment at the hands of security forces.

The war struck women across the political spectrum. Women on the right, especially those in high income brackets, had to live with the constant fear of being kidnapped by guerrillas. These women restricted their own mobility and that of family members in an effort to safeguard their families. Meanwhile, women who were part of any organizational effort or opposition group were targets for brutal repressive tactics implemented by the Salvadoran security forces and the armed forces. As Lynn Stephen notes, "Women prisoners [were] . . . punished uniformly with rape, sexual brutality, and often death."[5] Stephen goes on to say that during the 1980s, the army and governmental security forces reacted negatively to women who were politically active or seen participating in marches. These women were categorized as subversive and, when illegally detained, were often subjected to torture. It will take decades of careful planning and development to rebuild a peaceful, democratic Salvadoran society. The role of women has been particularly important.

- ## Preconflict Women's Organizations (1930s to 1980): Joining the Opposition Movement

Women organizing around women's issues in El Salvador can be traced to the 1932 strike that led to the Matanza that year. In 1947, some of the women who had participated in the strike and who had been later forced to hide their organizational activities formed the Women's League (La Liga Feminina). The Women's League focused on improving conditions for women in prison, establishing orphanages, and advocating women's right to vote, which was finally recognized in 1950. In the 1960s and early 1970s, several other women's organizations emerged and were associated with the labor and professional sectors. Thus, women's organizations in El Salvador before the civil war were most often tied to other oppositional struggles, particularly labor. This trend continued in the

1970s in the period building up to the conflict, with women's groups forming within the opposition movement mid-decade.

The first women's group to grow out of the opposition movement in the 1970s was the Association of Progressive Women of El Salvador (Asociación de Mujeres Progresistas de El Salvador, or AMPES), in 1975. Emerging from the trade union movement, this organization was closely associated with the Communist Party. The Association of Salvadoran Women (Asociación de Mujeres Salvadoreñas, or AMES) was formed a few years later, defining itself as "a channel for the incorporation of those sectors of women who, on account of their specific conditions (housewives, professionals, some teachers, slum dwellers, and students), have not yet incorporated into the popular struggle."[6]

In a document published in 1980, AMES emphasized women's disadvantaged economic condition over their collective gender identity.[7] By 1981, however, the group increasingly stressed gender oppression, flagging a shift in organizational focus that became more generalized in women's organizations by the mid-1980s. Seen as a threat by the Salvadoran government because of their ties to the FMLN, both AMPES and AMES were forced underground by the early 1980s, though the organizations continued to operate in exile.

- ### Early-Conflict Women's Organizations (1980 to 1985): Supporting the Popular Struggle

The changing positions of women in the Salvadoran economy both before and during the war affected their modes of organization. Women were active economically, socially, and politically in many of the sectors that were mobilized in the grass-roots opposition organizations that reinvigorated Salvadoran society before the peace accords in 1992. As women's involvement increased in the workplace, neighborhoods, and rural communities, popular organizations were forced to redefine their organizing strategies to attract and retain female recruits. Across the spectrum of the popular movement, women's committees *(comités femininas)* were formed.

Although this process attracted more women to the organizations, it initially led to the development of separate women's committees. For instance, FENASTRAS (Federación Nacional de Trabajadores Salvadoreños, or the Salvadoran National Workers Federation) began working with female factory workers as early as 1981, particularly in the textile industry. In 1986, a women's committee, CO-FENASTRAS

(Comité Feminina, or the Women's Committee of FENASTRAS), was created. Its projects included opening a childcare center and medical clinic, providing strike support for women workers, countering domestic violence, and denouncing human rights violations.

As women's committees were formed across different sectors, they began to affiliate with one another within the political coalitions that mirrored the structure of the FMLN. In 1986, for example, the National Coordinating Committee of Salvadoran Women (Coordinadora Nacional de Mujeres Salvadoreñas, or CONAMUS) was formed. Its members represented a hospital workers union, the women's committee of a teachers union, and an artists and cultural workers union. Other members hailed from the Eastern Confederation of Workers, the Confederation of Community Health Institutions, the women's committee of an organization for the displaced, and other women's committees. CONAMUS was one of five women's organizations that sponsored the conference, Primer Encuentro de la Mujer Salvadoreña, held in September 1988.

By 1989, there were nine different women's organizations in El Salvador, most of them federations such as CONAMUS. In addition, there existed groups that represented specific sectors, such as the Association of Indigenous Women (Asociación de Mujeres Indígenas Salvadoreñas) and University of El Salvador Women United (Mujeres Universitarias de El Salvador).

A final important arena that women's organizations worked in during the war was in the area of human rights. The group that best exemplifies this type of work is CO-MADRES (Committee of Mothers and Relatives of the Political Prisoners, Disappeared, and Assassinated of El Salvador "Monseñor Romero"), a women's group formed as a result of government repression and civil-war brutalities. CO-MADRES organized women to denounce publicly the disappearances, arrests, and assassinations of their children, spouses, and other family members during the war. Combining key elements of the ideology of motherhood with liberation theology and the discourse of the international human rights movement, CO-MADRES carved out a new political identity and practice. Like the Mothers of the Plaza de Mayo in Argentina, the organization took to the streets to denounce human rights abuses when no other groups dared. Increasingly, repression against CO-MADRES hardened: its offices were bombed and its members—many of whom ultimately "disappeared"—were detained, captured, and tortured. Despite the repression, CO-MADRES remained active throughout the 1980s and early 1990s. Its activities included taking out paid newspaper ads denouncing disappearances, demonstrating in the streets, and occupying foreign embassies, cathedrals, and government buildings. CO-MADRES also reached out internationally for political and material support, traveling to Europe, Australia, Canada, the United States, and elsewhere in Latin America.[8]

- **Late-Conflict and Postconflict Women's Organizations (1986 to Present): The Emergence of a Gendered Discourse on Women's Rights and Coalition Building**

The shift in women's organizations from supporting ongoing grass-roots groups to focusing specifically on women's issues and rights was subtle but evident by the late 1980s. The identification of "rights specific to women" marked the emergence of a gendered discourse in El Salvador's women's organizations and, ultimately, of declarations of autonomy from sponsoring FMLN parties. Although it would be another year before organizations would surface defining themselves as feminist, by the late 1980s individual Salvadoran women had begun to use a feminist analysis of gender in their work. The best example was CONAMUS, which had set up a clinic in 1986 for women who had been battered, raped, or tortured. The clinic provided not only medical treatment but psychological care and legal assistance as well, including services for women detained and tortured by the armed forces. However, in the aftermath of the FMLN offensive of 1989, the clinic was destroyed and the popular movement driven underground. (Although the FMLN was able to take and hold sections of San Salvador, the government's bombing of FMLN neighborhood strongholds forced the guerrillas to retreat after a few days.)

The Salvadoran women's movement reemerged more powerful after the 1989 offensive, when the FMLN tried to recruit more women directly into its organizations to build strength for the transition process to come after the war. In 1990, the CONAMUS clinic reopened. That same year, the organization began a campaign against domestic violence, which resulted in the opening of a shelter for battered women.[9] Also that year, the first women's groups to define themselves explicitly as feminist emerged: Women for Dignity and Life (Mujeres por la Dignidad y la Vida, or the Dignas) and the Center for Women's Studies "Norma Virginia Guirola de Herrera" (Centro de Estudios de la Mujer "Norma Virginia Guirola de Herrera," or CEMUJER).

As women's groups continued to mobilize to advocate their own interests, their ideas about women's struggles began to change. The signing of the peace accords created distinctly different conditions for women's organizational efforts. With the end of armed conflict and the increasing support and influence of transnational feminism, women's organizations openly challenged sexism in the FMLN and other mixed organizations, such as labor unions and peasant federations. They asserted their rights to define their struggle as being centered around women and issues specific to their own life experiences. The peace process resulted in significantly lower levels of open oppression and created room for women's organizations to forge a new path—that of working with both opposition sectors and agencies of the government. The Dignas offers an example of such an organization.

The women who started the Dignas in 1990 were all associated with the National Resistance (Resistencia Nacional, or RN), one of the five parties affiliated with the FMLN. Although their efforts to start a women's organization were initially supported by the RN leadership, the relationship soon became contentious. As the Dignas resisted direction from the top, they found their work increasingly being sabotaged by party leaders. According to Morena Herrera, one of the group's founding members, accusations of sexual promiscuity and lesbianism were also used against them. Faced with such devastating marginalization, the Dignas turned to other feminists, particularly those from Latin America. Feminist activists from Mexico and Nicaragua provided Dignas members with the feminist terminology that allowed them to understand and describe their predicament from a new perspective. By 1992, the Dignas had declared their independence from the FMLN and began to collaborate with a broad range of organizations, agencies, and institutions. For instance, in 1996 they worked with the Attorney General's Office, the Ministry of Education, and the Salvadoran Institute for the Protection of Minors to educate the groups about gender issues and help create programs that would increase the payment of child support by negligent fathers.

Not all Salvadoran women's groups have followed the same trajectory as the Dignas. Some have chosen to expel the more militant feminists from their ranks while remaining associated with (though often publicly proclaiming their independence from) the FMLN party organizations. These groups generally refer to themselves as "women's" rather than "feminist" organizations. Regardless of how they identify themselves, the overwhelming majority of Salvadoran women's organizations have struggled to gain autonomy from the FMLN parties or from organizations closely associated with the FMLN. Many of the organizations remain connected to the FMLN financially, organizationally, or at least ideologically.

In the postconflict period, one of the most significant ways Salvadoran women's organizations have exercised widening influence has been through coalition building. Every year, a wide range of women's organizations collaborate to recognize International Women's Day and the International Day Against Violence Against Women. In June 1997, many of these organizations came together in a series of workshops called "La Ley Contra la Violencia Intrafamiliar" (the Law Against Family Violence), which was supported by USAID through World Learning and Development Associates.

Although one-day events and workshops help connect women's organizations in present-day El Salvador, one of the most important ways for such groups to expand their reach is through the formation of long-term coalitions. Perhaps the most significant coalition-building process that took place among women in El Salvador in the 1990s was the organization of Mujeres '94, or Women in 1994. This effort can be linked to increasing participation of Salvadoran women in electoral politics at the local and national levels.

Mujeres '94 grew out of an effort by the women's movement to develop its own political platform during the 1994 election campaign. The media had labeled the 1994 elections as "the elections of the century," because they marked the first time since the signing of the peace accords that the FMLN was allowed to campaign as a legal political party. In addition, local, state, and national elections were held simultaneously that year, an event that occurs only every fifteen years.

Mujeres '94 brought El Salvador's women's organizations into a dialogue with national political parties and helped to solidify a sense of a women's movement among different organizations. Over the course of eight months, more than thirty-two women's organizations participated in creating a common platform that called for women's inclusion in development, drastic improvement in working conditions for women in all sectors, educational reform, programs to prevent violence against women, improvements in the healthcare system, reproductive rights, and gay rights. Changes to eliminate sexism from the legal code generally were also called for, as were reforms addressing domestic violence and discrimination in labor laws and agrarian reform. Finally, the platform demanded the establishment of quotas for women holding political office and positions of authority in political parties. These demands challenged the boundaries of the gender system in El Salvador.

Another significant political experience for women's organizations in El Salvador involved the hosting of the Sixth Latin American and Caribbean Feminist Encuentro in El Salvador in 1993. The *encuentros* (or meetings), which began in 1981, have brought together women from throughout the Latin American and Caribbean region to discuss issues, ideas, and strategies.[10] These encuentros have become increasingly diverse (by region, age, class, and race) with time and have raised some major issues now being debated in many countries.

The women who worked on organizing the feminist encuentro in El Salvador tended to be those who were the most independent and critical of the political parties. Many were also simultaneously involved in the Mujeres '94 women's political platform. In the month before the conference, the Salvadoran right wing launched a lesbophobic campaign to prevent the encuentro. Fortunately, despite the government's initial refusal to admit some foreign participants, the encuentro took place, with more than fifteen hundred women in attendance. The meeting achieved a higher level of racial, ethnic, and class diversity than previous encuentros, with significant participation from black women from the Caribbean, indigenous women from Andean countries and Guatemala, and many poor women from the cities and countrysides of Central America. The experience provided many Salvadoran women with their first opportunity to network with other Latin American women struggling with similar issues.

• Activities of Postconflict Women's Organizations

The activities of postconflict women's organizations can be grouped into five key areas: (1) health; (2) labor, work, land, and economic conditions; (3) domestic gender relations; (4) political participation; and (5) education and outreach.

Health projects of postconflict women's organizations in El Salvador have concentrated on several areas: reproductive health, birth control, maternal health and infant care, nutrition, and the prevention of AIDS/HIV and other sexually transmitted diseases. In the arena of reproductive health, for example, the Dignas founded a Casa de las Parteras (Midwives House) in the village of Nombre de Jesús, Chalatenango, and a Casa Materna (Maternal House) in the rural community of Talpatates, Belín. Postconflict women's organizations have been making a concerted effort to link with government health services for women and children. It appears that changing the perception of what women's health issues are is the biggest battle—for example, recognizing domestic violence as a public health issue and therefore including its prevention as part of public health campaigns.

The most recent and innovative work being done in the arena of health by women's organizations in El Salvador concerns the detection, treatment, and prevention of HIV and other sexually transmitted diseases.

Just as abortion is an extremely difficult public issue in El Salvador, so is the topic of sexually transmitted diseases. While contraception use has gone up significantly during the past twenty years, almost all of the methods used depend on women. Female sterilization has been the primary method used, although injections are becoming increasingly popular, as women can use this method without their partners being aware of it.[11] Condom use is minimal. While HIV rates for women in El Salvador are low, rates of other sexually transmitted diseases are not. As elsewhere, one of the groups of women most affected by HIV and other sexually transmitted diseases are prostitutes.

Mental health projects focusing on post-traumatic stress syndrome induced by women's experiences during the war have also been important. The long-term scars of rape, threatened rape, and other forms of physical violence and torture require the most prolonged, expensive, and labor-intensive treatment. Because so many members of opposition organizations in El Salvador were victims of violence, members of the staff and membership of many women's organizations continue to deal with the scars of violence and torture. Almost all groups have undergone some workshops, therapy, or other approaches to try to deal with the psychological and emotional wounds of the war.

Women's insertion into the political economy of El Salvador and their roles as workers, consumers, and procurers of households goods and services is the most traditional focus of Salvadoran women's organizations. Many organizations that now specialize in other activities previously had a strong emphasis on women's role in production. In the postconflict period, economic projects for women are most likely to be conceptualized as microenterprises and efforts to promote entrepreneurship among women, providing them with training in very concrete business skills.

Two other important areas should be included in women's organizations' activities that focus on women's roles in the economy. The first is questioning a land reform system that has largely excluded women from access to land. In some cases, efforts at increasing women's access were successful, most often at the local level where connections were made with local politicians such as mayors and city councilors who pushed for women's inclusion in land reform. The second area is new training that postconflict-era women's organizations are offering in nontraditional trades. In this area as well, women's organizations have attempted to link their efforts to government programs and to influence the state to expand the kind of job training that is available for women.

A major theme crosscutting most of the major women's organizations in postconflict El Salvador is domestic violence, which forms an important part of larger organizing efforts focused on questioning the physical subordination of women and children to men at the level of households and, by extension, in the larger society. CONAMUS did pioneering work in combating domestic violence. CONAMUS and CEMUJER also took out television advertisements to promote their organization and work against domestic violence. Another organization, MAM (Movimiento de Mujeres "Mélida Anaya Montes"), has also done important work to prevent violence against women, organizing Casas de las Mujeres (Women's Houses) across the country that serve as orientation centers. These centers provide individual attention to survivors of violence, whether it is family violence, sexual abuse, or workplace harassment. The Casas also serve as training centers for community leaders and counselors who dispense advice on legal issues, mental health, and women's health.

Work in domestic violence, which led women to question unequal power relations between men and women in the family, has also led to a new movement that focuses on pressuring men to pay child support. The Association of Women Seeking Child Support (Asociación de Madres Demandantes, or AMD) has organized women who rely on the state to collect child support. The AMD has created a new political identity, that of mothers who demand support from "deadbeat dads," as they are called in the United States. The AMD has made the issue of "irresponsible fatherhood" a national concern, succeeded in pressuring for better services for the mothers, and secured passage of legislation that prevents politicians from taking office if they are behind in their child-support payments.

Increasing women's political participation at local, regional, and national levels, as well as effecting change through the legislative system, has been another important focus of many postconflict women's organizations. A key component of strategies to increase women's political participation has been to bring women's political issues into mainstream politics. This has been done at local and national levels through developing women's municipal political platforms, which may include demands such as electricity, potable drinking water, education, responsible fathering, healthcare, housing, and an end to violence against women. It can also be done at the national level by creating a women's platform and pressuring mainstream political parties to adopt it, as seen in the efforts of the Mujeres '94 coalition described above. The Dignas, MAM, and other organizations have participated in these efforts.

A number of women's organizations have made considerable efforts in the postconflict period to promote women's election to municipal and national offices. They have been more successful at the municipal level, significantly increasing the number of female mayors and city councilors. The Dignas, in coordination with other groups, is now organizing women who have been elected to municipal councils. They estimate that number in late 1999 to be five hundred women. Through organizing women on municipal councils throughout the country, the Dignas and other women's organizations hope to formulate specifically gendered components into local development plans. While such efforts are being carried out locally, there is also an attempt to coordinate them nationally. All municipal governments are required to submit plans for a gendered component to local development efforts. Thus, mainstreaming women's issues into rural and urban planning requires not only electing female officials, but making sure that these officials will be respected and heard with regard to making women's issues a part of "regular" planning.

Efforts of women's organizations in the arena of education and outreach have included the development of nonsexist educational and training materials for literacy purposes as well as trying to sensitize government employees to gender issues. They have developed specific gender-sensitive training literature for this work. CEMUJER and other organizations have also used the media as education and outreach tools. A number of organizations have equipment and studios for producing radio programs and videos. Television commercials are used to give issues such as domestic violence higher visibility. A number of women's organizations also have long track records in developing literacy programs for women, an effort that can be traced back to the conflict period when schools were shut down. Using models of popular education (built on the ideas of Paolo Friere), the Dignas and other women's organizations have organized literacy circles. These small groups of mostly adult students were taught by literacy promoters, often young people, who had only completed their own basic education. While the efforts of such literacy programs are important for the women they serve, more important efforts include improving the overall level of funding for education in El Salvador and integrating a gendered perspective into the general education program.

• Overall Impact of Women's Organizations on Women's Empowerment

The transition of Salvadoran women's organizations from serving the needs of popular movements to articulating women's issues and then organizing projects on reproductive rights, education, health, housing, violence against women, economic inequality, and women's land rights has been critical to the actual and potential empowerment of Salvadoran women. By 1991, more than a hundred different women's organizations existed in El Salvador, each generating specific local and regional projects, and frequently working in the national political arena as well.

In the postconflict period, women's organizations have built national and international coalitions. They have also joined in a major push to increase women's participation in electoral politics and to influence the political platforms of the major parties. Some have also developed and implemented projects to meet their own needs by using less-restrictive funding channels, such as solidarity committees, small international foundations, and NGOs.

All of these accomplishments are important to improving conditions for Salvadoran women, for several reasons. First, thousands of Salvadoran women have gained important practical skills, leadership experience, and organizational abilities through their participation in projects with women's organizations. This reverberates into other areas of women's lives as well, in their homes and communities. One of the clearest influences of women's organizations has been that more women are running for mayor, city councilor, and other local offices. In addition, women have begun to include their issues in local political platforms, incorporating their demands into the mainstream political process.

Second, El Salvador now has a corps of hundreds of extremely articulate, well-educated, politically skilled female leaders who come from women's organizations formed in the 1980s and 1990s. Many of them have lobbied for women at international, national, and local levels. They are a largely untapped resource who can be integrated into the larger development process. Additionally, they can be the source of additional policy change to benefit women nationally through the legislature, government agencies, and links to the private sector and NGOs. Although a few of these women have entered formal politics, many remain attached to the organizations they helped form or in which they came of age. Their existence is very important for the further empowerment of women.

Third, the continued emphasis of women's organizations on the ways women are economically marginalized has spurred discussion of how women can be considered in land reform, industrial development, and other noneconomic areas affected by economic policy. This is so despite the government's forced adoption of structural adjustment policies, which has prevented women's groups from significantly improving women's economic situation.

Fourth, women's organizations have begun to hold government agencies accountable for considering women's issues. Through working with agencies such as the Ministry of Public Health and Social Assistance, the Attorney General's Office, the Ministry of Education, the Ministry of Agriculture, and the Salvadoran Institute for Women's Development, women's organizations are influencing government policy and training government employees to integrate gender concerns into their areas of service. This new development is a direct result of women's organizational efforts since the end of the conflict.

Perhaps the most important impact Salvadoran women's organizations have had on the empowerment of women during and after the war has been to enlarge the arena of public debate on a wide range of women's issues. The organizations have brought to the table for discussion issues such as abortion, reproductive rights, domestic violence (including marital rape), irresponsible fatherhood, unequal working conditions for women, and many others. These issues had never been raised consistently before the conflict, whether in the legislature, political parties, town meetings, or private and public settings.

• Factors Affecting the Autonomy of Women's Organizations

The experience of Salvadoran women's organizations is perhaps unique. Women's organizations in El Salvador began to form before the conflict terminated. Because they achieved clear agendas and identities during that time, their existence was not threatened by the end of the war. By the time the postconflict period had begun, many of the organizations had already established their autonomy. In many other contexts, women's organizations formed during a conflict go through a period of demobilization after the conflict ends. If such organizations are focused only on needs associated with the conflict, when the conflict ends, their influence may decrease. Because many Salvadoran women's organizations established strategic agendas for projects that went well beyond the needs generated by the war, they were able to move forward with their work rather than simply react to the end of the conflict. Some clues as to how this happened are found in funding patterns that evolved during the war.

In the late 1980s, funding from international development agencies became available for women's projects. As a result of this availability and the desire to recruit as many women as possible into the FMLN structure, women's committees were created in the various branches of the FMLN. In order to obtain financial support for women's projects, it was necessary for women in the FMLN to take an active role in conceptualizing and presenting these projects to potential funding entities. By allowing these women to develop and promote projects that specifically addressed women's needs, the FMLN provided the initiative for women to begin to investigate and identify the material basis for their subordination. This process also enabled women to move from working clandestinely to assuming an open and legal role as individuals responsible for nonmilitary development projects. The process of developing programs that would capture the funds designated for women's projects also fueled an awareness that women's needs are distinct from men's.

Another important external force that contributed to the emerging autonomy of some women's organizations from the FMLN was their ongoing contact with women's solidarity committees through tours, sister-city programs, and idea exchanges. From 1980 until the Salvadoran elections in April 1994, approximately six thousand U.S. citizens went to El Salvador as part of solidarity delegations.[12] Such delegations continued in smaller numbers after 1994. European countries, as well as Australia and New Zealand, also sent tours and formed support committees. Women made up a majority of participants in the U.S. solidarity tours.

Although no systematic study has been carried out on the politics of women involved in solidarity organizing, it appears a significant number of them "self-identify" as feminists. One U.S. solidarity organization in 1989 began running annual tours for women focused on International Women's Day (8 March). Each tour brings ten to fifteen women to El Salvador and puts them primarily in contact with women's organizations. Other solidarity groups have also sponsored women's tours.

Between the large number of women who went on mixed solidarity tours as well as those who participated specifically in women's tours, it is probably safe to say that at least a thousand women who identify with feminist politics have come into sustained contact with Salvadoran women and men. In many cases, tours that brought women together resulted in U.S. or European women inviting Salvadoran women to their countries for extended tours of one week to two months. This created a means for U.S. feminists and Salvadoran women to exchange ideas. Today, some Salvadoran women's organizations are strongly encouraging the continued exchange of ideas and interaction with U.S. and European women.[13]

These exchanges also led to funding for women's organizations from small solidarity committees in Europe and the United States. In other cases, people on the solidarity committees introduced leaders from Salvadoran women's organizations to funding sources such as Oxfam International and the Ford Foundation. Solidarity funds and small agencies such as Oxfam allowed women's organizations more autonomy in setting up projects than did larger, multilateral donors or the FMLN parties with which some of the women's organizations were affiliated.

Unlike other women's movements in Latin America, the Salvadoran women's movement has grown during the postconflict period (a period tied to a democratic transition). This suggests that the timing of the emergence of an independent, autonomous women's movement may be crucial to that movement's success. When women take political roles in opposition movements (such as the FMLN) during a conflict, the existence of an autonomous women's movement can be critical to ensuring that the women continue to occupy those roles after the conflict. Thus, helping women's groups establish their autonomy during, rather than following, a conflict may be crucial to ensuring the future of women's activism and a vital civil society. This is an important lesson to be learned from El Salvador.

• International Assistance to Women's Organizations

Salvadoran women's organizations currently subsist primarily on donations from private foundations in Western Europe, Canada, and the United States. (Some funds also come from embassies in El Salvador.) Most of the funding is packaged in short-term cycles and aimed at one-year projects.

International assistance to Salvadoran women's organizations has had a significant impact on the organizations as well as on the women they serve. Small, progressive foundations committed to a gender focus have extended more horizontal lines of communication with their Salvadoran counterparts than have large international donors, thereby increasing mutual learning on topics of common interest, such as reproductive rights, lessons learned by working in mixed organizations with men, and how to influence national culture and political systems. Many Salvadoran women's organizations have received support from small women's groups throughout North America and Europe.

Since the signing of the peace accords in 1992, Salvadoran women's organizations have also had access to bilateral or large international donors, such as USAID and the United Nations Development Program, as well as to funds from the European Union. This is a significant change from the pre-1992 period. The large bilateral donors have encouraged Salvadoran women's organizations to professionalize organizational features such as accounting controls, report writing, and legal status. Although this is a positive development in some ways, it has also limited the amount of autonomy women's organizations have in setting their project agendas. In part, some of the current strength of the women's organizations stems from the period before they began to receive funding from large international donors. Having smaller amounts of aid but greater control over what it was spent on allowed the groups to develop a strong and independent profile.

Given the dependency of Salvadoran women's organizations on donor funds, the organizations are seldom in a position to challenge donor requirements. Though organizations that have a wider donor base can decline to work with donors seen as overly demanding, other organizations have had to learn many difficult lessons about donor priorities and trends in the international funding of women's projects.

Given the limited amount of funds available for all Salvadoran NGOs and organizations in general, competition for support is often fierce. However, most of the Salvadoran women's organization directors interviewed agreed that there is less competition between women's organizations than between women's organizations and mixed (men and women) organizations. Perhaps partly as a response to the competition for international donor funds, many of the directors and fund-raising staff at Salvadoran women's organizations have carved out different funding spaces in terms of types of projects or kinds of donors.

Increasingly, Salvadoran women's organizations are experiencing competition from mixed organizations whose fund-raisers have learned the language of gender-focused proposal writing. Many of these organizations have not actually incorporated a gendered perspective into their mission and project implementation, but, nonetheless, they write project proposals using gender-sensitive language, hoping to gain funding at a time when funding sources are drying up.

Many of the women's organization directors whom the authors interviewed agreed that close working relationships with bilateral donors have led to mutual learning across several areas.[14] Although these relationships have also been characterized by tension, the directors acknowledge that donor support for institutional strengthening and strict requirements for accounting procedures and financial reporting have increased their organizations' professionalization and transparency. These are viewed as gains for women's organizations.

Salvadoran women's organizations experience both tensions and important lessons in their relationships with donors. Project monitoring and accounting procedures were mentioned as areas of tension by most of the women interviewed. Several women indicated that some donors have imposed onerous monitoring systems. Donors may send consultants to criticize how accounting procedures are carried out, but then provide no guidance on how to improve them.

Many project coordinators felt that women's organizations and projects often get lost in the "Big Picture" of development. Funding usually involves short-term, small funds for individual projects. The problem for Salvadoran women's organizations is they are not considered for bigger development projects. Work with women has to be seen as an integral, complementary part of big development projects, not as marginal.

Another frequent complaint among the women interviewed was that project time lines are geared toward the needs of donor agencies and do not match the political and social reality of organizing women in El Salvador. Political and organizational processes in El Salvador are not always compatible with the financial cycles of donor agencies. More attention needs to be paid to the political and social reality of local and regional circumstances in determining project implementation schedules.

Many of the directors interviewed commented on the benefit their organizations received from training in accounting, administration, and management procedures. Donor requirements have forced some groups to professionalize their administrative and accounting systems. Many wish, however, that there were a more horizontal relationship between donors and their beneficiaries, thus facilitating mutual learning instead of vertical power relationships.

• Recommendations

The current situation in El Salvador presents funding entities and planners interested in facilitating women's empowerment with a unique opportunity: to build on more than two decades of hard work and progress by women's organizations that have successfully negotiated a bloody civil war and a postconflict period. The following recommendations thus recognize the impact women's organizations have already had in the country. Women's organizations in El Salvador are carrying out critical development work that needs to be integrated into the overall process of recovering from the conflict and constructing an economically, socially, and politically sound country. Gendered perspectives are key to all these areas of development. When key projects are defined in the areas of democratization, the environment, rural development, education, and health, Salvadoran women's organizations should be part of their national project planning and evaluation process. Better incorporation of women's organizations into large development initiatives may also help eliminate some of the funding competition between mixed organizations and women's organizations.

Many women's organizations in El Salvador have existed for almost a decade, some for much longer. They bring a wealth of experience and expertise in a wide range of areas that are important to government institutions, including child-support payments, domestic violence, reproductive health, literacy, and gender-sensitivity training. This expertise should be recognized and used as a resource in the reconstruction of Salvadoran society. Comprehensive gender-sensitivity training and gender-focused programs are needed in almost every branch of government and in many private-sector institutions as well. The efforts of groups that work with specific government agencies to train personnel in gender sensitivity should be encouraged and expanded.

Improving the position of women in Salvadoran society will require continuous efforts to integrate women into the political system, at both the local and the national levels. In addition, all women need support to conduct grass-roots organizing and build political platforms and demands that reflect their needs and that are taken seriously by elected officials. This type of work also results in more women being elected as officials. Leaders from women's organizations are beginning to get involved in electoral politics at local and national levels and should be encouraged in this effort.

El Salvador is distinguished by the highest homicide rate in Latin America. The capital city of San Salvador is now identified by the World Bank as the most crime ridden city in Latin America. Violent crime is one of the most basic problems faced by women and families in the country. Rates of domestic violence appear to be on the rise. Crime prevention efforts that look specifically at how violent crime affects women are desperately needed. This involves not only putting more female police officers on the street and training police departments in gender sensitivity, but also building crime prevention efforts at the block and neighborhood levels. Until violent crime rates fall, other types of basic improvements in women's lives will be difficult to achieve.

Many women's organizations have a good track record and valuable experience in combating domestic violence. Although these efforts are admirable, the services available to women who are victims of domestic and other violence are still minimal. In addition to suffering ongoing violence, many Salvadoran women still face long-term psychological trauma from the war. Yet, few mental health services are available to them. Efforts to combat present-day violence and help women cope with a past history of violence are desperately needed.

Some evidence suggests that Salvadoran women's literacy rates may be declining.[15] It is crucial that women and girls who were not educated during the war receive access to basic literacy training. Instead of creating new networks, existing networks should be used.

Successful funding efforts that bring women's organizations together to work on one topic should be built upon, such as the series of workshops on the Law Against Family Violence that USAID supported through World Learning and Development Associates in June 1997. This effort successfully pulled together a wide range of women's organizations. Building horizontal ties between women's organizations is important to empowering women in the larger Salvadoran society.

Most Salvadoran women work in the informal economy with no benefits, low wages, and irregular hours. Even those in the *maquila* industry earn low pay. Salvadoran women need adequate employment to recover economically from the devastating impact of the war. Although some women have received access to land through postconflict land reform, a majority of rural women remain landless. For those in areas with no other employment options, title to subsistence plots is critical to their survival. Land reform should be applied equally to men and women. Single mothers should be granted priority in land redistribution. Women's names should be included on the titles of redistributed land along with their husbands' (whether legally married or not) to ensure that the women do not lose access to the land in cases of abandonment or separation.

The case study of women's organizations in El Salvador suggests that forming independent women's organizations during a conflict period can result in an important set of leaders, resources, and institutional experiences that can be key to empowering women following a sustained armed conflict. The lessons that women's organizations have already learned and their many accomplishments should serve as the basis for future development programs aimed at improving the lives of Salvadoran women. The case of El Salvador is also instructive in looking for positive trends to try to replicate in other postconflict societies that are trying to improve the lives of women.

• Notes

1. Murray, *El Salvador,* p. xvii.
2. See Stephen, *Hear My Testimony,* for one account.

3. See Arnson, *El Salvador;* Booth and Walker, *Understanding Central America;* Montgomery, *Revolution in El Salvador;* North, *Bitter Grounds;* Pearce, *Promised Land;* and Armstrong and Shenk, *El Salvador,* for descriptions of popular mobilization, government repression, and the formation of armed guerrilla organizations in the 1970s.

4. For a summary of how economic conditions were affecting Salvadoran women, see Pearce, *Promised Land,* and Ready, *Between Transnational Feminism.*

5. Stephen, *Women and Social Movements,* p. 37.

6. Thomson, *Women of El Salvador,* p. 95.

7. Golden, *Hour of the Poor,* p. 110.

8. See Stephen, *Hear My Testimony.*

9. The CONAMUS battered-women's shelter closed recently because of a lack of funding.

10. See Sapporta Sternback et al., "Feminisms in Latin America"; Miller, *Latin American Women;* and Stephen, *Women and Social Movements,* pp. 15–20, for a discussion of the other meetings.

11. FESAL–98, *Encuesta nacional,* p. 7.

12. This estimate comes from Van Gosse, a political scientist who has studied the U.S. solidarity movement with El Salvador. His estimate was checked against the records of CISPES (Committee in Solidarity with the People of El Salvador), the Center for Global Education, Witness for Peace, and CRISPES (Christians in Solidarity with the People of El Salvador). The delegations of CISPES include those associated with the Sister Cities and Sister Parishes projects as well as those put together by Share and Nest, two foundations that, along with CISPES, directed their delegations and aid to organizations and communities linked to Fuerzas Populares de Liberación (Popular Forces for Liberation, or FPL). The Center for Global Education and CRISPES were not aligned with any particular part of the FMLN.

13. See Stephen, *Women and Social Movements.*

14. This case study draws upon a combination of published sources, fieldwork by the three primary researchers over the past eight years (through July 1999), and telephone interviews the researchers conducted with staff members of Salvadoran women's organizations who have worked with international donor agencies. The interviews covered ten different topics regarding the women's experiences with donors. The researchers believe these conversations yielded a high degree of honesty and frankness because of their prior positive relationship with the interviewees.

15. One source suggests that the gap between female and male illiteracy has not been reduced since the war, but instead has grown. In 1994, female illiteracy was 5.3 percent higher than male illiteracy; in 1997, it was 5.8 percent higher. See Mujeres por la Dignidad y la Vida, *Informe institucional,* p. 6.

8

International Assistance to Women's Organizations

Krishna Kumar

Several factors have led the international donor community to support women's organizations both during and after conflict. One obvious factor is that because of lack of resources, shortage of skilled personnel, and general decline in the morale of the staff, public bureaucracies become extremely fragile in war-torn societies. They are often unable to provide urgently needed social services to the suffering populace. Therefore, the international community tends to develop partnerships with voluntary organizations, including women's organizations, to provide essential assistance to the needy people. There are two additional reasons for the international donor community to support women's organizations. First, by virtue of their leadership and commitment, these organizations are better able to reach women than are male-dominated or mixed civil-society organizations. Their staff members can easily empathize with the intended women beneficiaries, who in turn feel more at ease in sharing their problems with them. Second, the international community also sees in women's organizations potential for empowering women. In addition to channeling assistance, they contribute to the social and psychological empowerment of women by teaching self-reliance and leadership skills.

• Nature of International Assistance

The international community provided extensive assistance to women's organizations in all case-study countries. Precise data are not available, but it is safe to assume that most, if not all, of the money for national and umbrella organizations came from international sources. Funders included bilateral and multilateral donor agencies, private foundations, trade unions, international charitable organizations, religious and church organizations, professional organizations, and other NGOs in case-study countries.

International donors provided general grants for institutional development and for specific activities of women's organizations. Donors also contracted with these organizations to carry out specific projects and programs. Often foundations, religious organizations, NGOs, and small bilateral agencies (particularly from Scandinavian countries) gave grants for institutional development and activities. Such grants were flexible and did not involve any monitoring by the funding agency. However, USAID and major bilateral agencies preferred to tie assistance to specific projects and activities. Women's organizations were held accountable for the progress of these interventions.

The most common form of assistance was financial. Both donors and women's organizations preferred the flexibility of financial aid. International donors also gave in-kind assistance. For example, during conflict, USAID, the World Food Program, and the UN High Commissioner for Refugees provided food, medicines, and other essential commodities to women's organizations to distribute among targeted populations. Such programs usually ended when peace was established. Many international organizations also donated typewriters, computers, copiers, audiovisual equipment, and even automobiles to aid women's organizations.

In addition, the international community provided considerable technical assistance. Such assistance was necessary because the staffs of women's organizations usually lacked managerial and technical expertise. The international community routinely supported short- and long-term training programs in accounting, management, and technical fields. Donors also arranged overseas trips for senior officials of women's organizations who visited technical and educational institutions or attended international meetings and conferences. Some donors funded short-term consultants and long-term expatriate experts who helped solve specific managerial and technical problems. The cost of expatriate experts is exceptionally high, so international donors have become more reluctant to provide them.

• Contributions of International Assistance

The experiences of the case-study countries show unequivocally that international assistance has contributed to the growth, activities, and survival of women's organizations. Officials from the international community, leaders of women's organizations, host government officials, and academic experts all agree on this general conclusion. They emphasized four vital contributions of international assistance.

First, a slight majority of all women's organizations in all case-study countries would not have emerged—or at least not have survived—without international assistance. In fact, international donors generally went further than providing support. They often helped establish women's organizations to deliver assistance. For example, the UN High Commissioner for Refugees was instrumental in forming many volunteer women's groups during the conflict in Bosnia and Herzegovina. With the establishment of peace, many of these groups expanded their activities, establishing themselves as full-fledged women's organizations. Many international private voluntary organizations, such as CARE, Oxfam, and the Catholic Relief Society, prompted women to form organizations, develop their own projects, or to serve as subcontractors of the international donor agencies.

Factors specific to each country determined the nature of international efforts to foster the growth of women's organizations. In Bosnia and Herzegovina, the international community could easily mobilize large numbers of highly educated women professionals who had become unemployed because of the conflict. A similar course was not feasible in Cambodia, where the Khmer Rouge had wiped out the entire educated, middle class. Therefore, international donors depended on a small group of educated women, drawn from expatriates, refugees, and former leaders of state-run women's organizations. Several women's organizations emerged in El Salvador and Guatemala during the prolonged conflict, which received international support. In Rwanda, where genocide and massive migration destroyed practically all women's organizations, international donors helped revive some of them and started new ones in partnership with the government. In Georgia, international donors primarily targeted women's organizations to help internally displaced families and promote women's political participation.

Second, international assistance enabled most women's organizations to initiate projects and programs that benefited women and contributed to their empowerment. In none of the case-study countries could a majority of women's organizations raise necessary resources locally. Because of desperate economic situations, only a few local religious organizations, philanthropic groups, and political patrons could provide more than token help. Some women's organizations did receive local in-kind assistance, such as free office space and the services of professional staff, but these donations were hardly adequate to carry out effective programs. International assistance was essential in pursuing the ongoing activities of these organizations. Almost all the projects undertaken by women's organizations in vocational training, microenterprises, family planning, health services, social services, and electoral assistance have depended entirely on international assistance.

Third, foreign assistance contributed to legitimizing women's organizations. In many cases, international recognition also protected women's organizations from interference from the various arms of the government. For example, before the peace process began, many women's organizations fighting for the rights of victims of political oppression in El Salvador and Guatemala survived through the material and moral support of the international community.

Finally, international assistance contributed to the growth of managerial and technical skills. Many women's organizations in the case-study countries received training or technical assistance from the international community. In Bosnia and Herzegovina and in Cambodia, donors encouraged independent local organizations to assist women's organizations and other civil-society organizations. In addition, to qualify for funding from international donors, women's organizations often had to learn appropriate managerial and budgetary procedures. Most women's organizations established during or after conflict did not have even rudimentary managerial structures. To get international assistance, they had to establish management procedures, keep necessary records, and follow appropriate budgetary practices for their programs. The cumulative effect was that, over time, their managerial and technical capacities improved.

From their association with the international community, women's organizations seem to have acquired three sets of skills: (1) expertise in preparing and submitting proposals to international agencies; (2) accounting and budgeting skills, particularly in former communist countries where such skills were not common; and (3) management practices, such as work plans, job descriptions, individual assignments, management systems and controls, and monitoring and evaluation systems.

• Sustainability and International Assistance

The above discussion leads us to the question of sustainability of women's organizations. The question often is asked whether these organizations will survive or languish as foreign assistance wanes. There is no simple answer to this question since conditions vary from country to country and organization to organization. However, a few general observations can be made here.

The sustainability of women's organizations can be assessed with reference to three dimensions: financial, managerial, and outside linkages.[1] Financial sustainability indicates that an organization is able to survive without external funding, while managerial sustainability implies that women or their hired staff can effectively manage and lead the organization. Finally, linkage sustainability means that an organization is able to forge functional relationships with external actors to achieve its objectives.

As far as financial sustainability is concerned, the future of women's organizations remains questionable. Most of the organizations reviewed, particularly the national and umbrella women's organizations, were largely, if not exclusively, dependent on international assistance. Most of them were unable to charge fees for their services. There were, however, exceptions. Organizations that lent money for microenterprises were able to keep a small percentage of the interest paid by borrowers for administrative expenses. A few organizations created businesses. These usually sold various handicrafts—produced by members, for sale to the international community—though one Rwandan NGO opened a paper and school-supply store to help support its work. In addition, a few organizations (such as the Association of Salvadoran Women) had established partnerships with the government to run specific programs. But an overwhelming majority of women's organizations were not in a position to be self-sufficient and would not survive without outside funds. In the words of a women's organization founder in Cambodia, "Frankly, we cannot survive without international assistance. It is simply not possible."

There are several reasons for the lack of financial sustainability of women's organizations. Women's groups in postconflict societies lacked expertise in fund-raising and faced other significant obstacles. Governments were (and probably will remain) under pressure to reduce public expenditures. Thus they will not be in a position to support women's organizations financially for years to come. Even if government funding were available, some organizations might not want it because such funding could undermine their autonomy. Private-sector funding cannot fill the gap because private enterprise remains in a nascent stage in all case-study countries, with the possible exception of El Salvador. Those private firms that do exist have not yet developed a tradition for philanthropy and public service. It is unrealistic to expect women's organizations to raise enough money for their activities from local sources.

Smaller women's organizations are in the most precarious position. They are unlikely to have the resources and expertise to compete with large organizations, which have succeeded well in soliciting funds from the international community. Many small organizations also face stiff competition from mixed or men's voluntary organizations that have started developing projects specifically for women.

Managerial sustainability is not as significant a problem as financial sustainability. Women invariably led and managed all organizations examined in this study. Even though many organizations suffered from managerial problems, they were acquiring experience and expertise. Moreover, in all case-study countries, women were expanding their experience managing public institutions, and their technical capabilities were growing. A new generation of professional leaders is taking charge of many organizations, and there is no reason to believe there will be a shortage of well-trained and committed women managing these organizations in the future.

Linkage sustainability is the capacity of an organization to develop and maintain linkages with stakeholders. In the case of women's organizations, three stakeholders are important. The first—and undoubtedly most important—stakeholders are the organization's women beneficiaries. Most of the women's organizations examined in the case-study countries have established a rapport with their beneficiaries through deep commitment and empathy. In this they had (and will continue to have) a comparative advantage over male-dominated organizations. The second category of stakeholders includes government agencies and departments. A good working relationship with government is essential for women's organizations so they can obtain political and perhaps financial support and to avoid duplication of effort. Most women's organizations in the case-study countries have begun paying attention to local and national public institutions. Even the organizations that wanted at first to remain aloof from the government came to recognize the value of maintaining a good relationship. Cambodia is a case in point. During the late 1980s and early 1990s, when donor agencies were vying with one another to fund Cambodian women's organizations, the organizations adopted an attitude of benign neglect toward the government. With a decline in external funding and improvements in public bureaucracy, those organizations began reconsidering their earlier postures. The last category of stakeholders is external funding agencies. Most of the women's organizations that received funds from international donors had acquired a good understanding of those funders. Whether those organizations will be able to tap other philanthropic resources in their own countries remains to be seen.

The international development community recognizes that many women's organizations will not survive. The level of international funding and humanitarian assistance has declined over time in the case-study countries. Moreover, many of the problems that plagued these societies—including women refugees, demobilized women combatants, and separated children—have been resolved, at least partially, and are no longer acute. Consequently, the need for certain types of programs related to these problems has diminished, leading some women's organizations to reduce their activities, find different mandates, or close down. Even so, as these countries make economic, social, and political progress, new women's organizations will arise that are more sustainable and responsive to the changing needs of their societies. Those new organizations will, of course, build on the foundations laid by their elder sisters.

• Economic Dependence Versus Autonomy

Because of their economic dependence on international assistance, the question of the autonomy of women's organizations requires some discussion. There is a genuine concern among some donors and women leaders that dependence may prevent organizations from responding to the distinctive needs and aspirations of their targeted populations. The reasoning is simple. Given the organizations' overwhelming dependence on international assistance, their agendas, projects, and activities are likely to be determined not by their own assessment of needs or their organizational capabilities and strengths, but by the priorities and concerns of the international donor community.[2] For example, after the Dayton Accords, many women's organizations in Bosnia and Herzegovina closed their psychosocial healing projects against their own judgment, when international donors shifted their attention to economic growth and development. In the late 1990s in Cambodia, women's organizations found that funds were available for projects against domestic violence, so many began venturing into this field. Lacking alternative sources of funding, many considered it a prudent choice.

While there is substance in this reasoning, the reality of the relationship between funding and autonomy is complex. Interviews with informants suggest wide variation among countries and organizations, and

> **Differing Views on Autonomy**
> "Our main objective is to help suffering women. It is immaterial from what source we get our resources. Let academicians debate the issue."
> *—A woman leader from Cambodia*
>
> "What autonomy? Most of the women's organizations are the extension arm of international donors."
> *—A scholar from El Salvador*

over time. For example, during the early stages of conflict in Bosnia and Herzegovina, when women's organizations were fewer and international assistance was plentiful, women's groups enjoyed considerable autonomy in determining their activities. The international community supported their programs without any reservation. But conditions changed as the volume of international assistance declined and the number of women's organizations grew. The same phenomenon occurred in Cambodia. In El Salvador, however, many groups have established their own priorities and received donors' funds to support those priorities.

Some critics have argued that the practice of subcontracting with women's organizations leaves them little choice but to become an extension of the international community.[3] The important point to emphasize is that even when they contracted projects for international donors, women's organizations enjoyed considerable freedom and flexibility in shaping programs. In most cases, international donors identified priorities, and organizations developed their own programs and plans. There was much give-and-take between international donors and women's organizations during negotiations because each side needed the other. Although international donors had the financial leverage, women's organizations had bargaining power because of their local roots and capacity to deliver goods and services to the targeted women.

Finally, many international donors (particularly those from Scandinavian countries) and private foundations continue to give grants to women's organizations to develop and put into effect their own programs reflecting their priorities and understanding of local conditions. Major donor agencies such as USAID are also helping postconflict societies develop an institutional infrastructure for the civil society that will indirectly help women's organizations in strengthening their institutional capacities and tapping local resources for their programs.

• Critical Issues in International Assistance

International assistance suffered from six significant problems in the case-study countries. The first was the inability of international donors to make long-term commitments. The maximum donor commitment was for five years. But in most cases the grant was renewed every year. Because of shrinking levels of assistance to postconflict societies, renewals were not necessarily automatic. Thus, many organizations carried out activities in an environment of uncertainty and were unable to engage in long-term planning. Such uncertainty did nothing to help the morale of staff facing the prospect of unemployment. Nor did it help in developing sectoral specialization.

A second problem was the cumbersome and often unnecessary requirements for proposals, progress reports, and monitoring information imposed by international donor agencies. These had high opportunity costs for women's organizations. USAID provides a good example. USAID once required voluntary organizations applying for agency grants to register with USAID/Washington or meet the same requirements established for U.S.–based private voluntary organizations (PVOs). (This requirement was dropped in 2000.) Thus only a small number of women's organizations could obtain direct grants from USAID or its missions. Instead, funds were channeled to them through U.S. or international PVOs.[4] Moreover, USAID and its development partners often required detailed progress reports and, in some cases, information on the effects of the funded programs. Most smaller women's organizations had to spend considerable resources and time in meeting such requirements.

A third problem, related to the second, was that large, well-established women's organizations—usually led by well-connected women leaders—received the lion's share of international assistance. This was particularly true when international assistance began to decline and the competition for funds became intense. International donor agencies were aware of the problem, but they could do little about it. Because they were accountable for results, donors did not want to take risks with small, relatively unknown organizations. It made more sense to go with established ones. Moreover, reaching out to small organizations at the grass-roots level was difficult and involved more management time and resources. Some international donors tried to solve this problem by channeling resources through international PVOs or by establishing local voluntary organizations to assist small women's organizations.

Fourth, there has been little or no donor coordination. Donor agencies tended to work independently without adequate information and understanding of one another's programs. During the early postconflict phase, there was even competition among donors to fund suitable projects developed by women's organizations in Bosnia and Herzegovina, Cambodia, and Rwanda. Similar projects were funded by two or more agencies for the same community or region, resulting in a waste of precious resources. Even when one donor was not satisfied with the progress of a program and discontinued funding, others picked it up, resulting in the continuation of ineffective programs. The situation improved over time in almost all case-study countries. The decline in levels of international funding and corresponding reductions in the number of international actors operating in the country facilitated increased contacts, if not coordination, among the donors.

Fifth, international donors were unable to disseminate information about resource availability to all interested women's organizations. Limited information, language and geographical barriers, and time constraints contributed to this problem. A few organizations received a majority of the international resources, while many deserving organizations were denied assistance.[5] Organizations located in capital cities or those whose leaders were politically connected clearly enjoyed an advantage over smaller organizations based farther from metropolitan areas.

Finally, international assistance to women's organizations also suffered because the international community has yet to develop a coherent policy framework for assisting women and promoting gender equality in postconflict societies. Although the community has undertaken a wide range of programs, these have been established in an opportunistic manner without a carefully formulated policy framework.

• Notes

1. Carr, Chen, and Jhabvala, *Speaking Out,* p. 197.
2. This issue is generally discussed in the context of international assistance to civil-society organizations. For recent debate on this subject, please see Carothers, *Aiding Democracy Abroad,* and Hudock, *NGOs and Civil Society.*
3. This issue is generally discussed in the context of international assistance to civil-society organizations. For recent debate on this subject, please see Hudock, *NGOs and Civil Society.*
4. USAID has generally preferred to channel assistance through PVOs for other reasons as well. Direct assistance to local organizations is management-intensive, and USAID's overseas missions lack personnel to manage it. Because of their long involvement with grass-roots organizations, PVOs are in a better position to deal with women's organizations.
5. Alice Morton has made this point and suggested that the donor community should be sensitive about the problem.

9

Lessons and Recommendations for the International Community

Krishna Kumar

This volume has covered a vast territory. The first chapter and the five profiles therein examined the social, economic, and political effects of civil wars on women and gender relations. They also discussed the assistance programs that the international donor community has supported to alleviate the problems created by conflicts as well as to promote gender equality. The second chapter examined refugee camp and repatriation experiences and their impact on women. The five subsequent chapters analyzed the growth, activities, and contributions of women's organizations that emerged or reemerged in the aftermath of civil wars. The last chapter focused on the role of international assistance to women's organizations and identified a set of problems that plague the assistance programs. Taken together, these chapters have illuminated different dimensions of the complex relationships between civil wars and gender relations, raising a wide range of issues.

This chapter explores the policy implications of the findings and conclusions that emerge in the previous chapters for the international community. The first section presents the lessons and recommendations for international assistance to promote women's welfare and gender equality, while the second section offers lessons and recommendations for improving international assistance programs to women's organizations. The last section outlines a strategic framework for international assistance.

- **Lessons and Recommendations to Support Women and Gender Relations**

◦ Build on Women's Economic and Political Gains

Not all effects of intrastate conflicts on women and gender relations have been negative. In fact, in all case-study countries conflict undermined the traditional sexual division of labor, creating new economic and political opportunities for women. In most countries women were able to enter occupations that had been closed to them previously. Women's political participation in community and local affairs increased. In many cases they assumed the leadership of grass-roots civic and political institutions.

Because the postconflict era provides an opening to build on the progress made by women during conflict, it makes sense for the international community to capitalize on this opportunity by designing and implementing programs to ameliorate the negative conditions women endure and to help promote gender equality.

° **Pay Greater Attention to Civilian Security**

The decline of social control, the disintegration of community, the presence of demilitarized soldiers, and the ineffectiveness of law enforcement agencies all tend to increase lawlessness and violence in postconflict societies. Poverty and unemployment are exacerbating factors. Though all strata of society suffer, women and children are the most frequent victims. The international community has generally supported demobilization of ex-combatants, police reforms, and international monitoring of human rights to reform the security sector. But the primary target of its efforts has been political rights rather than civilian security. Consequently, while the human rights situation had improved in all case-study countries, civilian security remained a major problem.

The international community should help postconflict societies in addressing the problem of civilian security and assist them in devising and carrying out programs that can enhance physical security for women. Such programs could include security-sector reforms, greater representation of women in police forces and judicial processes, training of security staff on women's rights, establishment of peace committees to prevent the eruption of violence, and special interventions for vulnerable youth.

° **Emphasize Cost-Effective, Indigenous Approaches**

International programs for dealing with traumatized women have suffered from many limitations. The programs tend to ignore the cultural and social contexts of trauma and propose solutions that may not be relevant to victims. Programs are often short-lived and spotty because of inadequate funding and their experimental nature. Finally, because they concentrate on women and children, and not on men, these programs are ineffective in reducing domestic violence. Women often become the victims of aggression by traumatized men.

The international community should support innovative programs, based on indigenous approaches to psychosocial healing, to deal with traumatized men and women. For example, USAID has funded a few innovative projects that used traditional purifying rituals for the rehabilitation of child soldiers in Angola. It would be useful for the agency to examine its experience and explore the possibility of expanding these programs to include, on an experimental basis, both men and women. The international donor community should also consider funding research efforts that identify and evaluate the effectiveness of traditional modes of psychosocial healing in traditional societies.

◦ Step Up Efforts to Prevent Sexual Abuse

The international community has implemented many programs for helping sexually abused women in postconflict societies. Because of the nature of sexual crimes and the social stigma attached to them, these programs do not reach most victims. Nonetheless, they are important and should be supported. But the most important role for the international community is to support initiatives to educate people about these crimes and to prevent their recurrence.

International experts have put forward several proposals for consideration by the international community: protect witnesses; train international peacekeepers in gender issues; promote more women to international judicial posts; raise the awareness of and punishment for international trafficking in women; and treat sexual violence within the definition of torture under the UN 1994 Convention Against Torture and Other Cruel, Inhuman, and Degrading Treatment or Punishment. The concerned organizations and nations should carefully review these proposals and, when appropriate, endorse them.

◦ Promote Microcredit with Caution

The experience in many case-study countries indicates that microcredit programs have been quite effective. Though not exclusively targeted to women, the overwhelming majority of loans went to women. These programs appeared to achieve the dual objectives of relief and economic development. However, such programs are no cure for all economic problems facing women in postconflict societies. They do not address structural barriers to women's economic advancement. Although microcredit programs can prevent abject poverty, they do not promise sustained economic advancement.

While supporting microcredit programs, the international community should not ignore their limitations. The international community should advocate the removal of structural barriers to the economic advancement of women and treat microcredit programs only as short-term measures.

∘ Support Implementation of Property Rights Reforms

Women's lack of access to agricultural land and other productive assets is a major problem in postconflict societies. Women are usually denied legal rights to land and other resources owned by their dead husbands, fathers, or other close relatives. Consequently, widows and single women are unable to engage in many productive activities. Thus they often suffer deprivation and abject poverty.

The international community should vigorously push for property rights for women in postconflict societies. It should press not only for constitutional and legislative reforms, but for their implementation. It should support initiatives designed to build public support for women's property rights and to help resolve bureaucratic inertia and resistance.

∘ Promote Greater Women's Electoral Participation

With the exception of Rwanda, all case-study countries held postconflict elections at the national level.[1] Their main purposes were to form governments that enjoyed national and international legitimacy and to promote the rehabilitation and reconstruction of the society. USAID and other donors provided assistance in conducting postconflict elections. Although women constituted half or more of the electorate, only a small proportion were elected to national legislatures.

The international community should promote greater representation of women in postconflict elections, encourage political parties to field women candidates, and assist women candidates on a nonpartisan basis.

∘ Promote Political Participation of Women

Postconflict societies offered openings for women's political participation. Often democratic constitutions were adopted that provided for equality between men and women. Such constitutions also provided a legal framework for women's participation in the political arena. During conflict some women not only acquired leadership skills and experience, but also became aware of their political rights and responsibilities. The international community has provided assistance to encourage women to participate in political affairs. Despite all these developments, women's political participation has been limited.

The international community should support women's political participation with increased vigor. It should consider providing long-term technical and material assistance to nonpartisan women's advocacy organizations that engage in promoting women's participation in local and national affairs.

- **Lessons and Recommendations to Strengthen Women's Organizations**

○ Continue to Foster Women's Organizations

International agencies have supported the establishment and growth of women's organizations in postconflict societies for several reasons. Women's organizations represent an essential element of civil society and therefore are critical to consolidating nascent democracies. Further, they promote women's leadership, contributing to gender equality. Finally, women's organizations are instrumental in channeling humanitarian and development assistance to targeted populations, particularly women. The findings of this assessment show that the expectations of USAID and other donors were fully justified. Despite obvious limitations, women's organizations have made contributions toward the achievement of all these objectives. Moreover, the findings demonstrate that the international community can foster women's organizations in postconflict conditions.

The international community should continue with greater vigor its policy of fostering women's organizations as an integral part of efforts to rehabilitate and reconstruct postconflict societies. It also should encourage its development partners to support women's organizations.

○ Review Funding Requirements for Women's Organizations

Women's organizations encountered many problems obtaining funds from large international donors such as USAID. Many organizations viewed reporting requirements for projects and program activities as onerous. They had to furnish all kinds of information that was not easily available and required considerable time and resources to collect.

Major international donors should review their funding requirements and mechanisms. Wherever possible, it is advisable to impose minimal requirements and provide some funds to cover the costs of essential data collection and analysis.

○ Consider Multiyear Funding

A major problem women's organizations faced in all case-study countries was the short duration of funding. Most projects funded under humanitarian assistance spanned only six to nine months. The life-span of other projects was longer but was subject to annual reviews. Women's organizations were forced to spend considerable time and resources on proposal writing. Even after a project was funded, a cloud of uncertainty hung over it because funds for the subsequent years were not ensured.

The international donors should consider a longer funding duration for projects implemented by women's organizations. The assurance of long-term assistance would boost staff morale and help build institutional capacity.

○ Promote Sustainability of Women's Organizations

International donors and women's organizations generally agreed that most women's organizations cannot survive without international assistance. Most postconflict societies faced severe shortages of economic resources. They lacked a well-developed private sector, which could fund such organizations. Moreover, women's organizations themselves have limited technical and managerial capacity to diversify funding sources.

To promote the sustainability of some women's organizations that have done noteworthy work in areas where needs continue, the international community could: (1) provide technical assistance, when necessary, to improve management; (2) consider funding a portion of core costs, in addition to program costs, for a limited time; and (3) help the organizations become self-reliant by improving skills in advocacy, fund-raising, coalition building, strengthening local political networks, and networking with governmental and nongovernmental organizations. In addition, it should consider facilitating training and assistance to help women's organizations create viable businesses that support their core activities over the long term.

○ Integrate Women's Organizations in
Large-Scale Development Initiatives

The international community has tended to treat women's organizations—because of their gender emphasis and small size—as peripheral rather than mainstream. The development community generally entrusts them with initiatives that target women exclusively. It is important to move beyond this tendency for two reasons. First, a gender framework should inform all development projects—not merely those that help women. Second, integration of women's organizations into large development initiatives can strengthen the organizations' institutional capabilities.

International donors should explore the possibility of integrating women's organizations into large-scale development initiatives in post-conflict societies. Such integration could entail awarding them contracts for development initiatives and encouraging large development organizations to include women's organizations as partners in bidding for contracts for international projects.

• **Strategic Framework for International Assistance**

Although international donors have successfully designed and implemented a host of interventions to help women and promote gender equality, no strategic framework exists to inform these assistance programs. A strategic framework not only can provide an overall rationale for policy and program coherence, but also can promote meaningful donor coordination.

It should be recognized at the outset that the purpose of international assistance is not merely to mitigate the harmful effects of conflict, but also to transform gender relations by seizing opportunities for women's advancement. Therefore, any framework should be designed to achieve two objectives: (1) address the urgent and immediate problems that women face in the aftermath of conflict; and (2) contribute to women's social, economic, and political empowerment, thereby promoting more balanced gender relations. Although related, these are distinct objectives.

On the basis of the preceding discussion, the outline of a strategic framework is proposed here. The proposed framework has three elements: enhancing physical security, increasing access to resources, and promoting political empowerment.[2] These elements are represented graphically in Figure 9.1.

Figure 9.1   Strategic Framework for International Assistance

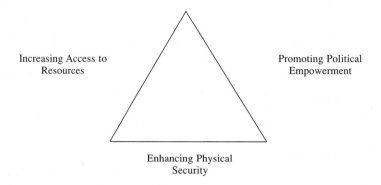

Increasing Access to
Resources

Promoting Political
Empowerment

Enhancing Physical
Security

○ **Enhancing Physical Security**

Physical security includes protection from violence and protection from hunger, both critical to women's welfare. Although both men and women are susceptible to lingering violence from a conflict, women are more vulnerable. They often are easy targets for those seeking revenge, particularly in ethnic conflicts. Women are more often the victims of sexual abuse and exploitation both during and after the conflict. Moreover, domestic violence often increases in the aftermath of conflicts. The international community has thus far limited its involvement in protecting women from violence. It should do more in the future.

Hunger is a primary form of insecurity for women. Women are particularly susceptible to food insecurity in postconflict societies because of abject poverty, additional economic pressures as single heads of households, and the addition of separated children to families. The international community has undertaken a host of programs to prevent hunger and starvation both during and after conflicts. These include the bulk distribution of food, food-for-work programs to generate employment, nutritional support programs for children, and the provision of seed and tools for agriculture. The international community has also developed mechanisms to ensure that women get their reasonable share of such assistance.

○ **Increasing Access to Resources**

Productive assets include not only physical assets but also technical skills and knowledge. Even in peaceful times, women do not receive equal access to productive assets. The situation tends to worsen in post-conflict periods because of the destruction of physical and institutional infrastructure, economic recession, and general social disorganization. It is therefore essential that concerted efforts be made early during post-conflict transition to give women increased access to and control of productive assets. Without such efforts, women can neither become productive members of their societies nor improve their social and economic status. Any economic gains they made during the conflict might even be undermined.

The international community has undertaken many programs to increase women's access to productive assets. First, in rural areas, the community provides seeds, pesticides, agricultural tools, and livestock so farmers can start or resume agricultural production. Experience has shown that women farmers often are underrepresented in such assistance. Second, international donors fund microenterprise programs. The major beneficiaries of such credit programs have been women. Third, the international community supports training and educational programs. Depending on the level of the country's development, such programs may range from literacy training to training in computer and business skills. Fourth, international donors also assist postconflict societies in restoring communal assets and improving people's access to them. Examples of this sort of assistance are projects to remove land mines, clean the environment, and repair and construct roads. Finally, international donors have supported legal reforms to enable women to inherit and own productive assets. All these efforts are valuable, but they should be pursued with greater vigor.

◦ Promoting Political Empowerment

The last element of the strategic framework is political empowerment. The gains to be made by increasing women's access to and control of productive resources cannot be consolidated without women sharing political power. Nor can traditional structures of discrimination and subjugation be eradicated without women's political leadership. The international development community has often underestimated the importance of political participation and power sharing by women in postconflict societies. Thus, political empowerment of women should be an essential element of a strategic framework for international assistance.

The international community has already supported many activities that directly or indirectly increase women's participation in public affairs.

For one, international donors have fostered the formation of women's organizations that not only provide an array of services to targeted women, but also nurture self-confidence and activism. These programs can and often do prepare women to assume leadership roles in the polity. For another, many international NGOs and donor agencies have provided assistance to women's groups working for increased political participation. Such groups articulate agendas, provide support to women candidates, and sometimes work with legislative bodies to fight discrimination.

This strategic framework is, at best, tentative and is designed to promote further dialogue on the subject. Nevertheless, its three elements are essential to advancing women's progress after major societal upheaval. Any framework incorporating these elements will help policymakers and program managers design and integrate coherent interventions that address women's most urgent problems and help establish gender equality and women's empowerment.

• Notes

1. Rwanda did hold local elections.
2. This framework is in many ways similar to that proposed by the World Bank in its *World Development Report 2000/2001: Attacking Poverty.*

Bibliography

Abashidze, Tamara, and Irine Zhvania. 1998. *Social Psychological Research on the State of Women in Georgia.* Tbilisi, Georgia: Women in Development, UN Development Program.

Abashidze, T., et al. 1998. *Women, Economic Development, and Conflict.* Tbilisi, Georgia: UN Development Program.

Academy for Educational Development. 1998. *Caucasus Women's Leadership Conference.* Final Report. Washington, D.C.

Acosta-Belen, Edna, and Christine E. Bose. 1990. "From Structural Subordination to Empowerment: Women and Development in Third World Contexts." *Gender & Society: Official Publication of Sociologists for Women in Society* 4 (3): 299.

Adams, Mark, and Mark Bradbury. 1995. *Conflict and Development: Organizational Adaptation in Conflict Situations.* Oxfam Discussion Paper 4. London: Oxfam England.

Afsharipour, Afra. 1999. "Empowering Ourselves: The Role of Women's NGOs in the Enforcement of the Women's Convention." *Columbia Law Review* 99 (1): 129.

Allison, Lincoln. 1996. "Problems of Democratization in the Republic of Georgia." *Democratization* 3 (4) (winter): 517–529.

Allison, Lincoln, Alexander Kukhanidze, and Malkhaz Matsaberidze. 1993. "The Georgian Election of 1992." *Electoral Studies* 12 (2): 174–179.

Amadiume, Ifi. 1987. *Male Daughters, Female Husbands: Gender and Sex in an African Society.* Atlantic Highlands, N.J.: Zed Books.

Anderson, Thomas. 1971. *Matanza: El Salvador's First Communist Revolt of 1932.* Lincoln: University of Nebraska Press.

André, Catherine, and Phillip Platteau. 1998. "Land Under Unbearable Stress: Rwanda Caught in the Malthusian Trap." *Journal of Economic Behavior and Organization* 34: 1–47.

Arcellana, Nancy Pearson. 1998. "Country Report: Cambodia." *Women in Action* 1 (72).

Area de Derechos de la Mujer (CALDH). 1998. "Informe nacional sobre la situación de los derechos humanos de las mujeres guatemaltecas. A presentarse ante la Comisión Interamericano de Derechos Humanos en su visita en loco a Guatemala del 6 al 11 de agosto de 1998." Guatemala: CALDH.

Armstrong, Robert, and Janet Shenk. 1982. *El Salvador: The Face of Revolution.* Boston: South End Press.

Arnson, Cynthia. 1982. *El Salvador: A Revolution Confronts the United States.* Washington, D.C.: Institute for Policy Studies.

Arnvig, Eva. 1994. "Women, Children, and Returnees." In Peter Utting, ed., *Between Hope and Insecurity: The Social Consequences of the Cambodian Peace Process.* Geneva: United Nations Research Institute for Social Development.

Aron, Adrianne, et al. 1991. "The Gender-Specific Terror of El Salvador and Guatemala: Posttraumatic Stress Disorder in Central American Refugee Women." *Women's Studies International* 37: 37–47.

Asociación Mujeres Vamos Adelante. 1999. "Attachment 2, Program Description Reducing Violence Against Women." Re: Award #520-A-00-99-00089-00 to Asociación Mujeres Vamos Adelante, 29 September 1999. Guatemala: Asociación Mujeres Vamos Adelante.

Aves, Jonathon. 1996. *Georgia: From Chaos to Stability?* London: Royal Institute of International Affairs.

Baden, Sally. 1997. *Postconflict Mozambique: Women's Special Situation, Population Issues, and Gender Perspectives to Be Integrated into Skills Training and Employment Promotion.* International Labor Office Program on Skills and Entrepreneurship Training for Countries Emerging from Armed Conflict. Geneva: International Labor Office.

Baldwin, Hannah, and Catharine Newbury. 1999. "An Evaluation of USAID/OTI's Women in Transition Initiatives in Rwanda." Office of Transition Initiatives and CDIE. Washington, D.C.: USAID.

Barrett, Jacqueline K., and Jane A. Malonis, eds. 1993. *Encyclopedia of Women's Associations Worldwide: A Guide to Over 3,400 National and Multinational Nonprofit Women's and Women-Related Organizations.* Detroit: Gale Research.

Bell, Patrick, Paul Kobrak, and Herbert F. Spirer. 1999. *State Violence in Guatemala, 1960–1996: A Quantitative Reflection.* Washington, D.C.: AAAS Science and Human Rights Program. From web site: http://hrdata.aaas.org/ciidh/qr/english/.

Bennett, Olivia, et al., eds. 1995. *Arms to Fight, Arms to Protect: Women Speak Out About Conflict.* London: Panos.

Booth, John, and Thomas W. Walker. 1989. *Understanding Central America.* Boulder, Colo.: Westview Press.

Boua, Chanthou. 1992. "Cambodia: Can Women Survive the New 'Peace'?" *Ms.,* July: 19.

Boutroue, Joel, and Stephen Jones. 1997. *Prospect for the Return of Internally Displaced Persons and Refugees to Abkhazia: A UNHCR Review of the Situation in Georgia.* Tbilisi, Georgia: UN High Commissioner for Refugees.

Boyden, Jo, and Sara Gibbs. 1997. *Children of War: Response to Psychosocial Distress in Cambodia.* Geneva: UNIRIST.

Bracewell, W. 1995. "Mothers of the Nation." In *Warreport.* London: Institute of War and Peace Reporting.

Brandt, Michele, and Chantol Oung. 1996. "Cambodia's Obligation to End Violence Against Women." *Cambodian Journal of International Affairs* 1 (1): 35.

Bringa, T. 1995 *Being Muslim the Bosnian Way: Identity and Community in a Central Bosnian Village.* Princeton: Princeton University Press.

Buck, Thomas. 1999. *Women, War, and Displacement in Georgia.* (PN–ACF– 180) Academy for Educational Development. Washington, D.C.: USAID.

Buck, Thomas, with Alice Morton, Susan Allen Nan, and Feride Zurikashvili. 2000. "Aftermath: Effects of Conflict on Internally Displaced Women in Georgia." Working Paper No. 310. Washington, D.C.: USAID/CDIE.

Bujra, J. 1986. "Urging Women to Redouble Their Efforts: Class, Gender, and Capitalist Transformation in Africa." In C. Robertson and I. Berger, eds., *Women and Class in Africa,* pp. 117–140. New York: Holmes & Meiers, 1986.

Bunch, Charlotte, and Roxanna Carrillo. 1992. *Gender Violence: A Development and Human Rights Issue.* Dublin: Center for Women's Global Leadership.

Burnet, Jennie E., and Jacqueline Mukandamage. 2000. "Réseau des Femmes Oeuvrant pour le Développement Rural: An Organizational Case Study." Washington, D.C.: Center for Development Information and Evaluation, USAID.

Byrne, Bridget. 1995. "Gender, Conflict, and Development: Volume I." *Briefings on Development and Gender* No. 34. Sussex, UK: Institute for Development Studies.

Byrne, Bridget, R. Marcus, and T. Power-Stevens. 1996. "Gender, Conflict, and Development: Volume II: Case Studies: Cambodia, Rwanda, Kosovo, Algeria, Somalia, Guatemala, and Eritrea." *Briefings on Development and Gender* No. 34. Sussex, UK: Institute for Development Studies.

Byron, G., and M. Walsh. 1998. "Beyond Reach: An Assessment of CARE's REACH Program for the Elderly." Unpublished report for CARE.

Cabarrús Molina, Carolina, Dorotea Gómez Grijalva, and Ligia Gónzalez Martínez. 2000. "Guatemalan Women Refugees and Returnees: Challenges and Lessons Learned from the the Refugee Camps and During Repatriation." Washington, D.C.: International Center for Research on Women and Centre for Development and Population Activities.

"Cambodia: Reconstructing the Fabric of Women's Lives." 1994. *Connexions* (46): 29.

Cambodia Women's Crisis Center. 1998. *Helping Women Help Themselves: Bi-Annual Report.* Phnom Penh: Cambodia Women's Crisis Center, August.

Cambodian NGO Support Network (CNSN). 1997. *Moving Forward Together: A Dialog on the Partnership Between Cambodian NGOs and Support Agencies.* Report on the CNSN Partnership Workshop held 3–4 September. Phnom Penh.

Camey Huz, María Rosenda. 2000. "Estrategia de desarrollo comunitario, a partir de programas de reparación psicosocial: Un estudio con viudas y huérfanos, mas afectados por la violencia política. El caso de la Aldea Las Lomas, San Martín Jilotepéque, Chimaltenango." Maestria en Gerencia para del Desarrollo Sostenible: Instituto Chi Pixab', Universidad Autónoma de Madrid.

Carothers, Thomas. 1999. *Aiding Democracy Abroad: The Learning Curve.* Washington, D.C.: Carnegie Endowment for International Peace.

Carr, Marilyn, Martha Chen, and Renana Jhabvala. 1996. *Speaking Out: Women's Empowerment in South Asia.* London: Intermediate Technology Publications.

Catholic Relief Services. 1989. "Report of a CARITAS–CRS Mission to Honduras: January 13–19, 1989." Unpublished report submitted to the UN High Commissioner for Refugees.

Catolico, Olivia. 1997. "Psychological Well-Being of Cambodian Women in Resettlement." *ANS, Advances in Nursing Science* 19 (4): 75.

Caucasus Women's Research and Consulting Network. 1999. *To Study of [sic] All Kinds of Discrimination Toward Women (Georgian Case).* Unpublished study conducted by the Caucasus Women's Research and Consulting Network with the support of the Global Fund for Women. Tbilisi, Georgia.

Chandler, David P. 1991. *Tragedy of Cambodia History.* New Haven: Yale University Press.

————. 1996. *A History of Cambodia.* 2d ed. Boulder, Colo.: Westview Press.

Chassen–Lopez, Francie R. 1997. "From Casa to Calle: Latin American Women Transforming Patriarchal Spaces." *Journal of Women's History* 9: 174.

Chirikba, Viacheslav A. 1998. "The Georgian–Abkhaz Conflict: In Search of Ways Out." *Caucasian Regional Studies* 3 (2). From web site: http://poli.vub.ac.be/publi/Georgians/chp0301.html.

Clayton, Michael. 1997. "Georgia's NGO Movement Flourishes, but Continued Support Is Needed." *Surviving Together* 15 (4): 4–6.

Cockburn, Cynthia. 1998. *The Space Between Us: Negotiating Gender and National Identities in Conflict.* London: Zed Books.

Cohen, Jonathan. 1997. "Civil Society Under Construction: A Challenge for Europe." In *OSCE—A Need for Co-operation: Toward the OSCE's Common and Comprehensive Security Model for Europe for the Twenty-first Century*, pp. 73–85. Copenhagen: Danish UN Association. From web site: http://www.una.dk/osce/essays/contents.html.

————. 1998. "Peace Postponed." *Transitions* 5 (7): 66–73.

Cohen, Roberta. 1995. *Refugees and Internally Displaced Women: A Development Perspective.* Washington, D.C.: Brookings Institution.

Colby, Benjamin N., and Lore M. Colby. 1981. *The Daykeeper: The Life and Discourse of an Ixil Diviner.* Cambridge, Mass.: Harvard University Press.

Colom, Yolanda. 1998. *Mujeres en la Alborada.* Guatemala: Artemis & Edinter.

————. 2000. Fundación Colom and Unidad Revolucionaria Nacional Guatemalteca (URNG). Interview, March.

Commission for Historical Clarification. 1999. *Guatemala: Memory of Silence.* Washington, D.C.: AAAS Science and Human Rights Program. From web site: http://hrdata.aaas.org/ceh/report/english/concl.html.

Commission on Human Rights and Reception of Complaints. 1997. *Report on the Problem of Sexual Exploitation and Trafficking in Cambodia.* Phnom Penh.

Conseil de Concertation des Organisations d'Appui aux Initiatives de Base. 1993. "Textes de base." Kigali, Rwanda.

Consejería en Proyectos. 2000 Interview, March.

Copelon, Rhonda. 1994. "Surfacing Gender: Reconceptualizing Crimes Against Women in Time of War." In Alexandra Stiglmayer, *Mass Rape: The War Against Women in Bosnia–Herzegovina*. Lincoln: University of Nebraska Press.

Coppieters, Bruno. 1999. "The Roots of the Conflict." In Jonathon Cohen, ed., "A Question of Sovereignty: The Georgia–Abkhaz Peace Process," in *Accord: An International Review of Peace Initiatives* (7): 14–19.

Cosgrove, Serena. 1995. *Women, Credit, and the Urban Informal Sector of El Salvador: An Ethnography of Two Communal Banks.* Master's thesis, Department of Sociology and Anthropology, Northeastern University, Boston.

COSYLI (Conseil National des Organisations Syndicales Libres au Rwanda). 1998. "Rapport des séminaires sur 'les normes, la legislation des femmes travailleuses et le syndicalisme.'" Kigali, Rwanda: COSYLI.

Date–Bah, Eugenia. 1996. *Sustainable Peace After War: Arguing the Need for Major Integration of Gender Perspectives in Postconflict Programming.* Geneva: International Labor Office.

De Keersmaeker, François, and Gerard Peart. 1997. *Children and Women of Rwanda: A Situation Analysis of Social Sectors.* Kigali, Rwanda: UNICEF.

De Lame, Danielle. 1996. *Une colline entre mille ou le calme avant la tempête: Transformations et blocages du Rwanda rural.* Tervuren: Musée Royal de l'Afrique Centrale.

De Smedt, Johan. 1998. "Child Marriages in Rwandan Refugee Camps." *Africa* 68 (2): 211–237.

Delphi International/MEET. 1998. *Special Report on Women's Participation Levels in Microcredit Programs in BiH.* Sarajevo: Delphi International.

Dercon, Stefan, and Pramila Krishnan. 1999. "Vulnerability, Seasonality, and Poverty in Ethiopia." Cambridge: Oxford University, Center for the Study of African Economies.

Dersham, Larry D., et al. 1996. *Food, Nutrition, Health, and Nonfood Vulnerability in Georgia, 1996: A Household Assessment.* Tbilisi, Georgia.

Des Forges, Alison. 1999. *Leave None to Tell the Story: Genocide in Rwanda.* New York: Human Rights Watch and International Federation of Human Rights.

Development Assistance Committee (DAC). 1997. *DAC Guidelines on Conflict, Peace, and Development Cooperation.* Organization for Security and Cooperation in Europe. Paris: DAC.

Donia, R. J., and J.V.A. Fine. 1994. *Bosnia and Herzegovina: A Tradition Betrayed.* London: Hurst and Company.

Dourglishvili, Nino. 1997. *Social Change and the Georgian Family.* Discussion Paper Series 3. Tbilisi, Georgia: UN Development Program.

Ebihara, May M. 1974. "Khmer Village Women in Cambodia." In C. Matthiasson, ed., *Many Sisters: Women in Cross-Cultural Perspective,* pp. 305–347. New York: Free Press.

Ebihara, May M., Carol A. Mortland, and Judy Ledgerwood. 1994. *Cambodia Culture Since 1975: Homeland and Exile.* Ithaca, N.Y.: Cornell University Press.

Edición Mujeres. 1994. *Suplemento especial. Edición mujeres.* San Salvador, El Salvador, March.

Einhorn, B. 1993. *The Impact of the Transition from Centrally Planned Economies on Women's Employment in East Central Europe.* Brighton: BRIDGE, Institute of Development Studies.

El-Bushra, Judy, and Cécile Mukaruguga. 1995. "Women, War, and Transition." *Gender and Development* 3 (3): 16–22.

El-Bushra, Judy, and E. Piza–Lopez. 1993. *Development in Conflict: The Gender Dimension.* London: Oxfam.

Equipo de Antropología Forense de Guatemala (EAFG). 1995. "Las masacres en Rabinal: Estudio histórico-antropológico de la masacres de Plan de Sánches, Chichupac, y Río Negro." Guatemala City: EAFG.

Etienne, Margareth. 1995. "Addressing Gender-Based Violence in an International Context." *Harvard Women's Law Journal* 18: 139–170.

Falla, Ricardo. 1992. *Masacres de la selva: Ixcán, Guatemala (1975–1982).* Guatemala: Editorial Universitaria.

Fane, Daria. 1993. "Soviet Census Data, Union Republic and ASSR, 1989." In Ian Bremmer and Ray Taras, eds., *Nations & Politics in Soviet Successor States.* New York: Cambridge University Press.

Federation of Bosnia and Herzegovina. 1996. *Health Reform and Reconstruction Programme of the Federation of Bosnia and Herzegovina.* Sarajevo: Ministry of Health.

Fernando, Jude L. 1997. "Nongovernmental Organizations, Microcredit, and Empowerment of Women." *Annals of the American Academy* 554: 150–177.

Ferris, Elizabeth G. 1993. "Women in Uprooted Families." *Journal of the Society for International Development* 4: 30–34.

FESAL–98. 1999. *Encuesta nacional de salud familiar: 1998, informe preliminar.* San Salvador, El Salvador: Asociación Demográfica Salvadoreña and Centers for Disease Control, Division of Reproductive Health.

Findlay, Trevor. 1995. *Cambodia: The Legacy and Lessons of UNTAC.* New York: Oxford University Press.

Fiske, Edward B. 1995. *Using Both Hands: Women and Education in Cambodia.* Manila: Asian Development Bank.

Foro Nacional de la Mujer. 1999a. "Plan de acción mujeres y desarrollo. Enero 2000–diciembre 2001." Foro Nacional de la Mujer, 10 December.

———. 1999b. "Reforma constitucionales y las mujeres, compromiso #29, acuerdos de paz." Guatemala: Kamaer Editorial.

Foundation for the Development of Human Resources. 1996. *Psychosocial Rehabilitation of IDPs in Georgia: 15 June 1995–15 June 1996.* Tbilisi, Georgia.

———. 1997. *Psychosocial Rehabilitation of IDPs in Georgia: 15 December 1996–15 December 1997.* Tbilisi, Georgia.

Frieson, Kate G. 1998. "The Role of Women's Organizations in Postconflict Cambodia." Washington, D.C.: USAID/CDIE.

Gachechiladze, Revaz. 1995. *The New Georgia: Space, Society, Politics.* London: University College of London Press.

Gaprindashili, Lela. 1999. "Women's Initiative for Equality." Email correspondence, 19 November.

García, Ana Isabel, and Enrique Gomariz, eds. 1989. *Mujeres centroamericanas 1.* San José, Costa Rica: FLACSO.

Garrard-Burnett, Virginia. 2000. "Aftermath: Women and Gender Issues in Postconflict Guatemala." Working Paper No. 311. Washington, D.C.: USAID/CDIE.

Gender Development Association. 1999. *Conditions of Women in Georgia.* A report for the United Nations Development Program. Tbilisi, Georgia.

Georgian Young Lawyers Association, Feminist Women's Club, International Fund of Medical Women, and the Women's Employment Association. 1999. *Report of Non-Governmental Organizations on the Status of Women in the Republic of Georgia Under CEDAW Articles* (CEDAW Shadow Report). Report submitted in preparation for the 21st CEDAW session. Tbilisi, Georgia.

Golden, Renny. 1991. *The Hour of the Poor, The Hour of Women: Salvadoran Women Speak.* New York: Crossroad.

Green, Edward C., and Alcinda Honwana. 1999. "Indigenous Healing of War-Affected Children in Africa." World Bank IK Notes #10. Washington, D.C.: World Bank.

Green, Linda. 1994. "Fear as a Way of Life." *Cultural Anthropology* 9 (2): 227–256.

———. 1999. *Fear as a Way of Life: Mayan Widows in Rural Guatemala.* New York: Columbia University Press.

Greene, Thomas. 1998. "Internal Displacement in the North Caucasus, Azerbaijan, Armenia, and Georgia." In Roberta Cohen and Francis M. Deng, eds., *The Forsaken People: Case Studies of the Internally Displaced,* pp. 233–311. Washington, D.C.: Brookings Institution Press.

Haguruka. 1999. "Rapport annuel 1998." Kigali, Rwanda: Haguruka.

Hashemi, Syed, Sidney Rush Schuler, and Ann Riley. 1996. "Rural Credit Programs and Women's Employment in Bangladesh." *World Development* 24 (4): 635–653.

Hayden, William. 1998. "Georgia." In Janie Hampton, ed., *Internally Displaced People: A Global Survey,* pp. 169–173. Norwegian Refugee Council Global IDP Survey. London: Earthscan.

Heise, Lori, Mary Ellsberg, and Megan Gottemoeller. 1999. "Ending Violence Against Women." *Population Reports.* Series L, No. 11. Baltimore: Johns Hopkins University School of Public Health, Population Information Program.

Helland, Anita, Kari Karamé, Anita Kristensen, and Inger Skjelsbæk. 1999. *Women and Armed Conflicts.* A study for the Norwegian Ministry of Foreign Affairs. Oslo: Norwegian Institute of International Affairs.

"Her Choice: In Cambodia's Highlands, Women Are the Ones at the Top." 1993. *Asiaweek* 19 (8) (22 September): 35.

Hilhorst, Dorothea, and Mathijs van Leeuwen. 1999. "Imidugudu: Villagisation in Rwanda: A Case of Emergency Development." *Disaster Sites,* no. 2. The Netherlands: Wageningen University.

Horizonti Foundation. 1998. *Caucasus Women's NGOs Needs Assessment.* Tbilisi, Georgia: Research and Analysis Project, Information Program of the Horizonti Foundation.

Howes, Ruth, and Michael Stevenson. 1993. *Women and the Use of Military Force.* Boulder, Colo.: Lynne Rienner Publishers.

Hudock, Ann. 1999. *NGOs and Civil Society: Democracy by Proxy.* Cambridge, Mass.: Polity Press.

Human Rights Watch. 1996. *The Commonwealth of Independent States: Refu-gees and Internally Displaced Persons in Armenia, Azerbaijan, Georgia, the Russian Federation, and Tajikistan.* New York: Human Rights Watch, May.

Human Rights Watch/Africa, Human Rights Watch Women's Rights Project, and the Fédération Internationale des Lingues des Droits de l'Homme. 1996. *Shattered Lives: Sexual Violence During the Rwandan Genocide.* New York: Human Rights Watch.

Hunt, Kathleen. 1995. *Forced Migration: Repatriation in Georgia.* New York: Open Society Institute.

INADES Formation Rwanda. 1985. "Inventaire O.N.G. 1985." Kigali, Rwanda: UNICEF.

Inter-American Development Bank. 1990. *Economic and Social Progress in Latin America.* Washington, D.C.: Inter-American Development Bank.

International Human Rights Law Group (IHRLG). 1999. *Women's Rights in BiH.* Sarajevo: IHRLG.

Irwin, Carol V. 1993. "Gender, Cash Cropping, and Land Purchase Programs in Guatemala." Produced for the Land Tenure Center, University of Wiscon-sin, Madison, Land Tenure Center.

IWACU. n.d. "Do You Know IWACU?" Kigali, Rwanda: IWACU.

Jacquette, Jane S., ed. 1994. *The Women's Movement in Latin America: Partic-ipation and Democracy.* Boulder, Colo.: Westview Press.

Jamail, Milton, and Margo Gutierrez. 1986. *Israel's Military Involvement in Central America.* Belmont, Md.: Association of Arab-American University Graduates.

Jefremovas, Villia. 1991. "Loose Women, Virtuous Wives, and Timid Virgins: Gender and the Control of Resources in Rwanda." *Canadian Journal of African Studies* 25 (3): 378–395.

Johnsson, Anders. 1989. "The International Protection of Women Refugees: A Summary of Principal Problems and Issues." *International Journal of Refugee Law* 221: 225–228.

Jones, Lynne, ed. 1983. *Keeping the Peace: A Women's Peace Handbook.* Lon-don: Women's Press.

Jones, Stephen. 1996. "Georgia's Return from Chaos." *Current History* 95 (603): 340–345.

Kabeer, Naila. 1995. "Targeting Women or Transforming Institutions? Policy Lessons from NGO Antipoverty Efforts." *Development in Practice* 5 (2): 108–117.

———. 1994. *Reversed Realities: Gender Hierarchies in Development Thought.* London: Verso Press.

Karl, Marilee. 1994. "Paths to Empowerment: Women and Political Participa-tion." *Women in Action* 1 (7).

———. 1995. *Women and Empowerment: Participation and Decision-Making.* London: Zed Books.

Kharashvili, Julia. 1995. *Psychosocial Examination of IDP Children and Women—Victims of Military Conflicts on the Territory of the Georgia.* A survey sponsored by Oxfam. Tbilisi, Georgia: Oxfam.

Khomeriki, Lela, Nino Chubinidze, and Nino Berekashvili. *Women's NGOs in Georgia.* 1998. A report for the International Center for Civic Culture. Tbilisi, Georgia. From web site: http://www.osgf.ge/wie/2.html.

Kibiriti, Christine. 1999. "Stratégies facilitant l'application de l'approche genre dans les différents secteurs de développement." In République Rwandaise, Ministère du Genre et de la Promotion de la Femme, "Atelier sur l'approche genre et le statut juridique de la femme rwandaise." Rapport provisoire, May.

Kiernan, Ben. 1996. *The Pol Pot Regime: Race Power and Genocide in Cambodia Under the Khmer Rouge: 1975–79*. New Haven: Yale University Press.

Kumar, Krishna, ed. 1997. *Rebuilding Societies After Civil Wars: Critical Areas for International Assistance*. Boulder, Colo.: Lynne Rienner Publishers.

———. 1998. *Postconflict Elections, Democratization, and International Assistance*. Boulder, Colo.: Lynne Rienner Publishers.

———. 2000. *Women and Women's Organizations in Postconflict Societies:* Washington, D.C.: USAID.

Kumar, Krishna, Hannah Baldwin, and Judy Benjamin. 2000. "Aftermath: Women and Women's Organizations in Postconflict Cambodia." Working Paper No. 307. Washington, D.C.: USAID/CDIE.

Kusakabe, Kyoko, Wang Yunxian, and Govind Kelkar. 1995. "Women and Land Rights in Cambodia." *Economic and Political Weekly* 30 (43): WS87.

Ledgerwood, Judy. 1992. *Analysis of the Situation of Women in Cambodia: Research on Women in Khmer Society*. Washington, D.C.: UNICEF.

———. 1994. "Economic Transformations and Gender in a Cambodian Village." Paper presented at the Northwest Regional Consortium for Southeast Asian Studies, Seattle, November.

———. 1996. "Politics and Gender: Negotiating Conceptions of the Ideal Woman in Present-Day Cambodia." *Asia Pacific Viewpoint* 37 (2): 139.

Lemarchand, René. 1995. "The Rationality of Genocide." *Issue* 23 (2): 8–11.

———. 1999. "The Crisis in the Great Lakes." In John W. Harbeson and Donald Rothchild, eds., *Africa in World Politics: The African State System in Flux,* pp. 324–352. Boulder and Oxford: Westview Press.

Levine, Corey. 1999. "The Gender Dimensions of Peacebuilding." Paper presented at the conference "Human Security: Policy Implications for the 21st Century," 18–19 September. Norman Paterson School of International Affairs, Carleton University, Ottawa.

Lewis, Shelby. 1997. *Women in Transitioning Societies*. A report for the Office of Transition Initiatives, Bureau of Humanitarian Response. Washington, D.C.: USAID.

Light, Deborah. 1992. "Healing Their Wounds: Guatemalan Refugee Women as Political Activists." *Women & Therapy* 13: 297.

"Lista oficial de diputados al congreso de la republica, noviembre 25 de 1999." 1999. From web site: http://www.c.net.gt/ceg/doctos/listadiput.html.

Lorentzen, Lois Ann, and Jennifer Turpin, eds. 1996. "Women and War." *Peace Review* 8: 315–421.

Loughna, Sean. 1998. "The Role of Women's Organizations During and After Intrastate Conflict in Guatemala." Washington, D.C.: USAID/CDIE.

Loughna, Sean, and Gema Vicente. 1997. *Population Issues and the Situation of Women in Postconflict Guatemala*. Geneva: International Labor Office.

Luciak, Ilja A. 1998. "Gender Equality and Electoral Politics on the Left: A Comparison of El Salvador and Nicaragua." *Journal of Interamerican Studies and World Affairs* 40 (1).

Lucy, T. V. 1995. "Empowerment of Women for Sustainable Development." *Social Action* 45 (2): 224.

Lykes, M. Brinton, Mary M. Brabeck, Theresa Ferns, and Angela Radan. 1993. "Human Rights and Mental Health Among Latin American Women in Situations of State-Sponsored Violence." *Psychology of Women Quarterly* 17: 525–544.

MacFarlane, S. Neil, Larry Minear, and Stephen D. Shenfield. 1996. *Armed Conflict in Georgia: A Case Study in Humanitarian Action and Peacekeeping.* Occasional Paper 21. Providence, R.I.: Thomas J. Watson Jr. Institute for International Studies, Brown University.

Malcolm, N. 1996. *Bosnia: A Short History.* Macmillan: London.

Marcus, Rachel. 1995. "Cambodia Case Study." Unpublished report. Phnom Penh.

Mars, Gerald, and Yochanan Altman. 1983. "The Cultural Basis of Soviet Georgia's Second Economy." *Soviet Studies* 35 (4) (October): 546–560.

Martin, Marie Alexandrine. 1994. *Cambodia: A Shattered Society.* Berkeley: University of California Press.

Martin, Susan. 1992. *Refugee Women.* London: Zed Books.

McNulty, Susan. 1998. *Women's Organizations During and After War: From Service Delivery to Policy Advocacy.* Academy for Educational Development. Washington, D.C.: USAID (PN-ACF-180).

Medica Zenica. 1996. "Surviving the Violence: War and Violence Against Women Are Inseparable." Information Bulletin. Zenica: Medica Zenica.

Medica Zenica Infoteka. 1999. "A Second Look: To Live Without Violence." Zenica: Medica Zenica.

Mehra, Rekha, ed. 1996. *Taking Women into Account: Lessons Learned from NGO Project Experiences.* Washington, D.C.: Interaction.

———. 1997. "Women, Empowerment, and Economic Development." *Annals of the American Academy of Political and Social Science* 554: 136.

Menchú, Rigoberta. 1984. *I . . . Rigoberta. An Indian Woman of Guatemala.* Trans. Elizabeth Burgos-Debray. London: Verso.

———. 1992. "The Quincentennial—A Gift of Life: A Message from the Indigenous People of Guatemala." *Social Justice* 19: 63.

———. 1998. *Crossing Borders.* Trans. Ann Wright. London: Verso.

Mendez, J. 1980. "Testimonies of Guatemalan Women." *Latin American Perspectives* 7: 160–168.

Meskhi, Marina. 1999. Women's Rights Study Group of the Georgian Young Lawyers Association. Interview, 20 October.

Metonidze, Veronika. 1998. "Woman and War in Abkhazia." Tbilisi, Georgia: Georgian Young Lawyers Association.

Metreveli, Tamar. 1997. "Innovations Introduced by the New Civil Code in Public Sector." *Horizonti: The Magazine for the Third Sector in Georgia* (1) (autumn): 3–5.

Migdal, Joel S., Atul Kohli, and Vivienne Shue, eds. *State Power and Social Forces: Domination and Transformation in the Third World.* Cambridge, Mass.: Cambridge University Press, 1994.

Miller, Francesca. 1991. *Latin American Women and the Search for Social Justice.* Hanover, Mass.: University Press of New England.

Ministry of Health (Cambodia). 1994. *Special Report.* Phnom Penh.

Ministry of Women Affairs (Cambodia). 1996. *Physical Abuse.* Phnom Penh.

Molina, Carolina Cabarrús, Doratea Gómez Grijalva, and Ligia González Martínez. 1999. "Guatemalan Women Refugees and Returnees: Challenges and Lessons Learned from the Refugee Camps and During Reintegration." Project Report, Promoting Women in Development Program. Washington, D.C.: International Center for Research on Women and Centre for Development and Population Activities.

Montenegro, Nineth. 2000. Grupo de Apoyo Mutuo and ANN. Interview, March.

Montgomery, Tommie Sue. 1995. *Revolution in El Salvador: Origins and Evolution.* 2d ed. Boulder, Colo.: Westview Press.

Morales Trujillo, Hilda. 1997. "Las obligaciones legislativas a favor de las mujeres derivadas de los acuerdos de paz." Oficina Nacional de la Mujer (ONAM), Ascrita al Ministerio de Trabajo y Prevision Social, Proyecto Mujer y Reformas Juridicas. Guatemala: Cooperación Holandesa, Cooperación Sueca, UNIFEM y PNUD through Proyecto GUA 96/010-PNUD.

Morgan, Betsy, and Laura Jackson, eds. 1993. "El Salvador: Special Report: Women and the Peace Process." *Connexions* 41: 28.

Morgan, Betsy, and Serena Cosgrove. 1994. "Seizing History in El Salvador." *Broadsheet: New Zealand Feminist Magazine* 203: 18.

Morton, Alice. 2000. "Women's Organizations and Empowerment in Transitional and Postconflict Societies." Unpublished paper. Washington, D.C.: USAID/CDIE.

Moser, Caroline. 1993. *Gender Development and Planning: Theory, Practice, and Training.* New York: Routledge Press.

Mossberg, Bjorn. 1999. Chief of Mission for SIDA. Personal communication, July.

Mujeres por la Dignidad y la Vida. 1993. *Hacer la política desde las mujeres.* San Salvador, El Salvador: Mujeres por la Dignidad y la Vida.

———. 1998. *Informe institutional.* San Salvador, El Salvador: Mujeres por la Dignidad y la Vida.

Murray, Kevin. 1997. *El Salvador: Peace on Trial.* An Oxfam Country Profile. London: Oxfam UKI.

Nagarajan, Geetha. 1997. *Developing Financial Institutions in Conflict-Affected Countries: Emerging Issues, First Lessons Learnt, and Challenges Ahead.* Geneva: International Labor Organization.

Nájera, Elisa Portillo. 1998. "Estadísticas sobre abusos a esposas, hijas, hermanas o convivientes de hombres que han sido parte de las furezas armadas o de seguridad." Congreso de la Republica de Guatemala: Comisión de Apoyo Tecnico Legislativo. Produced for Diputada Manuela Alvarado.

Nan, Susan Allen. 1999. "Civic Initiatives." In Johathon Cohen, ed., "A Question of Sovereignty: The Georgia–Abkhaz Peace Process," in *Accord: An International Review of Peace Initiatives* 7: 50–57.

———. 2000. "Aftermath: Cooperative Boosts Self-Respect of Displaced Georgian Women." Working Paper No. 306. Washington, D.C.: USAID/CDIE.

National Intelligence Council (NIC). 1999. *Global Humanitarian Emergencies: Trends and Projections, 1999–2000.* Washington, D.C.: NIC.

New American Press. 1989. *A Dream Compels Us: Voices of Salvadoran Women.* Boston: South End Press.

Newbury, Catharine. 1992. "Rwanda: Recent Debates over Governance and Rural Development." In Goran Hyden and Michael Bratton, eds., *Governance and Politics in Africa,* pp. 193–220. Boulder, Colo.: Lynne Rienner Publishers.

———. 1995. "Background to Genocide in Rwanda," *Issue* 23 (2): 12–17.

Newbury, Catharine, and David Newbury. 1999. "A Catholic Mass in Kigali: Contested Views of the Genocide and Ethnicity in Rwanda." *Canadian Journal of African Studies* 33 (2–3): 292–328.

Newbury, Catharine, and Hannah Baldwin. 2000. "Aftermath: Women in Postgenocide Rwanda." Working Paper No. 303. Washington, D.C.: USAID/CDIE.

Newbury, David. 1998. "Understanding Genocide." *African Studies Review* 41 (1) (April): 73–97.

———. 1999. "Ecology and the Politics of Genocide." *Cultural Survival Quarterly* 22 (4) (winter): 32–36.

NGO Forum on Cambodia. 1996. *Study on Differing Approaches to Development Assistance in Cambodia: NGO's and the European Commission.* Oxford: INTRAC, August.

Nguyen-Gillham, V. Q. 1999. "Bosnian Women and Social Reconstruction: Reweaving the Social Fabric." Unpublished Ph.D. dissertation. Boston University.

Niarchos, Catherine. 1995. "Women, War, and Rape: Challenges Facing the International Tribunal for the Former Yugoslavia." *Human Rights Quarterly* 17: 649–690.

Nikolic-Ristanvic, Vesna. 1996. "War, Nationalism, and Mothers." *Peace Review* 8: 359–364.

NIS–U.S. Women's Consortium. 1998. The Georgian Women's Leadership Training Program, Washington, D.C., 2–29 March.

Nodia, Ghia. 1995. "Georgia's Identity Crisis." *Journal of Democracy* 6 (1) (January): 104–116.

———. 1998. "The Conflict in Abkhazia: National Projects and Political Circumstances." *Caucasian Regional Studies* 3 (2). From web sites: http://poli.vub.ac.be/publi/Georgians/chp0201.htm; http://poli.vub.ac.be/publi/Georgians/chp0202.htm; http://poli.vub.ac.be/publi/Georgians/chp0203.htm, respectively.

North, Liisa. 1985. *Bitter Grounds: Roots of Revolt in El Salvador.* 2d ed. Westport, Conn.: Lawrence Hill.

Norwegian Refugee Council. 1995. *Survey on Internally Displaced People in Georgia.* Tbilisi, Georgia.

Nowrojee, Binaifer. 1996. *Shattered Lives: Sexual Violence During the Rwandan Genocide and Its Aftermath.* New York: Human Rights Watch.

Oficina de Derechos Humanos del Arzobispado de Guatemala (ODHAG). 1998. *Informe proyecto interdiocesano de recuperación de la memoria histórica (REMHI).* Vols. 1–4. Guatemala: Oficina de Derechos Humanos del Arzobispado de Guatemala.

OIM, FONAPAZ, SEPAZ, USAID. 1999. "Programa de asistencia a victimas de violaciones de los derechos humanos." Informe: Diagnóstico comunitario en cuatro municipalidaes del Departmento de El Quiché, Guatemala. (For internal distribution among participating organizations.)

Oloka-Onyango, J. 1996. "The Plight of the Larger Half: Human Rights, Gender Violence, and the Legal Status of Refugee and Internally Displaced Women in Africa." *Denver Journal of International Law and Policy* 24 (2–3): 349.

Organization for Economic Cooperation and Development (OECD). 1999. *Guidance for Evaluating Humanitarian Assistance in Complex Emergencies.* Paris: OECD/DAC Working Party on Aid Evaluation.

Organization for Security and Cooperation in Europe (OSCE). 1998. *Women's Representation in Bosnia and Herzegovina: A Statistical Overview 1986, 1990, 1996, 1997.* Sarajevo.

———. 1999a. *Employment Discrimination in Bosnia and Herzegovina,* Human Rights Department, Sarajevo.

———. 1999b. "Survey on the Role of Women in BiH Politics," Sarajevo.

Orvis, Pat. 1993. "Cambodia's Women: Shouldering the Burden." *Populi* 20 (3): 8.

Otzoy, Aura Marina. 2000. Frente Republicano Guatemalteco. Interview, March.

Palmer, Patrice. 1992. "The Empowerment of Women in Rural Bangladesh." *Canadian Woman Studies* 13 (1): 90.

Panhavichetr, P. 1993. "Case Studies: The Impact of Armed Conflict on Gender Relations, Case Study 1: Cambodia." In J. El Bushra and E. P. Lopez, eds., *Development in Conflict: The Gender Dimension.* Report of a workshop held in Thailand, February. Oxford Discussion Paper 3. London: Oxfam.

Pastor, Robert. 1986. National Security Council during Carter administration. Interview, May.

Pearce, Jenny. 1986. *Promised Land: Peasant Rebellion in Chalatenango, El Salvador.* London: Latin American Bureau.

Perez, Christina M. 1994. "Women's Liberation in El Salvador." *Humanity & Society* 18: 77–82.

Pietila, Hilkka, and Jeanne Vickers. 1994. *Making Women Matter: The Role of the United Nations.* London: Zed Books.

Pottier, Johan. 1989. " 'Three's a Crowd': Knowledge, Ignorance, and Power in the Context of Urban Agriculture in Rwanda." *Africa* 59 (4): 461–477.

Pradhan, Susanta Kumar. 1995. "The Role of Education in Empowerment of Women." *The Progress of Education* 69 (12): 252.

Prigoff, Arline. 1991. "Women, Social Development, and the State in Latin America: An Empowerment Model." *Social Development Issues* 14 (1): 56

Prism Research. 1998. *Women in the Bosnia and Herzegovina Economy: Current Status and Future Strategies.* Sarajevo.

Pro-Femmes/Twese Hamwe. 1996. "Campagne action pour la paix (Janvier 1997 à Mars 1998)." Kigali, Rwanda, November.

———. 1999. "Mieux connaître le collectif Pro-Femmes/Twese Hamwe." Kigali, Rwanda.

Pro-Niño y Niña Centroamericanos (PRONICE). 1998. *Violencia organizada y intervención psicosocial: Experiencia de 8 organizaciones que trabajan con comunidades, grupos, familias, y personas que han sido afectados por el conflicto armado y violencia organizada en Guatemala.* Guatemala: PRONICE.

————. 1999. *Efectos psicosociales en la niñez de comunidades de San Martín Jilotepéque, afectadas por la guerra.* Guatemala: PRONICE.

Prunier, Gérard. 1997. *The Rwanda Crisis: History of a Genocide.* 2d ed. New York: Columbia University Press.

Putnam, Robert D. 2000. *Bowling Alone: The Collapse and Revival of American Community.* New York: Simon and Schuster.

Putnam, Robert D., Robert Leonardi, and Raffaella Y. Nanetti. 1994. *Making Democracy Work: Civic Traditions in Modern Italy.* Princeton: Princeton University Press.

Radcliffe, Sarah, and Sallie Westwood, eds. 1993. *Women and Popular Protest in Latin America.* New York: Routledge.

Rapone, Anita, and Charles R. Simpson. 1996. "Women's Response to Violence in Guatemala: Resistance and Rebuilding." *International Journal of Politics, Culture, and Society* 10: 115–140.

Ready, Carol A. 1994. "It's a Hard Life: Women in El Salvador's Economic History." In Lynn Stephen, ed., *Hear My Testimony: Maria Teresa Tula, Human Rights Activist of El Salvador,* pp. 187–200. Boston: South End Press.

————. 1999. *Between Transnational Feminism, Political Parties, and Popular Movements: Mujeres por la Dignidad y la Vida in Postwar El Salvador.* Ph.D. dissertation. Graduate Faculty of Anthropology, City University of New York.

Reardon, Betty. 1993. *Women and Peace: Feminist Visions of Global Security.* Albany: State University of New York Press.

"Reflexion sobre la tema 'Mujer y derechos humanos.'" (Author, publisher, and date of publication unavailable.)

République du Rwanda, Ministère de la Santé. 1998. "Étude sur la prostitution et le sida. Rapport provisoire." Kigali, Rwanda, September.

République du Rwanda, Ministère des Finances et de la Planification Economique, Direction de la Statistique. 1998. "Enquête socio-démographique 1996, rapport final (abrégé)." Kigali, Rwanda, July.

République du Rwanda, Ministère du Travail et des Affaires Sociales. 1993. "Séminaire national sur la redynamisation du CCDFP." Kigali, Rwanda, 4–7 May .

Reyntjens, Filip. 1994. *L'Afrique des grands lacs en crise. Rwanda, Burundi 1988–1994.* Paris: Éditions Karthala.

————. 1995. *Trois jours qui ont fait basculer l'histoire.* Paris: L'Harmattan.

————. 1999. *La guerre des Grands lacs: Alliances mouvantes et conflits extraterritoriaux en Afrique centrale.* Paris: L'Harmattan.

Rice, Pranee. 1992. "Burdens, Risks and Mental Health of Cambodian Women: A Descriptive Paper." *Migration Monitor* (25–26) (June): 8.

Richters, Annemiek. 1994. *Women, Culture, and Violence: A Development, Health, and Human Rights Issue.* Leiden, Netherlands: Women and Autonomy Center.

"The Rights of Women." 1995. *Freedom Review* 26 (5). Special Issue.

Ríos Soto, Zury. 2000. Frente Republicano Guatemalteco. Interview, March.

Roche, Susan E. 1996. "Messages from the NGO Forum on Women, Beijing 1995." *Affilia* 11 (4) (winter): 484–494.

Roe, Michael D. 1992. "Displaced Women in Settings of Continuing Armed Conflict." *Women & Therapy* 12: 82–104.

Roman Catholic priest (anonymous by request), Alta Verapaz. 2000 Interview, March.

Roy, Debal, and K. Singha. 1995. "Peasant Movements, Grass-Roots Mobilizations, and Empowerment of Rural Women." *Economic and Political Weekly* 30 (37): 2306.

Rozee, Patricia D., and Gretchen van Boemel. 1989. "The Psychological Effects of War Trauma and Abuse on Older Cambodian Refugee Women." *Women & Therapy* 8: 23.

Rubenstein, Hiasaura Lawler, and K. Sharene. 1990. "Toward the Psychosocial Empowerment of Women." *Affilia* 5 (3): 27.

Rugiriza, Ephrem. 1998 "Démocratie: Á l'école des femmes de Gitarama." *La nouvelle reléve* (370) (October): 6.

Saint–Germain, Michelle A. 1997. "Mujeres '94: Democratic Transition and the Women's Movement in El Salvador." *Women & Politics* 18 (2): 75–98.

Saporta Sternback, Nancy, Marysa Navarro-Aranguren, Patricia Chuchryk, and Sonia E. Alvarez. 1992. "Feminisms in Latin America: From Bogotá to San Bernadino." In Arturo Escobar and Sonia Alvarez, eds., *The Making of Social Movements in Latin America,* pp. 207–239. Boulder, Colo.: Westview Press.

Sarayeth, Tive. 1998. *Women and the Media in Cambodia.* Phnom Penh: Women's Media Centre of Cambodia, November.

Save the Children Fund (UK). 1997. "Household Food Economy Analysis. Gikongoro and Butare, Rwanda," "Household Food Economy Analysis. Central Kibungo, Rwanda." Kigali, Rwanda: Food Assessment Unit, July-December.

———. 1998. "Household Food Economy Analysis, Gikongoro and Butare Prefectures High Population Density Area and Western Highland Area." Kigali, Rwanda: Food Assessment Unit, May.

Savjak, N. 1998. "Sexism and Equality: Women Between Stereotypes and Autonomy." In Bulletin of Women Today Roundtables, Helsinki Citizens Assembly and United Women, Banja Luka, unpublished.

Schirmer, Jennifer. 1993. "The Seeking of Truth and the Gendering of Consciousness: The Comadres of El Salvador and the Conavigua Widows of Guatemala." In Sarah A. Radcliffe and Sallie Westwood, eds.,*"Viva": Women and Popular Protest in Latin America.* London: Routledge.

Secretariat of State for Women's Affairs, Cambodia. 1995. *Women: Key to National Reconstruction: Cambodia's Country Report.* Phnom Penh.

Shawcross, William. 1994. *Cambodia's New Deal: A Report.* Washington, D.C.: Carnegie Endowment for International Peace.

Smillie, Ian. 1996. "Service Delivery or Civil Society? Nongovernmental Organizations in Bosnia and Herzegovina." A report for CARE Zagreb.

Sok, Chivy W. 1995. "Cambodian Women's Continuing Burden." *Freedom Review* 26 (5): 29–31.

Sørensen, Birgitte. 1998. *Women and Postconflict Reconstruction.* Occasional Paper No. 3. The War-Torn Societies Project. Geneva: United Nations Research Institute for Social Development.

Starr, S. Frederick. 1998. "The Era of Civil Society in Perspective." *Give & Take: A Journal of Civil Society in Eurasia* 1 (1) (summer): 5–7.

Steering Committee of the Joint Evaluation of Emergency Assistance to Rwanda. 1996. *Joint Evaluation of Emergency Assistance to Rwanda, The International Response to Conflict and Genocide: Lessons from the Rwanda Experience.* 4 vols. London: Overseas Development Institute Publications.

Stephen, Lynn, ed. 1994. *Hear My Testimony: María Teresa Tula, Human Rights Activist of El Salvador.* Boston: South End Press.

———. 1995. "Women's Rights Are Human Rights: The Merging of Feminine and Feminist Interests Among El Salvador's Mothers of the Disappeared (COMADRES)." *American Ethnologist* 22: 807–827.

———. 1997. *Women and Social Movements in Latin America: Power from Below.* Austin: University of Texas Press.

Stephen, Lynn, Serena Cosgrove, and Kelley Ready. 2000. "Aftermath: Women's Organizations in Postconflict El Salvador." Working Paper No. 309. Washington, D.C.: USAID/CDIE.

Stiglmayer, Alexandra, ed. 1994. *Mass Rape: The War Against Women in Bosnia–Herzegovina.* Lincoln: University of Nebraska Press.

Stoll, David. 1993. *Between Two Armies in the Ixil Towns of Guatemala.* New York: Columbia University Press.

Sullivan, Kathleen. 1996. "Constructing 'La Casa de la Mujer': The Guatemalan Refugee Women and the Midwives of Monja Blanca in El Porvenir Border Camp, Mexico." In Wenona Giles, Helene Moussa, and Penny Van Esterik, eds., *Development and Diaspora: Gender and the Refugee Experience,* pp. 268–279. Dundas, Ontario: Artemis Enterprises.

Taylor, Clark. 1998. *Return of Guatemala's Refugees: Reweaving the Torn.* Philadelphia: Temple University Press.

Thomson, Marilyn. 1986. *Women of El Salvador: Price of Freedom.* Philadelphia: ISHI.

Tilson, D., and C. M. Camino. 1997. *Reproductive Health Assessment and Health Education Project Gorazde.* New York: International Rescue Committee.

Tompkins, Tamara. 1995. "Prosecuting Rape As a War Crime: Speaking the Unspeakable." *Notre Dame Law Review* 70 (4): 845–890.

Townsend, Janet Gabriel, Emma Zapata, Joanna Rowlands, Pilar Alberti, and Marta Mercado. 1999. *Women and Power: Fighting Patriarchies and Poverty.* London: Zed Books.

Tripp, Aili Mari. 1998. "Expanding 'Civil Society': Women and Political Space in Contemporary Uganda." *Journal of Commonwealth and Comparative Politics* 36 (2) (July): 84–107.

Tsihinstavi, Nina. 1999. Caucasus Women's Research and Consulting Network. Interview, 11 October.

Tuyuc, Rosalina. 2000. CONAVIGUA and Frente Democrático Nueva Guatemala. Interview, March.

Twagiramariya, Clotilde, and Meredeth Turshen. 1998. "'Favours' to Give and 'Consenting' Victims: The Sexual Politics of Survival in Rwanda." In Meredeth Turshen and Clotilde Twagiramariya, eds., *What Women Do in Wartime: Gender and Conflict in Africa,* pp. 101–117. London: Zed Books.

Underwood, Penny. 1996. "Rebuilding Cambodia the Cambodian Way." *Community Quarterly: A Journal Focussing on Community Issues* (40): 48.

Unidad Revolucionaria Nacional Guatemalteca. 1999. "De la verdad histórica a la reconciliación." From web site: http://www.urng.com/120399.html.

United Nations. 1995. *The United Nations and the Situation in Georgia.* Reference paper. New York: United Nations.

———. 1998. *Guatemala: Los contrastes del desarrollo humano.* Guatemala: United Nations.

United Nations Development Program (UNDP). 1996. *Human Development Report: Georgia 1996.* Tbilisi, Georgia.

———. 1998a. *Cambodia Human Development Report.* National Assembly of Cambodia government report. Phnom Penh.

———. 1998b. *Human Development Report: Georgia 1998.* Tbilisi, Georgia.

———. 1999a. *Human Development Report: Bosnia and Herzegovina 1998.* Sarajevo.

———. 1999b. *Transition 1999 Human Development Report for Europe and the Commonwealth of Independent States.* From web site: http://www. undp.org/rbec/pubs/hdr99/pr.htm.

United Nations High Commissioner for Refugees (UNHCR). 1998. *1998 Global Appeal: The Former Yugoslavia and Albania.* From web site: http:// www.unhcr.ch.

———. 1999. *1999 Global Appeal: The Former Yugoslavia and Albania.* From web site: http://www.unchr.ch.

United Nations International Children's Emergency Fund (UNICEF). 1990. *Cambodia: The Situation of Women and Children.* Phnom Penh: U.N. Children's Fund, Office of the Special Representative.

———. 1998. *Women and Children: Bosnia and Herzegovina Situation Analysis.* Sarajevo.

———. 1999. *Women in Transition.* The Monee Project. CEE/CIS/Baltic. Regional Monitoring Report No. 6. Florence.

United Nations International Research and Training Institute for the Advancement of Women. 1996. *Women and Human Settlements in Conflict Zones.* Proceedings, Round Table, 11 June. Second United Nations Conference on Human Settlements, Habitat II. Istanbul.

"USAID Support for Implementation of the Guatemalan Peace Accords, June 1999." Author and publisher unavailable. Washington, D.C.

Utz, Kaslemal. 2000. "Caritas Diocesana del Quiché." Sr. Barbara Ford and Sr. Virginia Searing, coordinators. Interview, March.

Uvin, Peter. 1998. *Aiding Violence: The Development Enterprise in Rwanda.* West Hartford, Conn.: Kumarian Press.

van de Put, Wilem. *Individual and Collective Effects of Stress in the Cambodian Community: Assessment and Interventions.* Phnom Penh: Transcultural Psychosocial Organization (TPO).

van der Wijk, Dieneke. 1997. *The Human Side of Conflict: Coping Strategies of Women Heads of Households in Four Villages in Sri Lanka and Cambodia.* A report for the Gender and Learning Team of Oxfam UK. London: Oxfam.

Vázquez, Norma. 2000. "Refugees and Returnee Women: Skills Acquired in Exile and Their Applications in Peacetime." Washington, D.C.: Promoting

Women in Development Program/International Center for Research on Women and Centre for Development and Population Activities.

Vickers, Jeanne. 1993a. "The Impact of War on Women." *Journal of the Society for International Development* 4: 35–40.

———. 1993b. *Women and War.* London: Zed Books.

Visvanathan, Nalini, ed. 1997. *The Women, Gender, and Development Reader.* London: Zed Books.

Voss, Joachim. 1987. "L'Amélioration de la culture du haricot sur la base d'un diagnostic des contraintes de production, des pratiques et des potentiels des agriculteurs" In Augustin Nkundabashaka and Joachim Voss, eds., *Les Projets de développement rural: Réussites, échecs et stratégies nouvelles,* pp. 37–47. Butare: Université Nationale du Rwanda.

Walsh, Martha. 1997. *Postconflict Bosnia and Herzegovina: Integrating Women's Special Situation and Gender Perspectives in Skills Training and Employment Promotion.* Geneva: International Labor Organization.

———. 1998. "Mind the Gap: Where Feminist Theory Failed to Meet Development Practice—A Missed Opportunity in Bosnia and Herzegovina." *European Journal of Women's Studies* 5: 329–343.

———. 2000. "Aftermath: The Impact of Conflict on Women in Bosnia and Herzegovina." Working Paper No. 302. Washington, D.C.: USAID/CDIE.

Washington Office on Latin America (WOLA). 1984. *Security and Development Conditions in the Guatemalan Highlands.* Washington, D.C.: WOLA, Report on a Mission of Inquiry.

Waugh, Lisa Johnson. 1998. "Gender Issues in the Special Objective: Support the Implementation of the Peace Accords." Unpublished paper done for USAID, WorldWID Fellowship Program.

Waylan, Georgina. 1994. "Women and Democratization: Conceptualizing Gender Relations in Transition Politics." *World Politics* 46: 327–354.

Weiss Fagen, Patricia. 2000. *Refugee Women in El Salvador and Guatemala: Challenges and Lessons of Reintegration.* Washington, D.C.: International Center for Research on Women.

Wijk, Dieneke van der. 1997. *The Human Side of Conflict: Coping Mechanisms of Women Heads of Households in Four Villages in Sri Lanka and Cambodia.* Oxford: Oxfam.

Willame, Jean-Claude. 1995. *Aux sources de l'hécatombe rwandaise.* Paris: L'Harmattan.

Winch, Paula Emilia. 1999. "Maya Women's Organizing in Post-*Violencia* Guatemala: 'Tenemos el Derecho de Decir lo Que Pasó.'" Master's thesis. Austin: University of Texas.

Wipper, Audrey. 1975–1976. "The Maendeleo ya Wanawake Organization: The Co-optation of Leadership." *The African Studies Review* 18 (3): 99–120.

"Women in Site Two (Cambodia)." 1991. *Women in Action* (3): 24.

"Women Shoulder the Burden of Cambodia's Economy." 1994. *World of Work* (9) (September): 24.

Women's Commission for Refugee Women and Children. 1996. *The Struggle for Peace and Recovery in Former Yugoslavia: Move Women from Background to Foreground!* New York.

———. 1997. *Rwanda's Women and Children: The Long Road to Reconciliation.* New York.

————. 1998. *Women Displaced in the Southern Caucasus—an Examination of Humanitarian Assistance Needs in Azerbaijan, Armenia, Nagorno–Karabakh, and Georgia.* New York.

Women's Committee of Abkhazia. 1998. *Statement of the Women's Committee Mission of the Abkhazia Autonomous Republic.* Tbilisi, Georgia.

Worby, Paula. 1999. *Lessons Learned from UNHCR's Involvement in the Guatemala Refugee Repatriation and Reintegration Programme (1987–1999).* UNHCR Regional Bureau for the Americas and Evaluation and Policy Analysis Unit.

World Bank. 1998. *Bosnia and Herzegovina—The Priority Reconstruction Program: Achievements and 1998 Needs.* Washington, D.C.

————. 1999a. *Bosnia and Herzegovina: 1996–1998 Lessons and Accomplishments Review of the Priority Reconstruction Program and Looking Ahead Towards Sustainable Economic Development.* Washington, D.C.

————. 1999b. *Georgia: A Poverty Report.* Vol 1. Tbilisi, Georgia.

————. 2000. *World Development Report 2000/2001: Attacking Poverty.* New York: Oxford University Press.

Woroniuk, Beth. 1999. "Women's Empowerment in the Context of Human Security: A Discussion Paper." Background paper for the Joint Workshop of the United Nations Inter-Agency Committee on Women and Gender Equality and the OECD/DAC Working Party on Gender Equality, held 7–8 December in Bangkok.

Yudelman, Sally W. 1994. "A Week in Chiapas: February 20–27, 1994." Report of a delegation under the auspices of the International Council of Voluntary Agencies, Geneva, Switzerland.

Yudelman, Sally W., Dawn Calabia, and Holly Myers. 1992. *We Have a Voice and We Can Speak: Women and Children Refugees, Repatriates and Displaced in El Salvador, Guatemala, Nicaragua, and Mexico.* New York: Women's Commission for Refugee Women and Children.

Zamora de García, Gloria, and María Rosenda Camey. 2000a. "Gender in Guatemala: CONAVIGUA Case Study." Working Paper. Washington, D.C.: USAID/CDIE.

————. 2000b. "Informe de la organización a nivel nacional: Coordinadora Nacional de Viudas de Guatemala—CONAVIGUA." Guatemala: CDIE and USAID.

Zena Zenama. 1998. "Annual Report." Unpublished.

Zur, Judith N. 1998. *Violent Memories: Mayan War Widows in Guatemala.* Boulder, Colo.: Westview Press

Zurikashvili, Feride. 1998. *The Socioeconomic Status of Women with Children Among Internally Displaced Persons in Contemporary Georgia.* Tbilisi, Georgia: Women's Studies Center of Tbilisi State University.

————. 1999. "Georgia Background Study." Report submitted to USAID/CDIE. Washington, D.C.

————. 2000. "Report on a Survey of Internally Displaced Women and Their Families in Three Regions of Georgia." Unpublished paper. Washington, D.C.: USAID/CDIE.

The Contributors

Krishna Kumar is a Senior Social Scientist at the U.S. Agency for International Development. Dr. Kumar has directed a series of studies on the political rehabilitation of war-torn societies, two of which resulted in the edited volumes *Rebuilding Societies After Civil War* and *Postconflict Elections, Democratization, and International Assistance,* published by Lynne Rienner in 1997 and 1998, respectively. He has written or edited ten books on development and evaluation research and has authored numerous monographs, reports, and articles in professional journals.

Hannah Baldwin is the Democracy and Governance (D&G) Team Leader, U.S. Agency for International Development in Guinea, where her work emphasizes conflict resolution and decentralized self-governance of village-based cooperatives, among other D&G goals. Prior to her posting to Guinea, Ms. Baldwin served as a technical adviser to the Women in Development Program.

Judy Benjamin is Senior Technical Advisor on Gender for the Women's Commission for Refugee Women and Children, where she supervises the Commission's local capacity project, helping women's organizations respond to refugee emergencies. She also manages the organization's work in Afghanistan, including research and data collection on conditions of Afghan refugee women and girls. Her prior expeience includes directing CARE International's AIDS/HIV program for Rwandan refugees.

Thomas Buck is a Senior Research Analyst at the U.S. Agency for International Development's Center for Development Information and Evaluation. Mr. Buck has published several papers on problems of transition and democratization in Eastern Europe, including chapters on the effects of nationalism in the Russian and Macedonian transitions in separate volumes published by the Institute on East Central Europe at Columbia University.

Serena Cosgrove has lived in Central America for over a decade. Presently she co-coordinates project analysis for AVINA, a foundation investing in leadership for sustainable development in Latin America. Ms. Cosgrove has a master's degree in social anthropology and a Ph.D. in sociology. Her doctoral research focused on the impacts of development projects on Salvadoran women.

Patricia Weiss Fagen joined the UN High Commissioner for Refugees in 1988. During 1995–1996, she was on loan to the UN Research Institute for Social Development, as Senior Associate of the War-Torn Societies Project in Geneva. Subsequently she worked in the World Bank and the Inter-American Development Bank. Currently she is Senior Associate at the Institute for the Study of International Migration, Georgetown University.

Virginia Garrard-Burnett is Senior Lecturer in Latin American Studies and History at the University of Texas, Austin. She is the author of *Protestantism in Guatemala: Living in the New Jerusalem,* editor of *Religion in Latin America,* and coeditor of *Rethinking Protestantism in Latin America.* She has also published more than a dozen articles on ethnicity, gender, and religion in Latin America.

Alice L. Morton is a Ph.D. social anthropologist who has worked on gender and development for over twenty years, first in academia, then in USAID and at the World Bank. She attempts to include gendered analysis in sectoral and transsectoral settings in policies, programs, and policy domains.

Susan Allen Nan is Senior Program Associate in the Conflict Resolution Program at the Carter Center in Atlanta, Georgia. She serves as Vice-President of the Board for the Alliance for Conflict Transformation. She has worked over ten years as a conflict resolution project director, consultant, facilitator, trainer, evaluator, and researcher in intergroup conflicts in both the United States and abroad.

Catharine Newbury teaches in the Department of Political Science and the Department of African and Afro-American Studies at the University of North Carolina at Chapel Hill. Her earlier research focused on the historical development of ethnicity in Rwanda, and women and agrarian change in Central Africa. She is currently studying the roots to the politics of violence in this region. She is the author of *The Cohesion of Oppression: Clientship and Ethnicity in Rwanda, 1860–1960*—a study of the interplay between state building and the growth of ethnic cleavages during colonial rule—and has also written for journals such as *Cahiers d'études africaines, Africa, Comparative Politics, Canadian Journal of African Studies, African Studies Review,* and *Africa Today.*

Kelley Ready has been privileged to observe the Salvadoran women's movement since its growth over the last thirteen years. She has a Ph.D. in anthropology from the City University of New York and is currently a Visiting Assistant Professor of Anthropology at Northeastern University.

Lynn Stephen teaches at the University of Oregon. Her research has focused on gender, ethnicity, political economy, social movements, human rights, and nationalism in Latin America. She is the author of *Hear My Testimony: María Teresa Tula, Human Rights Activist of El Salvador; Women and Social Movements in Latin America: Power from Below;* and *Zapata Lives: Histories and Political Culture in Southern Mexico.*

Martha Walsh holds a master's degree in gender and development from the Institute of Development Studies at the University of Sussex. She has focused on the situation of women in postconflict societies, particularly Cambodia and Bosnia–Herzegovina. She has recently qualified as a barrister.

Sally W. Yudelman is a Senior Fellow at the International Center for Research on Women. She has been involved with development assistance, governance, and human rights programs of governmental and nongovernmental agencies and organizations for many years as a practitioner, donor, consultant, and volunteer.

Feride Zurikashvili is professor of human geography and head of the Women's Studies Center at Tbilisi State University in the Republic of Georgia. Dr. Zurikashvili has done extensive research on the conditions and status of internally displaced women throughout the Republic of Georgia.

Index

About the Book

Women typically do not remain passive spectators during a war, nor are they always its innocent victims; instead, they frequently take on new roles and responsibilities, participating in military and political struggles and building new networks in order to obtain needed resources for their families. Consequently, while civil war imposes tremendous burdens on women, it often contributes to the redefinition of their traditional roles and the reconfiguration of existing gender relations in the society.

This work presents a detailed analysis of how intrastate conflict affects women, and how women's networks and organizations respond in ways that increase their economic, social, and political power. The authors also consider policy implications for the international community.

Krishna Kumar is Senior Social Scientist with the U.S. Agency for International Development. His recent publications include *Rebuilding Societies After Civil War: Critical Areas for International Assistance,* and *Postconflict Elections, Democratization, and International Assistance.*